朝日新書

Asahi Shinsho 823

対訳　武士道

新渡戸稲造　著

山本史郎　訳

JN053341

朝日新聞出版

＊本書中には、第7章中の「士農工商」の身分制度に関する記述、また第14章 女性の教育と地位 など、今日では差別表現とみなすべき記述がありますが、本書が底本としている1905年の改訂版発表時（英語原文）の時代背景を考え合わせ、また著者が故人であるという事情を考慮し、原文通りとしました。

朝日新聞出版　書籍編集部

このささやかな書を

最愛の叔父

太田時敏に捧げる

過去を敬い

武士道を尊ぶべきことを

教えてくれたがゆえに

*

TO MY BELOVED UNCLE

TOKITOSHI OTA

WHO TAUGHT ME TO REVERE THE PAST

AND

TO ADMIRE THE DEEDS OF THE SAMURAI

I DEDICATE

THIS LITTLE BOOK

目次

CONTENTS

　　　　　　　　　　　　　　　　　あの道は

山を越えてゆくが、そこを歩む者は

真に道なのか疑いたくなる。

しかれども、荒れ地より望めば、

まぎれもなく、くっきりと、

底から頂へと上っている。荒れ野のことを思えば、

一、二度道が途切れても、それが何であろうか？

それというのも（ものの見方を変えるなら）、

あとから振り返って見えてくる。

道の断絶は、絶妙な仕掛け。

人の目を鍛え、信仰の何たるかを教えるためのもの。

　ロバート・ブラウニング「ブルグラム大司教の弁明」

時として海の上を移動し、人類の倫理的な感情とエネ
ルギーを衝き動かす動力となってきた力強い精神が三
つある。自由の精神、宗教の精神、そして名誉の精神
である。

　　　　　　　　　　ハラム『中世ヨーロッパ』

騎士道はそれ自体が人生の詩である。

　　　　　　　　　シュレーゲル『歴史の哲学』

—"That way
Over the mountain, which who stands upon,
Is apt to doubt if it be indeed a road;
While if he views it from the waste itself,
Up goes the line there, plain from base to brow,
Not vague, mistakable! What's a break or two
Seen from the unbroken desert either side?
And then (to bring in fresh philosophy)
What if the breaks themselves should prove at last
The most consummate of contrivances
To train a man's eye, teach him what is faith?"
—ROBERT BROWNING, *Bishop Blougram's Apology.*

"There are, if I may so say, three powerful spirits,
which have from time to time, moved on the face of
the waters, and given a predominant impulse to the
moral sentiments and energies of mankind. These
are the spirits of liberty, of religion, and of honor."
—HALLAM, *Europe in the Middle Ages.*

"Chivalry is itself the poetry of life."
—SCHLEGEL, *Philosophy of History.*

序

　十年ばかり前のことである。ベルギーの著名な法律学者であった、故ド・ラヴレー氏のお宅に泊めていただいたおり、あるときの散歩のおりに話題が宗教のことに及んだ。「まさか君、学校時代に宗教教育がなかったなどというんじゃなかろうね」と教授が言われた。

　いや、そうだと答えると、驚きのあまり足を止めて、「宗教教育がないだって！どうやって子どもに倫理を教えるのかね」と何度も言われたあの声が忘れられない。そう言われると私のほうも唖然として、すぐには答えが返せなかった。子どものころ学んだ倫理は学校で教わったわけではないからだ。そうして、私の正邪の観念を作り上げている諸々の要素をつらつら考えてみるに、それを心に吹き込んでくれたのは武士道だったのだということに気がついた。

About ten years ago, while spending a few days under the hospitable roof of the distinguished Belgian jurist, the lamented M. de Laveleye, our conversation turned, during one of our rambles, to the subject of religion. "Do you mean to say," asked the venerable professor, "that you have no religious instruction in your schools?"

On my replying in the negative he suddenly halted in astonishment, and in a voice which I shall not easily forget, he repeated "No religion! How do you impart moral education?" The question stunned me at the time. I could give no ready answer, for the moral precepts I learned in my childhood days, were not given in schools; and not until I began to analyze the different elements that formed my notions of right and wrong, did I find that it was Bushido that

この小著が書かれた直接のきっかけは、あれやこれやの考え方や習慣がなぜ日本にあるのかと、妻からたびたび質問されたことである。

ド・ラヴレー氏とわが妻に納得してもらえるような答えを出そうとするうち、私は現今の日本の倫理観を解き明かすには、封建制と武士道[1]の理解が不可欠であるということに思いいたった。

長わずらいのせいで養生を余儀なくされたのを機に、無聊のなぐさめに我が家庭内の会話の中で答えたことの一部を書き綴り、以下の本書の順に整理して並べてみた。私の幼少期、封建制がまだ続いている時代に教わったことがほとんどである。

片やラフカディオ・ハーンとヒュー・フレイザー夫人、そして他方アーネスト・サトウとチェンバレン教授というそうそうたる面々を左右に見ながら、日本のことを英語で書くのは勇気のいることだ。私に有利な点がたった一つあるとすれば、これらの著名人がせいぜいのところ弁護士のような代理の立場であるのに対して、私は自らの口で自国のために論述できるということである。

[1]「ブシドー」と発音される。日本語と日本名を英語になおすときは、ヘップバーン式による。母音はヨーロッパ言語、子音は英語式である。

breathed them into my nostrils.

The direct inception of this little book is due to the frequent queries put by my wife as to the reasons why such and such ideas and customs prevail in Japan.

In my attempts to give satisfactory replies to M. de Laveleye and to my wife, I found that without understanding Feudalism and Bushido,[1] the moral ideas of present Japan are a sealed volume.

Taking advantage of enforced idleness on account of long illness, I put down in the order now presented to the public some of the answers given in our household conversation. They consist mainly of what I was taught and told in my youthful days, when Feudalism was still in force.

Between Lafcadio Hearn and Mrs. Hugh Fraser on one side and Sir Ernest Satow and Professor Chamberlain on the other, it is indeed discouraging to write anything Japanese in English. The only advantage I have over them is that I can assume the attitude of a personal defendant, while these distinguished writers

---

[1] Pronounced *Boó-shee-doh'*. In putting Japanese words and names into English, Hepburn's rule is followed, that the vowels should be used as in European languages, and the consonants as in English.

「私に彼らの文才があれば、日本のためにもっと雄弁に弁じることができるのだが！」と私はよく思う。だが、他から借りた言語で語る者は意味が通じるように書ければ、それだけでもありがたいと思わねばならない。

　本書の全体を通じて、大事な点についてはヨーロッパの歴史と文学から類似の例を示して説明することを心がけた。そうすることによって本書のテーマが、外国の読者に理解されやすくなるだろうと思ってのことである。

　宗教的なテーマや、宗教にたずさわる人びとのことにも触れているが、まんがいち軽んじるような口ぶりに感じられることがあったとしても、私のキリスト教に対する態度が疑問に付されることはないものと信じている。教会のやり方や、キリストの教えを覆い隠してしまう形式主義は感心しないが、キリストの教えそのものは別である。キリストが教え、新約聖書によって伝えられてきた信仰、そして心に刻まれている律法を、私は心より是とする。それのみならず、神は、ユダヤ人か否か、キリスト教徒か否かにかかわらず、すべての民すべての国と、「旧約」と呼ばれる約束を取り交わされたのだと信じている。だが、これ以上ここで私の信仰についての考えを述べて、読者諸氏の忍耐をためす必要はないだろう。

are at best solicitors and attorneys. I have often thought,—"Had I their gift of language, I would present the cause of Japan in more eloquent terms!" But one who speaks in a borrowed tongue should be thankful if he can just make himself intelligible.

All through the discourse I have tried to illustrate whatever points I have made with parallel examples from European history and literature, believing that these will aid in bringing the subject nearer to the comprehension of foreign readers.

Should any of my allusions to religious subjects and to religious workers be thought slighting, I trust my attitude towards Christianity itself will not be questioned. It is with ecclesiastical methods and with the forms which obscure the teachings of Christ, and not with the teachings themselves, that I have little sympathy. I believe in the religion taught by Him and handed down to us in the New Testament, as well as in the law written in the heart. Further, I believe that God hath made a testament which maybe called "old" with every people and nation,—Gentile or Jew, Christian or Heathen. As to the rest of my theology, I need not impose upon the patience of the public.

この序文をしめくくるにあたって、わが友人アナ・
C・ハートショーン氏への感謝を述べさせていただこ
う。女史は数々の貴重な助言をくださり、この本のカバ
ーのためにとても日本的なデザインをしてくださったの
である。

　新渡戸稲造

　1899 年 12 月、ペンシルヴァニア州、モルヴァーンにて

In concluding this preface, I wish to express my thanks to my friend Anna C. Hartshorne for many valuable suggestions and for the characteristically Japanese design made by her for the cover of this book.

INAZO NITOBE.

Malvern, Pa., Twelfth Month, 1899.

第十版（改定版）への序

　この小著は六年以上前にフィラデルフィアで出版されて以来、予想もしなかった道を歩むこととなった。日本で八版を重ね、この英語版は第十版である。この新版と同時に、ニューヨークのジョージ・H・パットナムズ・サンズ出版社から、アメリカ版とイギリス版が出版される。

　いっぽう、『武士道』はカンデシュのデヴ氏によってマラーティー語へ、ハンブルクのカウフマン女史によってドイツ語に、シカゴのホーラ氏によってボヘミア語に、レンベルクの科学生命協会によってポーランドに翻訳されている。ただしこのポーランド語版はロシア政府によって検閲をうけた。ノルウェー語とフランス語への翻訳が現在進行中で、中国語版も計画されている。日本

TO THE TENTH AND REVISED EDITION

Since its first publication in Philadelphia, more than six years ago, this little book has had an unexpected history. The Japanese reprint has passed through eight editions, the present thus being its tenth appearance in the English language. Simultaneously with this will be issued an American and English edition, through the publishinghouse of Messrs. George H. Putnam's Sons, of New York.

In the meantime, *Bushido* has been translated into Mahratti by Mr. Dev of Khandesh, into German by Fräulein Kaufmann of Hamburg, into Bohemian by Mr. Hora of Chicago, into Polish by the Society of Science and Life in Lemberg,—although this Polish edition has been censured by the Russian Government. It is now being rendered into Norwegian and into French. A Chinese translation is under contem-

で捕虜となっているあるロシア軍士官が、ロシア語版の原稿を作っており、すぐにも出版可能だ。ハンガリーではこの本の一部が公刊され、ほとんど論文といってよいほどの詳しい書評が日本語で出版された。若い学生にも読めるように、学術的な注釈がわが友人のH・サクライ氏によって作成されている。そしてこのサクライ氏には、他の面でも様々にお世話になっている。

このささやかな本が、広く様々の読者の共感を呼んできたところから、このテーマは世界中の人びとの興味をひくものであると感じられるのが何よりも嬉しい。

ルーズベルト大統領が本書を読み、数十人の友人に本を配られたという知らせを公の筋からいただいた。過分の名誉にして、喜びこれにまさるものはない。

このエディションのために加筆修正を行ったが、その対象はほぼ具体例にかぎられる。ずっと気になっていたことだが、親孝行についての章を加えることが出来なかったのは、返す返すも残念である。親孝行は忠君と並んで、日本的倫理の車の両輪をなしているからである。それができなかったのは、日本人が親孝行についてどう感

plation. A Russian officer, now a prisoner in Japan, has a manuscript in Russian ready for the press. A part of the volume has been brought before the Hungarian public and a detailed review, almost amounting to a commentary, has been published in Japanese. Full scholarly notes for the help of younger students have been compiled by my friend Mr. H. Sakurai, to whom I also owe much for his aid in other ways.

I have been more than gratified to feel that my humble work has found sympathetic readers in widely separated circles, showing that the subject matter is of some interest to the world at large.

Exceedingly flattering is the news that has reached me from official sources, that President Roosevelt has done it undeserved honor by reading it and distributing several dozens of copies among his friends.

In making emendations and additions for the present edition, I have largely confined them to concrete examples. I still continue to regret, as I indeed have never ceased to do, my inability to add a chapter on Filial Piety, which is considered one of the two wheels of the chariot of Japanese ethics—Loyalty being the other. My inability is due rather to my ignorance of

じているかを知らないからではなく、それに対して西洋人がどのような感情を向けるのかが分からず、得心のいく比較例が私には出せないからである。このテーマを含めて、もっと多くの話題について詳しく述べる日がいつかおとずれることを願っている。本書で触れているテーマはどれももっと詳細に述べ、議論することが可能であるが、現時点では、これ以上分厚い本にするのは難しい。

　この序文が公正を欠く未完成の文章にならぬよう、ここに妻への感謝を記しておかねばならない。校正刷りを読み、有益な助言をくれ、何よりも終始かわらず私を元気づけてくれたのが妻だったのだから。

I.N.

京都
1905 年 5 月 22 日

the Western sentiment in regard to this particular virtue, than to ignorance of our own attitude towards it, and I cannot draw comparisons satisfying to my own mind. I hope one day to enlarge upon this and other topics at some length. All the subjects that are touched upon in these pages are capable of further amplification and discussion; but I do not now see my way clear to make this volume larger than it is.

This Preface would be incomplete and unjust, if I were to omit the debt I owe to my wife for her reading of the proof-sheets, for helpful suggestions, and, above all, for her constant encouragement.

I.N.

Kyoto,
Fifth Month twenty-second, 1905.

第1章

武士道は
人の道である

　武士道は日本の国の華。国の象徴である桜とともに、**日本の土壌**に生えた純潔の華である。それは過去の遺物となり、古代の徳の標本と化して歴史に埋もれるどころか、今なお日本人の心に、今を彩る美として、そして力として息づいている。形として目に見えず手に触れることもできないが、それは依然として人の倫の骨格をなし、我々は今もなおその強い磁場の中にいることを感じずにはいられない。武士道を生みはぐくんだ社会状況はとうに過去のものとなった。しかしながら、はるか遠くの恒星がそれ自身が消滅した後もなおも我らに光を注ぎ続けるのに等しく、武士道の燦きは、旧い**封建制度**によって生まれたものとはいえ、封建制度がなくなった現在でもなお**徳の道**を明々と照らしている。エドマンド・バークはヨーロッパの騎士道がいまや滅びさり、打ち捨てられているのを惜しみ、讃仰の思いを切々たる名文に託したことで世に知られているが、ここに、その同じ言語

CHAPTER 1

BUSHIDO AS
AN ETHICAL SYSTEM

Chivalry is a flower no less indigenous to **the soil of Japan** than its **emblem**, the cherry blossom; nor is it a dried-up specimen of an antique virtue preserved in the herbarium of our history. It is still a living object of power and beauty among us; and if it assumes no tangible shape or form, it not the less scents the moral atmosphere, and makes us aware that we are still under its potent spell. The conditions of society which brought it forth and nourished it have long disappeared; but as those far-off stars which once were and are not, still continue to shed their rays upon us, so the light of chivalry, which was a child of **feudalism**, still illuminates our **moral path**, surviving its mother institution. It is a pleasure to me to reflect upon this subject in the language of Burke, who uttered the well-known touching eulogy over the neglected bier

によって武士道を語ることができるのは、私の大いなる喜びとするところである。

　ジョージ・ミラー博士ともあろう碩学（せきがく）が、**騎士道**やそれに類する行動規範は、過去も現在も東洋には存在しなかったと断言してはばからない[2]。極東の国がいまだ十分世界に知られていないことは遺憾の極みであるが、このような無知はむりからぬことではある。博士の著述の第三版が出版されたのは、ペリー提督が鎖国していた日本の門を叩こうとする、まさにその時にあたっていた。そして、それから十年あまりの後、幕藩体制が**断末魔に喘いで**いたとき、カール・マルクスは『**資本論**』において、封建制度が世界で唯一日本に存続しており、社会的・政治的側面から研究することに意義があると指摘した。マルクスの顰（ひそ）みにならって、私は現在の日本に息づいている「騎士道」の研究を、西欧の歴史学や倫理学の学究に促したい。

　ヨーロッパの封建制度と騎士道を日本のそれと比較すれば、面白い歴史論文となるだろうが、そこに深入りすることは小著の目的ではない。本書ではまず第一に、**日本の「騎士道」の起源、及びそれを生み出した土壌**につ

---

[2] *History Philosophically Illustrated*, (3rd Ed. 1853), Vol. II, p.

of its European prototype.

It argues a sad defect of information concerning the Far East, when so erudite a scholar as Dr. George Miller did not hesitate to affirm that **chivalry**, or any other similar institution, has never existed either among the nations of antiquity or among the modern Orientals.[2] Such ignorance, however, is amply excusable, as the third edition of the good Doctor's work appeared the same year that Commodore Perry was knocking at the portals of our exclusivism. More than a decade later, about the time that our feudalism was **in the last throes of existence**, Carl Marx, writing his *Capital*, called the attention of his readers to the peculiar advantage of studying the social and political institutions of feudalism, as then to be seen in living form only in Japan. I would likewise invite the Western historical and ethical student to the study of chivalry in the Japan of the present.

Enticing as is a historical disquisition on the comparison between European and Japanese feudalism and chivalry, it is not the purpose of this paper to enter into it at length. My attempt is rather to relate, *firstly*, **the origin and sources of our chivalry**; *sec-*

いて触れる。第二にその特質、及びその教えの内容について述べる。第三に一般民衆への影響、そして第四にその影響が今に及び、今後も変わらざることへと論を進める。このうち第一の点については簡潔にすませよう。いたずらに読者諸氏を日本史の枝道に迷わせることは、私の本意ではない。ひるがえって、詳しく述べたいのは第二の点である。国際倫理や比較行動学の研究者がとくに関心があるのは、日本人の思考様式や行動の特質であろう。そしてその後の部分では、その**論理的帰結**について論じることにしよう。

　ここまで大まかに「騎士道」と呼んできたが、それに相当する日本語の意味するところは、「騎馬」（馬に乗ること）にはとどまらない。「武士道」を文字に分解すれば、「武器をもつ・貴人の・方法」である。すなわち、高貴な武人が日常の立ち居ふるまいと、本来の戦人（いくさびと）としての人格において守るべき諸々の作法を意味している。つまり「騎士の心得」、**武人**の「ノブレス・オブリージュ」のことである。以上、文字通りの意味を解説したので、ここからは原語を用いさせていただこう。原語がなぜ望ましいのかというと、日本の「武士道」は地理的に限定された、他に例を見ぬものであり、独特の精神と人格を育て上げる我が国に固有のものであるがゆえに、それ独自の表徴（かお）が文字の上にも表れるようにすべきだから

ondly, its character and teaching; *thirdly*, its influence among the masses; and, *fourthly*, the continuity and permanence of its influence. Of these several points, the first will be only brief and cursory, or else I should have to take my readers into the devious paths of our national history; the second will be dwelt upon at greater length, as being most likely to interest students of International Ethics and Comparative Ethology in our ways of thought and action; and the rest will be dealt with as **corollaries**.

The Japanese word which I have roughly rendered Chivalry, is, in the original, more expressive than Horsemanship. *Bu-shi-do* means literally Military-Knight-Ways—the ways which fighting nobles should observe in their daily life as well as in their vocation; in a word, the "Precepts of Knighthood," **the *noblesse oblige* of the warrior class**. Having thus given its literal significance, I may be allowed henceforth to use the word in the original. The use of the original term is also advisable for this reason, that a teaching so circumscribed and unique, engendering a cast of mind and character so peculiar, so local, must wear the badge of its singularity on its face; then,

である。どの国の言語にも、民族の特質と不可分の響き
をもった語が存在する。そのような語は、いかにうまく
翻訳しようと、完全な誤訳とはいわないにせよ、言葉本
来の響きがほとんど伝わらないというようなことが生じ
る。ドイツ語の Gemüth を誰がうまく訳せるだろうか？
英語の gentleman とフランス語の gentihomme は言語的
に近縁の関係にあるが、この二つの語の差異を感じない
者がいるだろうか？

　このように武士道は武人が教わり、それに従うことが
求められる**倫理規範**である。文書に書かれた規則ではな
い。格言の形で口から口へと伝えられたり、名のある武
人や賢者が筆に残した断章はあれど、基本的には、語ら
れず、書かれざる不文律である。そして、それがゆえに
一層、誠のこもった行いと、血のかよう胸に深々と刻印
された法によって裏打ちされているのである。それは一
個の優秀な頭脳や、一人の人格者の生き様から生み出さ
れたものではない。武家の心得が、数十年、数世紀の長
きにわたって樹木のごとく成長したのである。おそら
く、倫理の歴史の中で武士道が占める位置は、政治史に
おける英国の法制度に近いものがあるだろう。しかし、

some words have a national *timbre* so expressive of race characteristics that the best of translators can do them but scant justice, not to say positive injustice and grievance. Who can improve by translation what the German "*Gemüth*" signifies, or who does not feel the difference between the two words verbally so closely allied as the English *gentleman* and the French *gentilhomme*?

Bushido, then, is **the code of moral principles** which the knights were required or instructed to observe. It is not a written code; at best it consists of a few maxims handed down from mouth to mouth or coming from the pen of some well-known warrior or savant. More frequently it is a code unuttered and unwritten, possessing all the more the powerful sanction of veritable deed, and of a law written on the fleshly tablets of the heart. It was founded not on the creation of one brain, however able, or on the life of a single personage, however renowned. It was an organic growth of decades and centuries of military career. It, perhaps, fills the same position in the history of ethics that the English Constitution does in political history; yet it has had nothing to compare with **the**

<ruby>大憲章<rt>マグナカルタ</rt></ruby>や人身保護法に相当するものが存在するわけではない。十七世紀初頭には、武士の法典（武家法度）が公布されたが、その十三の短い条項はほとんどが縁組、城普請、徒党の禁止などに関わるもので、行動の規範については軽く触れるにとどまる。したがって特定の時代と場所を示して、「ここが武士道の<ruby>濫觴<rt>はじまり</rt></ruby>である」と述べることはできない。ただし時代については、武士道は封建時代に意識化されるようになったものなので、封建制度とともにはじまったと言えなくもない。ただ、その封建制度にしても単純な一本の直線はないので、武士道の歴史も複雑である。イギリスの封建体制は、**ノルマンの征服**にはじまると言えるだろう。同じく、日本では十二世紀の後半、源頼朝が幕府を開いたときに誕生したと言えるかもしれない。ただしイギリスでも、社会の中の封建制らしい部分は、すでに征服王ウィリアムよりもはるか以前に存在していたのと同じことで、日本でもいま述べた時代よりもかなり以前からその**萌芽**があったのである。

　ヨーロッパと同じく、日本でも、封建体制が制度として確立すると、当然のことながら武を事とする階級の者たちが社会の上層を占め、「さぶらい」と称されるよう

Magna Charta or the Habeas Corpus Act. True, early in the seventeenth century Military Statutes (*Buké Hatto*) were promulgated; but their thirteen short articles were taken up mostly with marriages, castles, leagues, etc., and didactic regulations were but meagerly touched upon. We cannot, therefore, point out any definite time and place and say, "Here is its fountain head." Only as it attains consciousness in the feudal age, its origin, in respect to time, may be identified with feudalism. But feudalism itself is woven of many threads, and Bushido shares its intricate nature. As in England the political institutions of feudalism may be said to date from **the Norman Conquest**, so we may say that in Japan its rise was simultaneous with the ascendency of Yoritomo, late in the twelfth century. As, however, in England, we find the social elements of feudalism far back in the period previous to William the Conqueror, so, too, the **germs** of feudalism in Japan had been long existent before the period I have mentioned.

Again, in Japan as in Europe, when feudalism was formally inaugurated, the professional class of warriors naturally came into prominence. These were

になった。この名称は古英語の cniht（knecht, knight）
と同じく、従者もしくは衛護の士の意にして、カエサル
がアキテーヌに存在すると記している soldurii や、タキ
トゥスが、当時のゲルマンの族長に付き従っていたと述
べている comitati と性質を一にする語である。もっと後
の時代に例をもとめるなら、中世ヨーロッパの歴史に出
てくる milites medii も同じものといえる。日本では、
漢文を起源とする「武家」や「武士」という呼称が一般
に用いられるようになる。この者たちは特権を有する階
級で、そもそもの出自は、戦いをなりわいとする荒くれ
者の集団である。戦乱の世で、社会の最下層の野心にあ
ふれた者たちが、おのずからの如く集団をなしたのがそ
の起源で、選別が進む中で肝のすわらぬ軟弱な者は容赦
なく淘汰され、エマソンの語を借りるならば「雄々し
く、獣の腕力をもった無骨な人種」が生き残って家門を
なし、**「武士」の階級**を築いたのである。彼らは自らが
大いなる名誉と特権を有する者であることを公言し、そ
れに伴う大いなる責任をも自任することで、**共通の行動
規範**の必要を感じるようになった。彼らはその出自から
して争いを好む階級であり、しかも多数の門や閥が反目
しあっていたからである。医師が同業者どうしの仁義に

known as *samurai*, meaning literally, like the old English *cniht* (knecht, knight), guards or attendants — resembling in character the *soldurii* whom Caesar mentioned as existing in Aquitania, or the *comitati*, who, according to Tacitus, followed Germanic chiefs in his time; or, to take a still later parallel, the *milites medii* that one reads about in the history of Mediaeval Europe. A Sinico-Japanese word *Bu-ké* or *Bu-shi* (Fighting Knights) was also adopted in common use. They were a privileged class, and must originally have been a rough breed who made fighting their vocation. This class was naturally recruited, in a long period of constant warfare, from the manliest and the most adventurous, and all the while the process of elimination went on, the timid and the feeble being sorted out, and only "a rude race, all masculine, with brutish strength," to borrow Emerson's phrase, surviving to form families and **the ranks of the samurai**. Coming to profess great honor and great privileges, and correspondingly great responsibilities, they soon felt the need of **a common standard of behavior**, especially as they were always on a belligerent footing and belonged to different clans. Just as physicians limit

よって無用の競争を避け、法曹が道義違反を訴えられると名誉を守るべく法廷に立たされるが如く、武家の者も、自らの不行跡を断罪する、最終審をえる手段がなければならなかったのである。

戦うならフェアプレイで！このいささか原始的で子どもじみた本能から、なんと豊かな道徳律が生み出されてくることだろうか。これこそが、軍人と市民のへだてなく、あらゆる徳義が生じてくる大本ではなかろうか。幼い英国人トム・ブラウンの、「小さな少年を虐めることなく、大きな少年を前にたじろぐこともなかったと後々賞賛されたい」という子どもじみた願望にたいして、我々は（自分はそんなことはとっくに卒業したというような顔で！）微笑みを向けるが、このような願望こそが倫理の礎石であり、その上にこそ広壮な館がそびえ立つのである。もっとも温厚で平和を愛する宗教ですら、このような野心をよしとするものだと言っておこう。イギリスの偉大さは、このようなトムの願望の上に打ち立てられたのであり、武士道も、これと同じ堅固な土台の上に立っていることがまもなく分かるであろう。攻撃であろうと防御であろうと、戦うことはまさしくクエーカー教徒の言うとおり野蛮な悪であるが、我々はレッシングの言うように「人間の徳義が、どんな道徳的欠陥から生じているかを知っている」[3]のである。健全で単純な

competition among themselves by professional courtesy, just as lawyers sit in courts of honor in cases of violated etiquette, so must also warriors possess some resort for final judgment on their misdemeanors.

Fair play in fight! What fertile germs of morality lie in this primitive sense of savagery and childhood. Is it not the root of all military and civic virtues? We smile (as if we had outgrown it!) at the boyish desire of the small Britisher, Tom Brown, "to leave behind him the name of a fellow who never bullied a little boy or turned his back on a big one." And yet, who does not know that this desire is the corner-stone on which moral structures of mighty dimensions can be reared? May I not go even so far as to say that the gentlest and most peace-loving of religions endorses this aspiration? This desire of Tom's is the basis on which the greatness of England is largely built, and it will not take us long to discover that *Bushido* does not stand on a lesser pedestal. If fighting in itself, be it offensive or defensive, is, as Quakers rightly testify, brutal and wrong, we can still say with Lessing, "We know from what failings our virtue springs."[3] "**Sneaks**" and

人々にとって、「陰口屋」や「臆病者」と言われるのは
もっとも恥ずべき不名誉である。人は早くもこうした考
えを抱いて子ども時代を生きるが、武人の道においても
しかりである。人生が広がり、多方面に関わりが生じて
くると、この幼少の信念は、より高い権威によって承認
されることを欲する。その正当性を保証し、安心立命の
うえに発展させることのできる、理性的な根拠を求め
る。**高度な倫理観**に裏打ちされることなく、**争いの利**の
みが横行すれば、武の道は騎士道の理想にはるか及ばぬ
ものとなるであろう！ヨーロッパにおいては、キリスト
教が本来の姿をわずかに変貌させ、騎士道に合わせた解
釈を加えることで、騎士道に精神的な内容を注ぎ込ん
だ。ラマルティーヌの言葉をかりるなら「宗教と戦争と
栄光は、**完全無欠のキリスト教騎士の三つの魂である**」
ということになったのである。

---

[3] ラスキンは人並みはずれて心優しく、争いを好まぬ人物であったが、生きること
はすなわち努力であるという人生観の持ち主らしく、戦争の重要性を認識していた。
『野生のオリーヴの冠』で以下のように述べている。「わたしは、戦争はあらゆる芸術
の礎であると言いたい。そしてこの言葉には、人間のあらゆる高潔な美徳と能力の礎
であるという意味をもこめている。これを思いついたとき違和感を感じ、恐ろしくも
あったが、それがまぎれもない事実なのだと悟った。(中略) 要するに、偉大な国家
は言葉の真実と思想の強さを、戦争によって学んできたということが分かったのであ
る。それは戦争の中で養われ、平和の中で失われること、戦争によって教えられ、平
和によって騙されること、戦争によって鍛えられ、平和によって裏切られること、す
なわち戦争で生まれ、平和で消滅することを、私は理解したのである」。

"**cowards**" are epithets of the worst opprobrium to healthy, simple natures. Childhood begins life with these notions, and knighthood also; but, as life grows larger and its relations many-sided, the early faith seeks sanction from higher authority and more rational sources for its own justification, satisfaction and development. If **military interests** had operated alone, without **higher moral** support, how far short of chivalry would the ideal of knighthood have fallen! In Europe, Christianity, interpreted with concessions convenient to chivalry, infused it nevertheless with spiritual data. "Religion, war and glory were **the three souls of a perfect Christian knight**," says Lamartine.

---

[3] Ruskin was one of the most gentle-hearted and peace loving men that ever lived. Yet he believed in war with all the fervor of a worshiper of the strenuous life. "When I tell you," he says in the *Crown of Wild Olive*, "that war is the foundation of all the arts, I mean also that it is the foundation of all the high virtues and faculties of men. It is very strange to me to discover this, and very dreadful, but I saw it to be quite an undeniable fact. ... I found in brief, that all great nations learned their truth of word and strength of thought in war; that they were nourished in war and wasted by peace, taught by war and deceived by peace; trained by war and betrayed by peace; in a word, that they were born in war and expired in peace."

第 2 章
武士道の源流

　日本に武士道を誕生させたものとして、いくつかの源流（みなもと）が考えられる。まずは**仏教**である。**運命を静観し、宿命を心静かに受忍し、危険や大惨事にも心乱さず、生を軽んじ死に親しむ**、という態度は、仏教に由来する。ある**剣豪**は、免許皆伝の弟子にむかって、「ここからはわたしではなく**禅の教え**に従いなさい」と諭した。禅は日本における「ディーアーナ」で、「**瞑想によって、言葉を超えた思考の境地に達しようとする人間のいとなみ**」である [4]。観想をその手段とし、森羅万象の奥にある原理、なろうことなら「絶対者」の存在を感得し、そのことを通じて「**絶対者」との合一**を達成するのが、その目的であると私は理解している。そのように定義するな

---

[4] Lafcadio Hearn, *Exotics and Retrospectives*, p. 84.

CHAPTER 2

SOURCES OF BUSHIDO

In Japan there were several sources of bushido, of which I may begin with **Buddhism**. It furnished a sense of calm trust in **Fate**, a quiet submission to the inevitable, that stoic composure in sight of danger or calamity, that disdain of life and friendliness with death. **A foremost teacher of swordsmanship**, when he saw his pupil master the utmost of his art, told him, "Beyond this my instruction must give way to **Zen teaching**." "Zen" is the Japanese equivalent for the Dhyâna, which "represents human effort to reach through **meditation** zones of thought beyond the range of verbal expression."[4] Its method is contemplation, and its purport, as far as I understand it, to be convinced of a principle that underlies all phenomena, and, if it can, of the Absolute itself, and thus to put oneself in **harmony with this Absolute**. Thus

ら、この教えは一宗派の**教義**を超えていると言えるだろう。「絶対者」の境地に達した者は、日常の瑣事雑事を超越し、「**新たなる乾坤**」に遊ぶようになるのである。

　ついで仏教からは得られないものを、神道がたっぷりと提供した。神道ほど、主君への忠誠、**先祖への尊崇**、そして**親孝行**を重んじる宗教はない。これらは神道の教えから武士道へと流れ込み、武士が奢る心を持たぬよう、謙譲の徳を伝えた。神道には「**原罪**」の観念はない。むしろ、人間の魂は生まれながらに善で、神のように純粋であると考えられている。心は**神の託宣**が出てくる、聖なる場所であるとされている。よく言われることだが、**神道の社**には崇拝のための物や道具がないのが、大きな特徴となっている。そして神域にかけられた一枚の素朴な鏡が、社の中心である。なぜ鏡があるのか、説明は簡単だ。それは心の象徴なのである。完璧に静かで澄みきっていれば、神の御姿がそこに映る。社の前にたって拝礼をすると、鏡のきらめく表面に自分自身を見る

defined, the teaching was more than the **dogma** of a sect, and whoever attains to the perception of the Absolute raises himself above mundane things and awakes, **"to a new Heaven and a new Earth."**

What Buddhism failed to give, Shintoism offered in abundance. Such loyalty to the sovereign, such **reverence for ancestral memory**, and such **filial piety** as are not taught by any other creed, were inculcated by the Shinto doctrines, imparting passivity to the otherwise arrogant character of the *samurai*. Shinto theology has no place for the dogma of **"original sin."** On the contrary, it believes in the innate goodness and God-like purity of the human soul, adoring it as the adytum from which **divine oracles** are proclaimed. Everybody has observed that the **Shinto shrines** are conspicuously devoid of objects and instruments of worship, and that a plain mirror hung in the sanctuary forms the essential part of its furnishing. The presence of this article, is easy to explain: it typifies the human heart, which, when perfectly placid and clear, reflects the very image of the Deity. When you stand, therefore, in front of the shrine to worship, you see your own image reflected

ことができるのであり、それゆえ拝礼は、「**汝自身を知れ**」というデルポイの神託に通じる行為なのである。しかし、この場合の自分自身を知るとは、ギリシャ、日本の教えのどちらにおいても、体の造作や器官、心の表層を知るということではない。それは倫理的な知であり、自らの心の内なる徳性を見つめることである。モムゼンはギリシャ人とローマ人を比較して、こう述べている。──礼拝のときにギリシャ人は天を仰ぐのに対して、ローマ人は顔にヴェールをかぶるという違いがある。ギリシャ人にとって礼拝は観想であるのに比して、ローマ人にとっては自らを見つめる**自省**の行為であるからだ、と。日本の宗教観はローマのものと基本的に似ており、自省することによって個人の徳性ではなく、国の意識が前面に出てくる。神道は自然崇拝であるところから、「くに」が我々の魂にとって親しみのあるものとなる。また先祖崇拝であるところから、万世一系の**天皇家**を「くに」の源とあおぐこととなる。日本人にとって国は、金を掘り出す土地、穀物を収穫する土壌であるにはとどまらない。神々、すなわち先祖たちの魂が宿る家なのである。天皇は単に「**法治国家**」の警察長官でも、「**文化国家**」のパトロンでもなく、この地上における天の化身

on its shining surface, and the act of worship is tantamount to the old Delphic injunction, **"Know Thyself."** But self-knowledge does not imply, either in the Greek or Japanese teaching, knowledge of the physical part of man, not his anatomy or his psycho-physics; knowledge was to be of a moral kind, the introspection of our moral nature. Mommsen, comparing the Greek and the Roman, says that when the former worshiped he raised his eyes to heaven, for his prayer was contemplation, while the latter veiled his head, for his was **reflection**. Essentially like the Roman conception of religion, our reflection brought into prominence not so much the moral as the national consciousness of the individual. Its nature-worship endeared the country to our inmost souls, while its ancestorworship, tracing from lineage to lineage, made **the Imperial family** the fountain-head of the whole nation. To us the country is more than land and soil from which to mine gold or to reap grain—it is the sacred abode of the gods, the spirits of our forefathers: to us the Emperor is more than the Arch Constable of a *Rechtsstaat*, or even the Patron of a *Culturstaat*—he is the bodily representative of Heav-

であり、天上の権威と慈悲をその一身にあわせ持っている。M. バウトミー[5]は、王とは「**権威の表象**であるにとどまらず、**国家の統合をもたらすそのシンボルでもある**」と述べたが、これがイギリスの王についてあてはまるなら——わたしはそのとおりだと思うが——日本の天皇には二重、三重にもあてはまる。

　神道の教義は、日本人の心情の二大特徴に関わっている。すなわち**愛国心**と**忠誠心**である。アーサー・メイ・クナップはいみじくもこう述べている。「ヘブライ文学では、著者の述べているのが神のことなのか、国のことなのか、天のことなのかエルサレムのことなのか、**救世主**のことなのか国家のことなのか、分からなくなることがある」と[6]。同様に、我が国の国家宗教の「神道」という名称にも、ある種の混乱がうかがえるだろう。ここで混乱といったのは、理詰めで考えようとすれば、この語が多義的であるところから、たしかにそのようにも見えるからである。しかし、神道は**国家観**と**民族的感情**の大枠ではあるものの、系統だった思想や、神学の理論を有しているわけではない。この宗教——むしろ、この宗教に表れている民族感情といったほうが正確だろうが

---

[5] *The English People*, p. 188.
[6] *Feudal and Modern Japan* Vol. I, p. 183.

en on earth, blending in his person its power and its **mercy**. If what M. Boutmy[5] says is true of English royalty—that it "is not only **the image of authority**, but **the author and symbol of national unity,**" as I believe it to be, doubly and trebly may this be affirmed of royalty in Japan.

The tenets of Shintoism cover the two predominating features of the emotional life of our race—**Patriotism** and **Loyalty**. Arthur May Knapp very truly says: "In Hebrew literature it is often difficult to tell whether the writer is speaking of God or of the Commonwealth; of heaven or of Jerusalem; of the **Messiah** or of the nation itself."[6] A similar confusion may be noticed in the nomenclature of our national faith. I said confusion, because it will be so deemed by a logical intellect on account of its verbal ambiguity; still, being a framework of **national instinct** and **race feelings**, Shintoism never pretends to a systematic philosophy or a rational theology. This religion—or, is it not more correct to say, the race emotions which this religion expressed?—thoroughly imbued Bushido

——から大きな影響をうけて、武士道は主君への忠誠と、愛国感情を特徴とすることとなった。これらの心情は教義というより、本能というべきものである。中世のキリスト教会では信者に信仰箇条（クレデンダ）を課したが、神道ではそのようなことはなく、単純素朴な行動規律を与えるのみであった。

　厳密な倫理体系という側面では、武士道は**孔子の教え**からきわめて大きな影響をうけている。孔子に挙げられている「五倫」、すなわち君臣の義、父子の親、夫婦の別、長幼の序、朋友の信は、孔子の書が中国から入ってくる以前から、民族の本能として存在していたのが、あらためて確認されたものである。政治と倫理にわたる孔子の教えは、冷静かつ慈愛にあふれ、世間知に富んでいるので、**支配階級**となった武士には、とくに相性よく感じられた。その貴族的で保守的な色調は、武によって立つ為政者のまさに必要とするところであった。孔子についで、**孟子**も武士道に大きな影をおとした。孟子の時として民衆擁護に淫する力強い学説は、**惻隠の情（同情**

with loyalty to the sovereign and love of country. These acted more as impulses than as doctrines; for Shintoism, unlike the Mediaeval Christian Church, prescribed to its votaries scarcely any *credenda*, furnishing them at the same time with *agenda* of a straightforward and simple type.

As to strictly ethical doctrines, **the teachings of Confucius** were the most prolific source of Bushido. His enunciation of the five moral relations between master and servant (the governing and the governed), father and son, husband and wife, older and younger brother, and between friend and friend, was but a confirmation of what the race instinct had recognized before his writings were introduced from China. The calm, benignant, and worldly-wise character of his politico-ethical precepts was particularly well suited to the samurai, who formed **the ruling class**. His aristocratic and conservative tone was well adapted to the requirements of these warrior statesmen. Next to Confucius, **Mencius** exercised an immense authority over Bushido. His forcible and often quite democratic theories were exceedingly taking to **sympathetic**

心）のゆたかな者にとってきわめて魅力的だが、現存の社会制度を脅かし、秩序潰乱のおそれがあるとすら考えられていたので、『孟子』はずっと批判のもとにあった。しかし、孟子の言葉は常に武士の心に宿っている。

　孔子と孟子の書は若年の者にとってはもっとも重要な教科書であり、大人にとっては物事の是非を論じるうえで最高の権威であった。ただしこれら聖人の書物といえども、日頃それに親しんでいるというだけでは尊敬されなかった。**孔子を頭だけで理解している**者をからかうことわざがある。「『論語』読みの『論語』知らず」という。文学の物知りのことを本の虫とけなした、いかにも武士らしい武士がいる。また、「学問は腐った野菜のようなもので、何度も煮なければ食えない。少し学問をした者は少し鼻につき、多く学問した者はひどく鼻につく。どちらも不愉快である」と言った武士もいる。これは、知識は**学ぶ者の心によく消化され、人格に現れ出て**こそ真の知識である、という意味である。頭で学ぶだけの者はただの機械である。知性は**倫理的感情**に従属すべ

natures, and they were even thought dangerous to, and subversive of, the existing social order, hence his works were for a long time under censure. Still, the words of this master mind found permanent lodgment in the heart of the samurai.

The writings of Confucius and Mencius formed the principal textbooks for youths and the highest authority in discussion among the old. A mere acquaintance with the classics of these two sages was held, however, in no high esteem. A common proverb ridicules one who has **only an intellectual knowledge of Confucius**, as a man ever studious but ignorant of *Analects*. A typical samurai calls a literary savant a book-smelling sot. Another compares learning to an ill-smelling vegetable that must be boiled and boiled before it is fit for use. A man who has read a little smells a little pedantic, and a man who has read much smells yet more so; both are alike unpleasant. The writer meant thereby that knowledge becomes really such only when **it is assimilated in the mind of the learner and shows in his character**. An intellectual specialist was considered a machine. Intellect itself was considered subordinate to **ethical emotion**. Man

きものと考えられていた。人も宇宙も魂をもち、倫理的なものとされていた。宇宙の過程は**人の道と無関係**であるというハクスリーの学説は、武士道とは無縁である。

　武士道は知識のための知識を軽蔑した。学問はそれ自体を目的とするのではなく、**一段高い叡智を得る**ための手段であった。よって、この目標に達せざる者は、求めれば詩や格言をひねり出せる便利な機械にすぎないと思われた。知は現実への応用と一致せねばならぬ、という考えであった。このようなソクラテス流の思想を主張した代表的な思想家として、中国の王陽明がいる。王陽明は「知行合一」を説いて飽くことがなかった。

　この問題を論じるついでに、しばし脱線をお許しいただきたい。もっとも高貴な武士たちは、この王陽明という思想家の教えに強い影響をうけた。西欧人が読めば、王陽明の学説には、**新約聖書**と共通するところが多いと感じるであろう。それぞれに特有の表現がなされているが、それを割り引いて考えるなら、「何よりもまず、神の国と神の義を求めなさい。そうすれば、これらのものはみな加えて与えられる」という一節に表されている思想は、王陽明の書物のほとんどどのページを開いても出

and the universe were conceived to be alike spiritual and ethical. Bushido could not accept the judgment of Huxley, that the cosmic process was **unmoral**.

Bushido made light of knowledge as such. It was not pursued as an end in itself, but as a means to **the attainment of wisdom**. Hence, he who stopped short of this end was regarded no higher than a convenient machine, which could turn out poems and maxims at bidding. Thus, knowledge was conceived as identical with its practical application in life; and this Socratic doctrine found its greatest exponent in the Chinese philosopher, Wan Yang Ming, who never wearies of repeating, **"To know and to act are one and the same."**

I beg leave for a moment's digression while I am on this subject, inasmuch as some of the noblest types of *bushi* were strongly influenced by the teachings of this sage. Western readers will easily recognize in his writings many parallels to **the New Testament**. Making allowance for the terms peculiar to either teaching, the passage, "Seek ye first the kingdom of God and his righteousness; and all these things shall be added unto you," conveys a thought that may be

てくる。王陽明に学んだある日本人[7] はこう述べている
——「万物を統べる天地の主は、人の心の中に住んでお
り、その心そのものとなる。よって心は生きており、常
に明々と輝いている」と。またこうも言う——「人の本
質の魂の光は純にして、意志によって濁らされることは
ない。それは人の心に自ずと灯り、正と邪をおしえ、良
心と呼ばれる。まさしく天の神よりきたる光である」
と。このような言葉は、まるでアイザック・ペニントン
など神秘思想家の書物から出てきたようではないか！単
純な神道の教えからも明らかにうかがえる**日本的な心性**
には、王陽明の学説を受け入れやすい素地があるのでは
ないかと思う。王陽明は、良心は絶対に誤ることがない
という考えを、極限にまで押しすすめた超越論的思想を
主張し、正邪を判別する能力にとどまらず、心理現象や
物理現象の本質を見抜く能力があると論じた。そしてバ
ークレーやフィヒテの観念論を超えているとはいわない
にしても、それに近いところまで行き、人間に知覚でき
ないものは存在しないとまで主張している。王陽明の思
想には**唯我論**につきものの**論理的誤謬**があるが、強い確

---

[7] 三輪執斎（みわしっさい）

found on almost any page of Wan Yang Ming. A Japanese disciple[7] of his says—"The lord of heaven and earth, of all living beings, dwelling in the heart of man, becomes his mind (*Kokoro*); hence a mind is a living thing, and is ever luminous:" and again, "The spiritual light of our essential being is pure, and is not affected by the will of man. Spontaneously springing up in our mind, it shows what is right and wrong: it is then called conscience; it is even the light that proceedeth from the god of heaven." How very much do these words sound like some passages from Isaac Pennington or other philosophic mystics! I am inclined to think that **the Japanese mind**, as expressed in the simple tenets of the Shinto religion, was particularly open to the reception of Yang Ming's precepts. He carried his doctrine of the infallibility of conscience to extreme transcendentalism, attributing to it the faculty to perceive, not only the distinction between right and wrong, but also the nature of psychical facts and physical phenomena. He went as far as, if not farther than, Berkeley and Fichte, in Idealism, denying the existence of things outside of human ken. If his system had all **the logical errors** charged to **Solip-**

信が人を動かし、**人格を鍛え乱れぬ心をつくる**という倫理的な意義のあることは否定できない。

　このように、源流が何であれ、武士道が影響をうけ、取り入れてきた**重要な原理**はほんの少数の、単純なものにすぎない。そして我が国の歴史でもっとも混乱し、きわめて危険の大きかった時代を、安全に生き抜くには、この少数の単純な原理でじゅうぶんだったのである。**武士の先祖たち**は健全で単純素朴な人々であったが、体系をなさない、一にぎりの平凡な教えから、精神を養うたっぷりの栄養を得た。それは**古代の思想**のいわば大街道や脇道から拾い集めてきた知恵であったが、時代の要求に応じ、それを基にして、独自の形で男性の理想を作り上げたのである。フランス学会の俊英であるM・ド・ラ・マゼリエールは、十六世紀について自分の印象をこのようにまとめている。——「十六世紀半ば、日本は政府も、社会も、教会もすべてが混乱の極みにあった。しかし、相次ぐ内乱に世の人の風儀が獣へと堕し、人それぞれが自らのために義をたてねばならなくなったとき、十六世紀のイタリア人にも比すべき大人物が形成されて

sism, it had all the efficacy of strong conviction and its moral import in **developing individuality of character and equanimity of temper** cannot be gainsaid.

Thus, whatever the sources, the **essential principles** which *Bushido* imbibed from them and assimilated to itself, were few and simple. Few and simple as these were, they were sufficient to furnish a safe conduct of life even through the unsafest days of the most unsettled period of our nation's history. The wholesome, unsophisticated nature of **our warrior ancestors** derived ample food for their spirit from a sheaf of commonplace and fragmentary teachings, gleaned as it were on the highways and byways of **ancient thought**, and, stimulated by the demands of the age, formed from these gleanings anew and unique type of manhood. An acute French savant, M. de la Mazelière, thus sums up his impressions of the sixteenth century: —"Toward the middle of the sixteenth century, all is confusion in Japan, in the government, in society, in the church. But the civil wars, the manners returning to barbarism, the necessity for each to execute justice for himself,—these formed men comparable to those Italians of the sixteenth century, in whom

きた。テーヌが『生命あふれる積極性、一瞬の決断と乾坤一擲の勝負に出る習慣、なみはずれた行動と忍耐を許容する器の大きさ』を賞賛したような人物が登場してきたのだ。イタリアと同じく日本でも、『中世の粗暴な気風が人間を鍛えて、武術にたけ、抵抗力が大であるすばらしい動物へと仕立てあげた』のである。そのために、**日本民族の一番の特質**が、十六世紀にきわめて顕著に現れでた。**気質**のみならず心も、人によって大きな違いがある。インドや中国では、主として活動力や知性に個人差があるが、日本では人格の面でも個々人で大きく異なっている。**個人の独自性**はすぐれた民族、発達した文明のあかしである。ニーチェの好んだ言い方を用いるなら、『人間のことを話すのに、アジアではあれこれの平野を比べるようなものだが、日本とヨーロッパでは、先ずもってどんな山があるかを語る』と言えるだろう」。

　では、M・ド・ラ・マゼリエールが上のように記した人々の、共通する特徴について考えてみることにしよう。

Taine praises 'the vigorous initiative, the habit of sudden resolutions and desperate undertakings, the grand capacity to do and to suffer.' In Japan as in Italy 'the rude manners of the Middle Ages made of man a superb animal, wholly militant and wholly resistant.' And this is why the sixteenth century displays in the highest degree **the principal quality of the Japanese race**, that great diversity which one finds there between minds (*esprits*) as well as between **temperaments**. While in India and even in China men seem to differ chiefly in degree of energy or intelligence, in Japan they differ by originality of character as well. Now, **individuality** is the sign of superior races and of civilizations already developed. If we make use of an expression dear to Nietzsche, we might say that in Asia, to speak of humanity is to speak of its plains; in Japan as in Europe, one represents it above all by its mountains."

To the pervading characteristics of the men of whom M. de la Mazelière writes, let us now address ourselves.

第3章

廉直、
または「義」

　まずは**廉直**（まっすぐ）であること、または**「義」**（正しい道）である。これは**武士の行動規律**のなかでもっとも力強い教えである。武士にとって忌むべきことの第一は、裏取引や曲がったふるまいである。ここで「廉直」という語を用いるとやや誤解を生じるかもしれない。意味が狭められるきらいがなくもないからである。ある著名な武士によれば「それは**決意する力である**」という。——「廉直とは、理性に基づいて**何らかの行動をとることを決意**し、そこからぶれない力である。死ぬことが正しい場合には死ぬ、打つことが正しい場合には打つことだ」と。また別の武士の言によればこうである。「廉直は、**堅忍不抜**の精神力をもたらす骨である。骨がなければ脊椎は首を支えず、手も動かず、足も立たないのと同様、廉直でなければ、いかに学問や才能があれども武士にはなれない。廉直であれば、才と学がなくても

CHAPTER 3

RECTITUDE OR JUSTICE

I shall begin with **rectitude** or **justice**, the most cogent precept in **the code of the samurai**. Nothing is more loathsome to him than underhand dealings and crooked undertakings. The conception of Rectitude may be erroneous—it may be narrow. A well-known bushi defines it as **a power of resolution**;—"Rectitude is the power of **deciding upon a certain course of conduct** in accordance with reason, without wavering;—to die when it is right to die, to strike when to strike is right." Another speaks of it in the following terms: "Rectitude is the bone that gives **firmness** and stature. As without bones the head cannot rest on the top of the spine, nor hands move nor feet stand, so without rectitude neither talent nor learning can make of a human frame a samurai. With it the lack of accomplishments is as nothing." Mencius calls

かまわない」と。人の心は**慈愛**であり、「廉直」あるい
は「**義**」とは人の道であると孟子は説いた。「この道を
忘れはて、心を失い、取り戻すことを知らぬとは、なん
と嘆かわしいことか! 鶏や犬を失えば、取り戻すすべを
知っているのに、心を失うと取り戻すすべを知らない」
という。これを読むとまさに「鏡を通しておぼろに」
(『コリントの信徒への手紙1 13：12』)の思いがする。
孟子の三百年後に、異なる土地で、人類の偉大な師であ
ったキリストが話した寓話も同じ趣旨である。キリスト
は自らのことを、人が失ったものを見出すための「義の
道」であると言ったのであった。話が少しわきにそれた
が、孟子によれば、「義」とは失われた楽園を回復する
ために人がとるべき、狭くてまっすぐな道のことであ
る。

　封建制の後期となり、平和の日々がつづくと武士階級
の生活にも余暇が生じ、さまざまの娯楽や、おとなしい
学芸が行われるようになったが、そんな時代になって
も、「**義士**」(まっすぐな人)と称されることは、学芸の
練達を意味するどんな褒辞にもまさると考えられてい
た。我が国の民衆教育で重んじられる四十七人の忠臣
は、「**四十七人の義士**」と一般に呼ばれている。

Benevolence man's mind, and Rectitude or **Righteousness** his path. "How lamentable," he exclaims, "is it to neglect the path and not pursue it, to lose the mind and not know to seek it again! When men's fowls and dogs are lost, they know to seek for them again, but they lose their mind and do not know to seek for it." Have we not here "as in a glass darkly" a parable propounded three hundred years later in another clime and by a greater Teacher, who called Himself the Way of Righteousness, through whom the lost could be found? But I stray from my point. Righteousness, according to Mencius, is a straight and narrow path which a man ought to take to regain the lost paradise.

Even in the latter days of feudalism, when the long continuance of peace brought leisure into the life of the warrior class, and with it dissipations of all kinds and gentle accomplishments, the epithet *Gishi* (**a man of rectitude**) was considered superior to any name that signified mastery of learning or art. The Forty-seven Faithfuls—of whom so much is made in our popular education—are known in common parlance as **the Forty-seven *Gishi*.**

狡猾な企みが戦略とみなされ、まっかな虚言が戦術と
して用いられる今の世の中にあって、この**嘘のないまっ
すぐな男の美徳**は、なによりも輝かしい、最高の賛辞に
あたいする宝石ではなかろうか。「廉直」は、もう一つ
の武士の徳である**「勇気」**と双子の関係にある。しか
し、「勇気」に話を進めるまえに、「廉直」から派生した
一つの表現に触れておこう。当初はほんの僅かなずれに
すぎなかったのが、しだいに大きく乖離し、今では一般
に曲解されて用いられるようになった語、すなわち「義
理」である。文字通りには「正しい理由」という意味で
あるにもかかわらず、今では世間をおもんぱかって何か
を果たさねばならない、**漠然とした義務感を意味する**よ
うになっている。しかし、まじりけのない文脈では、本
来純粋で単純な義務という意味であった。両親への「義
理」、目上の人への「義理」、部下への「義理」、社会全
体への「義理」などという場合はそうである。これらの
例では、「義理」は義務である。**「正しい理由」が求め、
命じることを行うことが、「義務」でなくて何であろう**
か。我々にとって、「正しい理由」こそが「定言的命令」
でなければならない。
　このように、本来の「義理」は、ただ義務を意味した
にすぎない。例えば我々の両親にたいするふるまいにお

In times when cunning artifice was liable to pass for military tact and downright falsehood for *ruse de guerre*, this **manly virtue, frank and honest**, was a jewel that shone the brightest and was most highly praised. Rectitude is a twin brother to **Valor**, another martial virtue. But before proceeding to speak of Valor, let me linger a little while on what I may term a derivation from Rectitude, which, at first deviating slightly from its original, became more and more removed from it, until its meaning was perverted in the popular acceptance. I speak of *Gi-ri*, literally the Right Reason, but which came in time to **mean a vague sense of duty** which public opinion expected an incumbent to fulfil. In its original and unalloyed sense, it meant duty, pure and simple,—hence, we speak of the *Giri* we owe to parents, to superiors, to inferiors, to society at large, and so forth. In these instances *Giri* is duty; for what else is duty than **what Right Reason demands and commands us to do**. Should not Right Reason be our categorical imperative?

Giri primarily meant no more than duty, and I dare say its etymology was derived from the fact that in

いては、愛情が唯一の動機であるべきだが、それを欠く場合、**孝心をむりにでも引き出す権威**がなければならない。そこで作られたのが「義理」である。これは妥当な考え方である。愛情が徳を果たさないなら、知にはたらきかけ、理によって正しい行為へと導かねばならない。その他の義務についても同じことである。「義務」が必要とあらば、「正しい理由」が乗り込んできて、怠慢をゆるさない。このような意味の「義理」はきびしい見張り人であり、ムチをふるってなまけ者を動かそうとする。ただし倫理的には、これはいわば**奥の手**である。人を動かす動機としては、愛が「法^{のり}」であるとするキリスト教の教義に比べると、はるかに劣っている。「義理」は、人工的に作られた社会の、諸条件によって生み出されたものであると思われる。**生まれた境遇や、根拠のない特権**によって**階層の序列**が生じているこの社会では、**家が社会単位**であり、年齢の上下が才能の上下より重要とされ、**自然の愛情**よりも**人が恣意的に作った習慣**が優先されることも多いのである。このように「義理」は不自然に架構された観念なので、やがて堕落し、行動のよ

our conduct, say to our parents, though love should be the only motive, lacking that, there must be some other **authority to enforce filial piety**; and they formulated this authority in *Giri*. Very rightly did they formulate this authority —*Giri*—since if love does not rush to deeds of virtue, recourse must be had to man's intellect and his reason must be quickened to convince him of the necessity of acting aright. The same is true of any other moral obligation. The instant Duty becomes onerous, Right Reason steps in to prevent our shirking it. *Giri* thus understood is a severe taskmaster, with a birch-rod in his hand to make sluggards perform their part. It is a **secondary power** in ethics; as a motive it is infinitely inferior to the Christian doctrine of love, which should be *the* law. I deem it a product of the conditions of an artificial society—of a society in which **accident of birth and unmerited favour** instituted **class distinctions**, in which **the family was the social unit**, in which seniority of age was of more account than superiority of talents, in which **natural affections** had often to succumb before **arbitrary man-made customs**. Because of this very artificiality, *Giri* in time degenerated into

しあしを漠然と判断する語になってしまった。例えば、やむをえない事情にせまられた母親が、長子を救うために他の子どもを犠牲にする理由を述べたり、父親の放蕩の穴埋めに、娘が自分を遊里に売って金をこしらえることを是認したりという場合に用いられるのである。元来の「義理」は「正しい理由」を意味したものの、いまや落ちぶれはて、**詭弁**に利用されていると私は思う。人の非難をむやみに恐れる、臆病者の隠れ蓑に堕している。スコットが愛国心について言ったことが、そのまま「義理」にもあてはまる。スコットいわく「それはもっとも美しいがゆえにもっとも怪しい、**他の感情を隠すための仮面である**」。「義理」は「正しい理由」をとびこえて、あるいはその下にもぐりこんで、その美しい名とは似ても似つかない奇々怪々な怪物となりはてた。その翼の下に、**詭弁と偽善**を隠しもっている。

a vague sense of propriety called up to explain this and sanction that,—as, for example, why a mother must, if need be, sacrifice all her other children in order to save the first-born; or why a daughter must sell her chastity to get funds to pay for the father's dissipation, and the like. Starting as Right Reason, *Giri* has, in my opinion, often stooped to **casuistry**. It has even degenerated into cowardly fear of censure. I might say of *Giri* what Scott wrote of patriotism, that "as it is the fairest, so it is often the most suspicious, **mask of other feelings**." Carried beyond or below Right Reason, *Giri* became a monstrous misnomer. It harbored under its wings every sort of **sophistry and hypocrisy**.

第4章

勇気、
勇猛心と不動の心

それ（義理）は臆病者の巣窟になりかねないところだったが、武士道はそれを許さなかった。武士道では、勇気、勇猛心、不動の心などの徳が、繊細かつ正しく理解されている。勇気は**正義のために用いる**のでなければ、徳とはみなされない。『**論語**』では、孔子がよく行うように、その逆が何かという形で「勇気」が定義されている。「義を見てせざるは勇なきなり」という。ひっくり返すと「**勇気とは正しいことをすることである**」ということになる。どんな危難にもひるまず、**身を危険にさらし**、死の顎に敢然ととびこんでいく――一般にこれが勇気とされ、武人のあいだでそんな無謀なふるまいが潔しとされるが、それはシェイクスピアが言うところの「生まれそこないの勇気」にほかならず、賞賛にはあたら

CHAPTER 4

COURAGE, THE SPIRIT OF DARING AND BEARING

It might easily have been turned into a nest of cowardice, if Bushido had not a keen and correct sense of courage, the spirit of daring and bearing, to the consideration of which we shall now return.Courage was scarcely deemed worthy to be counted among virtues, unless it was **exercised in the cause of Righteousness**. In his *Analects* Confucius defines Courage by explaining, as is often his wont, what its negative is. "Perceiving what is right," he says, "and doing it not, argues lack of courage." Put this epigram into a positive statement, and it runs, **"Courage is doing what is right."** To run all kinds of hazards, **to jeopardize one's self**, to rush into the jaws of death— these are too often identified with Valor, and in the profession of arms such rashness of conduct—what Shakespeare calls, "valor misbegot"—is unjustly applauded; but not

ず、武士道では厳に戒められている。**死ぬに価しないことのために死ぬ**のは、「犬死」だと軽蔑される。水戸光圀公は「戦いの渦にとびこんで死ぬのはかんたんなことだ。どんな雑兵にだってできる。生きることが正しいときに生き、死ぬのが正しいときにのみ死ぬのが真の勇気である」と述べている。光圀公は、プラトンが「恐れるべきものと恐れるべきでないものを区別できるのが勇気である」と述べたことは知らなかっただろう。西洋では**精神の勇気と肉体の勇気**が区別されるが、そのことは日本でも大昔から理解されていた。武士の子弟は、「大勇」と「蛮勇」という言葉を耳にたこができるほど聞かされていたのである。

　勇気、剛勇、敢為、勇猛、豪胆——これらは**若者の心にうったえやすく、手本と訓練により鍛えることができる**。いわばもっとも人気のある徳目であり、若年の者は競い合って身につけようとする。**いくさの手柄話**は、ほとんど男児が母親の乳房を離れもしない前から、くりかえし聞かされる。幼児が泣こうものなら、母親はこういって叱る——「そんなくらいで痛いといって泣くとは、

so in the Precepts of Knighthood. **Death for a cause unworthy of dying for**, was called a "dog's death." "To rush into the thick of battle and to be slain in it," says a Prince of Mito, "is easy enough, and the merest churl is equal to the task; but," he continues, "it is true courage to live when it is right to live, and to die only when it is right to die," and yet the Prince had not even heard of the name of Plato, who defines courage as "the knowledge of things that a man should fear and that he should not fear." A distinction which is made in the West between **moral and physical courage** has long been recognized among us. What samurai youth has not heard of "Great Valor" and the "Valor of a Villein?"

Valor, Fortitude, Bravery, Fearlessness, Courage, being the qualities of soul which **appeal most easily to juvenile minds**, and which **can be trained by exercise and example**, were, so to speak, the most popular virtues, early emulated among the youth. **Stories of military exploits** were repeated almost before boys left their mother's breast. Does a little booby cry for any ache? The mother scolds him in this fashion: "What a coward to cry for a trifling pain! What will

なんて弱虫だこと！いくさで腕を切り落とされたら、切腹を命じられたらどうするのですか」と。歌舞伎の『仙台萩』で、いたいけな若殿が小姓にむかって、「籠に寄りくる親鳥の、餌ばみをすれば小雀の、嘴さしよるありさまに、小鳥を羨む稚心にも、侍の子は、ひもじい目をするのが忠義じゃ」といって、けなげにも空腹をがまんする物語は世に広く知られている。勇猛心や肝っ玉の逸話は数知れず、幼児に語り聞かせて、おさな心に勇気と豪胆を教えこむが、方法はそれだけではない。親はほとんど情け容赦なく、子どもがありったけの勇気をしぼりだすよう、困難な試練をあたえることがある。ことわざに**「獅子は我が子を千尋の谷に落とす」**というが、武士の子は深い谷に落とされ、シジフォスのような試練をあたえられる。**ひもじい目にあわせ、寒さをがまんさせる**ことは、忍耐心を養うのによいと考えられている。幼い子どもが言伝を託され、見知らぬ他人のもとに遣られる

you do when your arm is cut off in battle? What when you are called upon to commit *hara-kiri*?" We all know the pathetic fortitude of a famished little boy-prince of Sendai, who in the drama is made to say to his little page, "Seest thou those tiny sparrows in the nest, how their yellow bills are opened wide, and now see! there comes their mother with worms to feed them. How eagerly and happily the little ones eat! but for a samurai, when his stomach is empty, it is a disgrace to feel hunger." Anecdotes of fortitude and bravery abound in nursery tales, though stories of this kind are not by any means the only method of early imbuing the spirit with daring and fearlessness. Parents, with sternness sometimes verging on cruelty, set their children to tasks that called forth all the pluck that was in them. **"Bears hurl their cubs down the gorge,"** they said. Samurai's sons were let down the steep valleys of hardship, and spurred to Sisyphus-like tasks. Occasional **deprivation of food or exposure to cold**, was considered a highly efficacious test for inuring them to endurance. Children of tender age were sent among utter strangers with some message to deliver, were made to rise before the sun, and before

ことがある。夜明け前に起こされ、朝食前に素読のけい
こに行くが、寒い冬でもはだしで師範のところへと通わ
される。学問の神の祭礼など、月に一、二度、数人が集
まり、**夜を徹して交代ごうたいで素読の練習をする**。ま
た少年たちは、**処刑場、墓地、幽霊が出るという家**など
様々の怖い場所に行って肝試しをする。斬首が公開で行
われていた時代に、幼い少年たちはその場面を見に行か
されるばかりか、暗闇のなか一人で処刑場をおとずれ、
たしかに来たという証拠に生首に印をつけるということ
までやらされたものだ。

　現代の教育者は、こんな風に**胆力を鍛えるスパルタ顔
負けのやり方**に嫌悪をおぼえ、そんな教育をすると粗暴
な子どもができてしまうのではないか、おさな心に芽生
えた**優しい感情**を摘み取ってしまうのではないかと、疑
いの目を向けるのではなかろうか。ここでさらに、武士
道で考えられている、胆力の他の側面を眺めてみよう。

　勇気ある心は、つねに**穏やか**にして、**冷静沈着**でいる
のがその証_{あかし}である。動かざるときは泰然としているの
が、勇気である。静にあっては泰然自若、動にあっては
豪胆敢為、それが勇気のありようだ。勇者の心はつねに

breakfast attend to their reading exercises, walking to their teacher with bare feet in the cold of winter; they frequently—once or twice a month, as on the festival of a god of learning,—came together in small groups and **passed the night without sleep, in reading aloud by turns**. Pilgrimages to all sorts of uncanny places—to **execution grounds**, to **graveyards**, to **houses reputed to be haunted**, were favorite pastimes of the young. In the days when decapitation was public, not only were small boys sent to witness the ghastly scene, but they were made to visit alone the place in the darkness of night and there to leave a mark of their visit on the trunkless head.

Does this **ultra-Spartan system of "drilling the nerves"** strike the modern pedagogist with horror and doubt—doubt whether the tendency would not be brutalizing, nipping in the bud the tender emotions of the heart? Let us see what other concepts Bushido had of Valor.

The spiritual aspect of valor is evidenced by **composure—calm** presence of mind. Tranquillity is courage in repose. It is a statical manifestation of valor, as daring deeds are a dynamical. A truly brave man is

明鏡止水である。ものに動じるということがない。こころの平静を乱されることはない。**戦いのさなかでも冷静である**。大惨事がおきても心は平らかである。地震に揺すぶられることなく、嵐にむかって莞爾と笑っている。身を脅かす危険や死がせまっても、**自己を失わない者**こそ、真に偉大であると賞賛される。例えば、危険がふりかかってきても詩歌をひねり、死に面しても句を唱える。手もふるえず声もかすれずそのように振る舞えるのが**器の大きな人間のあかし**であり、それが心の余裕というものである。そのように焦ることなく、雑念のない心は、つねに何かを受け入れる余地を残しているのだ。

　歴史上の真実として伝わっている逸話をご紹介しよう。江戸城を築いた太田道灌が槍で刺された。刺客は道灌の詩心を知っていたので、このような上の句を口ずさんだ。

　　かかる時さこそ命の惜しからめ

ever serene; he is never taken by surprise; nothing ruffles the equanimity of his spirit. **In the heat of battle he remains cool**; in the midst of catastrophes he keeps level his mind. Earthquakes do not shake him, he laughs at storms. We admire him as truly great, who, in the menacing presence of danger or death, **retains his self-possession**; who, for instance, can compose a poem under impending peril or hum a strain in the face of death. Such indulgence betraying no tremor in the writing or in the voice, is taken as an **infallible index of a large nature**—of what we call a capacious mind (*Yoyū*), which, for from being pressed or crowded, has always room for something more.

It passes current among us as a piece of authentic history, that as Ōta Dokan, the great builder of the castle of Tokyo, was pierced through with a spear, his assassin, knowing the poetical predilection of his victim, accompanied his thrust with this couplet—

> "Ah! how in moments like these
>   Our heart doth grudge the light of life;"

命の尽きようとしている道灌は、脇腹の致命傷にいささかもひるむことなく、下の句を詠んだのであった。

　　かねて無き身と思い知らずば

　勇者の心には軽みさえある。平凡な人間には大真面目なことでも、勇者にとっては戯れにすぎないこともある。例えば、昔の合戦では、敵味方が気の利いた言葉を投げかわし、和歌の応酬をはじめるなどということも稀ではなかった。**いくさとは腕力のみならず、知を競わせる場でもあったのだ。**

　そのような例として、十一世紀の末におきた衣川の合戦が挙げられよう。東軍が敗走し、大将の安倍貞任が逃げた。追ってきた敵の大将、源義家が「敵に背を向けるとは武士の風上にもおけぬやつ」と呼ばわると、貞任は手綱をひいた。そこで追っ手の将が、その場で浮かんだ歌で呼びかけた。

　　衣のたてはほころびにけり

whereupon the expiring hero, not one whit daunted by the mortal wound in his side, added the lines—

"Had not in hours of peace,
  It learned to lightly look on life."

There is even a sportive element in a courageous nature. Things which are serious to ordinary people, may be but play to the valiant. Hence in old warfare it was not at all rare for the parties to a conflict to exchange repartee or to begin a rhetorical contest. **Combat was not solely a matter of brute force; it was, as well, an intellectual engagement.**

Of such character was the battle fought on the bank of the Koromo River, late in the eleventh century. The eastern army routed, its leader, Sadato, took to flight. When the pursuing general pressed him hard and called aloud—"It is a disgrace for a warrior to show his back to the enemy," Sadato reined his horse; upon this the conquering chief shouted an impromptu verse—

"Torn into shreds is the warp of the cloth(*koromo*)."

するとすかさず、返しの句がすらすらと敗軍の将の口
から出てきた。

　　　年を経し糸のみだれの苦しさに

　これを聞いた義家は、つがえていた弓を下げ、馬の頭^{こうべ}
をめぐらせて相手を逃してやった。この不可解なふるま
いを人が不審がると、敵に追いつめられても平常心を失
わない者を殺すのは忍びないと答えたのであった。

　ブルータスの死に際してアントニウスとオクタヴィア
ヌスを襲った悲しみは、勇者一般の経験であろう。武田
信玄と十四年間戦った上杉謙信は、信玄の訃報を聞いた
とき「**かけがえのない敵**を失った」といって号泣した。
この謙信の信玄へのふるまいは、**時と世をこえ、気高い
模範として記憶されるべき**ものである。信玄の領地が海
から遠い山国であったため、塩を東海道の北条家の領地
から得ていた。ところが、北条は信玄といくさはしてい

Scarcely had the words escaped his lips when the defeated warrior, undismayed, completed the couplet—

"Since age has worn its threads by use."

Yoshiie, whose bow had all the while been bent, suddenly unstrung it and turned away, leaving his prospective victim to do as he pleased. When asked the reason of his strange behavior, he replied that he could not bear to put to shame one who had kept his presence of mind while hotly pursued by his enemy.

The sorrow which overtook Antony and Octavius at the death of Brutus, has been the general experience of brave men. Kenshin, who fought for fourteen years with Shingen, when he heard of the latter's death, wept aloud at the loss of **"the best of enemies."** It was this same Kenshin who had **set a noble example for all time**, in his treatment of Shingen, whose provinces lay in a mountainous region quite away from the sea, and who had consequently depended upon the Hōjō provinces of the Tokaido for salt. The Hōjō prince wishing to weaken him, al-

ないものの、武田の力を弱体化させることを狙って、信玄との塩の取引を禁じた。宿敵の苦難を聞き及んだ謙信は、自らの支配地の海岸で塩が採れるので、信玄に書状をおくって**北条の当主の了見のせまさ**を難じ、自分は貴殿といくさをしているが、貴殿に大量の塩を送るよう臣下の者に指示したと告げた。そして曰く、「**わたしは塩ではなく刀で戦っているのだ**」と。ローマの将カミルスが残した名言「我らは金ではなく鉄で戦う」とまるで同じではないか。また、「汝、敵を誇るべし。しからば、敵の勝利は汝の勝利とならん」というニーチェの言も、武士の心を代弁している。いくさに際しては、**平時にあって友と呼ぶにふさわしい者**と戦うべし、というのが勇気と名誉がともに命じるところなのである。

though not openly at war with him, had cut off from Shingen all traffic in this important article. Kenshin, hearing of his enemy's dilemma and able to obtain his salt from the coast of his own dominions, wrote Shingen that in his opinion **the Hōjō lord had committed a very mean act**, and that although he (Kenshin) was at war with him (Shingen) he had ordered his subjects to furnish him with plenty of salt-adding, **"I do not fight with salt, but with the sword,"** affording more than a parallel to the words of Camillus, "We Romans do not fight with gold, but with iron." Nietzsche spoke for the samurai heart when he wrote, "You are to be proud of your enemy; then, the success of your enemy is your success also." Indeed valor and honor alike required that we should own as enemies in war only such as **prove worthy of being friends in peace**.

第5章

仁、
惻隠の心

　勇気がこの高みに達することができたあかつきには、それは仁（慈悲）及び惻隠の心（不幸な人への共感）、すなわち他者への愛、同情と憐憫へと近づく。そしてこの仁愛こそが最高の美徳にして、人間の魂の最高の資質であることは、古往今来、万人の一致するところである。仁は二重の意味で美徳の王者と考えられている。高貴な魂にそなわっている様々の徳目のなかでも、それが最高のものであるというのが一つ。そして、とくに君主にこそふさわしい徳であるというのが第二の点である。シェイクスピアに指摘されるまでもなく――ただし、それを流麗な詩文にのせるにはシェイクスピアの筆を俟たねばならなかったが――王には王冠より仁のほうが似合い、仁の力は王笏をもしのぐのである。人の上に立つ者にもっとも必要なものが仁であると、孔子、孟子はくりかえし述べている。孔子は「王に徳をもたせよ。そうす

CHAPTER 5

BENEVOLENCE, THE FEELING OF DISTRESS

When valor attains this height, it becomes akin to **benevolence**, the feeling of distress, love, magnanimity, **affection for others**, **sympathy** and **pity**, which were ever recognized to be supreme virtues, **the highest of all the attributes of the human soul**. Benevolence was deemed a princely virtue in a twofold sense;—princely among the manifold attributes of a **noble spirit**; princely as particularly befitting a princely profession. We needed no Shakespeare to feel—though, perhaps, like the rest of the world, we needed him to express it—that **mercy became a monarch better than his crown**, that it was above his sceptered sway. How often both Confucius and Mencius repeat the highest requirement of a ruler of men to consist in benevolence. Confucius would say, "Let but a prince cultivate virtue, people will flock to

れば民はおのずから集まり、民とともに諸国もなびくだ
ろう。諸国がなびけば富が増すだろう。富が増せば風儀
がよくなる。徳が根で、富が果実である」と述べた。さ
らにまた「王が仁を愛すれば、民が義を愛さないという
ことはない」とも述べている。孟子もこれと符節を合わ
せるかのように、「小邦ならば仁のない者が最高の位に
たっした例はあるが、仁を欠く者が大国を手に入れた例
はいまだ聞いたことがない」と述べている。さらに「民
の心が従わない者が君主となることはできない」ともい
う。このように孔子、孟子のいずれも仁は君主に不可欠
の徳であるとし、「仁は人である」と言い切っている。
封建制はややもすれば軍事専制の国になりはてるが、
我々を君主の専横から救ってくれるのが仁である。支配
される者が「身命」をあまさず捧げれば、支配する者に
は自分勝手な意志のみが残り、その当然の結果として絶
対の専制政治が生じる。これはよく**「東洋的専制」**など

him; with people will come to him lands; lands will bring forth for him wealth; wealth will give him the benefit of right uses. Virtue is the root, and wealth an outcome." Again, "Never has there been a case of a sovereign loving benevolence, and the people not loving righteousness," Mencius follows close at his heels and says, "Instances are on record where individuals attained to supreme power in a single state, without benevolence, but never have I heard of a whole empire falling into the hands of one who lacked this virtue." Also,—"It is impossible that any one should become ruler of the people to whom they have not yielded the subjection of their hearts." Both defined this indispensable requirement in a ruler by saying, "Benevolence—Benevolence is Man." Under the régime of feudalism, which could easily be perverted into militarism, it was to Benevolence that we owed our deliverance from despotism of the worst kind. An utter surrender of "life and limb" on the part of the governed would have left nothing for the governing but self-will, and this has for its natural consequence the growth of that absolutism so often called **"oriental despotism,"**—as though there were no despots of

と呼ばれるが、西洋の歴史にだって事例には欠かない！

　専制政治を擁護するつもりは毛頭ないが、封建制と専制政治を同一視するのはあやまりである。フレデリック大王は「**王は国の第一の召使である**」と記したが、このとき法学者たちは自由発展の歴史の中で、**新たな時代のはじまり**を認識した。奇しくも時をおなじくして、東北日本の陬邑（いなか）で、米沢藩主、上杉鷹山はまったく同じことを述べ、封建制は、専制君主及び民の抑圧とは一線を画する必要のあることを示した。**封建制の主君**はたとえ**臣下の者への自らの責務**を忘れても、先祖と天への高邁な責務を感じていた。すなわち主君は臣民にとって父親であり、臣民は天からの預かりものであった。この擬似的な父子関係は、「武士道」のふつうの意味には含まれないものの、心地よいものとして受け止められていた。それは、これほど親身にはなってくれない、優しいおじさん（"サムおじさん"）の政治とは違うのである。**専制国家と父権的国家の違い**は、前者では人は**不承ぶしょう従う**のに対して、後者は「**誇り高き屈服、威厳ある服従**であり、心を他の支配下におくものの、自由であるとい

occidental history!

Let it be far from me to uphold despotism of any sort; but it is a mistake to identify feudalism with it. When Frederick the Great wrote that **"Kings are the first servants of the State,"** jurists thought rightly that **a new era was reached** in the development of freedom. Strangely coinciding in time, in the back-woods of North-western Japan, Yozan of Yonézawa made exactly the same declaration, showing that feudalism was not all tyranny and oppression. **A feudal prince**, although unmindful of **owing reciprocal obligations to his vassals**, felt a higher sense of responsibility to his ancestors and to Heaven. He was a father to his subjects, whom Heaven entrusted to his care. In a sense not usually assigned to the term, Bushido accepted and corroborated paternal government—paternal also as opposed to the less interested avuncular government (Uncle Sam's, to wit!). **The difference between a despotic and a paternal government** lies in this, that in the one the people **obey reluctantly**, while in the other they do so with "that **proud submission**, that **dignified obedience**, that subordination of heart which kept alive, even in servi-

う高揚感が胸に生き続ける」のである[8]。古いことわざがある。——英国王は「悪魔を治めている。英国民はしょっちゅう反乱をおこし、王を取りかえるから」。これに対してフランス王は「ロバを治めている。民にのほうずもなく税金と義務を背負わせるから」。スペイン王は「人間を治めている。臣民は嬉々として**服従している**から」。——なるほど一面の真理をついているが、話をもとにもどそう。

アングロサクソン系の人々には、「徳」と「絶対的権力」は**相容れない概念**であるように見えるかもしれない。ロシアの政治家ポベドノスツェフは、国家の成り立ちにおいて、イギリスとその他ヨーロッパの国々が対照的であることをはっきりと示してくれた。つまり、ヨーロッパの国々は、**共通の利害に基づいて秩序づけられて**いるのにたいして、イギリスは**独立独歩の個性が高度に発達している**点が特徴だという。ヨーロッパ大陸の国々に加えて、スラブ系の諸民族でとくに顕著だが、こうした地域では、個人が何らかの社会関係に依存し、最終的には国家目標に依存していると、ポベドノスツェフは述べているが、このことは日本に、二重にあてはまる。したがって日本人は、**君主による自由な権力の行使**につい

[8] Burke, *French Revolution*.

tude itself, the spirit of exalted freedom."[8] The old saying is not entirely false which called the king of England the "king of devils, because of his subjects' often insurrections against, and depositions of, their princes," and which made the French monarch the "king of asses, because of their infinite taxes and Impositions," but which gave the title of "the king of men" to the sovereign of Spain "because of his subjects' **willing obedience**." But enough!—

Virtue and absolute power may strike the Anglo-Saxon mind as terms which it is **impossible to harmonize**. Pobyedonostseff has clearly set before us the contrast in the foundations of English and other European communities; namely that these were organized on the basis of **common interest**, while that was distinguished by a **strongly developed independent personality**. What this Russian statesman says of the personal dependence of individuals on some social alliance and in the end of ends of the State, among the continental nations of Europe and particularly among Slavonic peoples, is doubly true of the Japanese. Hence not only is **a free exercise of monarchical power** not felt as heavily by us as in Europe,

て、ヨーロッパほどに重荷に感じないばかりか、**臣民の気持ちを思いやる父親のような配慮**を感じるがゆえに、なおさら重圧感が弱められている。ビスマルクは「絶対主義は先ず第一に、君主が**公平であること、正直であること、義務を果たすこと、努力を惜しまないこと、心が謙虚であること**を要請する」と述べている。もう一つ引用を許していただけるなら、ドイツ皇帝がコブレンツで行った演説をひいておきたい。「神の御はからいによって王となるが、王には重い責務があり、創造主なる神にとてつもない責任を負い、いかなる人、大臣、議会によっても解任されない」という。

　仁は慈しむ母のような徳である。まっすぐな「廉直」ときびしい「義」が男性的とするなら、「仁」には女性的な優しさと、なめらかさが感じられる。しかし、無際限に優しいのはいけない、義と廉直でひきしめなければならない、と言われる。正宗の有名な格言がある。**「義に過ぎれば固くなる。仁に過ぎれば弱くなる」**のである。

　幸いなことに、仁は美しいばかりか、普遍的でもある。**「もっとも勇ある者はもっとも優しく、愛する者は**

but it is generally moderated by **parental consideration for the feelings of the people**. "Absolutism," says Bismarck, "primarily demands in the ruler **impartiality**, **honesty**, **devotion to duty**, **energy** and **inward humility**." If I may be allowed to make one more quotation on this subject, I will cite from the speech of the German Emperor at Coblenz, in which he spoke of "Kingship, by the grace of God, with its heavy duties, its tremendous responsibility to the Creator alone, from which no man, no minister, no parliament, can release the monarch."

We knew Benevolence was a **tender virtue and mother-like**. If upright Rectitude and stern Justice were peculiarly masculine, Mercy had the gentleness and the persuasiveness of a feminine nature. We were warned against indulging in indiscriminate charity, without seasoning it with justice and rectitude. Masamuné expressed it well in his oft-quoted aphorism—**"Rectitude carried to excess hardens into stiffness; Benevolence indulged beyond measure sinks into weakness."**

Fortunately Mercy was not so rare as it was beautiful, for it is universally true that "**The bravest are the**

恐れを知らない」という。「**武士の情け**」という言葉には、人の高貴な心の琴線をただちに共鳴させる響きがある。といっても、武士の慈悲心が、他の人の慈悲心とは種類が異なっているというわけではない。ただし、それは単に**見境のない衝動ではなく**、義をきちんとわきまえたものである。ただ一つの感情であるにとどまらず、**生殺与奪の力**をそなえたものであるからだ。経済学者が需要について、有効か有効でないかなどというが、これとまったくおなじ意味で、武士の慈悲心は「有効である」と言っておこう。それを受ける者を幸にも不幸にもする力がそなわっているからである。

　武士は粗野な武力と、それを利用する特権を誇りとしてはいるものの、仁愛の力を説く孟子の教えにはまったく同意している。孟子いわく、「水が火を抑えるように、仁はその力を阻むものを抑える。水が炎を消す力のあることを疑うのは、コップ一杯の水で、荷車の干し草を焼く炎を消そうとする者のみである」。またこうも述べている。「**惻隠の心**は仁のはじまり。であるがゆえに、仁

tenderest, the loving are the daring." "*Bushi no na-sakê*"—**the tenderness of a warrior**—had a sound which appealed at once to whatever was noble in us; not that the mercy of a samurai was generically different from the mercy of any other being, but because it implied mercy where mercy was **not a blind impulse**, but where it recognized due regard to justice, and where mercy did not remain merely a certain state of mind, but where it was backed with **power to save or kill**. As economists speak of demand as being effectual or ineffectual, similarly we may call the mercy of bushi effectual, since it implied the power of acting for the good or detriment of the recipient.

Priding themselves as they did in their brute strength and privileges to turn it into account, the samurai gave full consent to what Mencius taught concerning the power of Love. "Benevolence," he says, "brings under its sway whatever hinders its power, just as water subdues fire: they only doubt the power of water to quench flames who try to extinguish with a cupful a whole burning wagonload of fagots." He also says that "**the feeling of distress** is the root of benevolence, therefore a benevolent man is ever

者は苦しみ悲しむ者のことをつねに懐っている」と。よって、孟子は、**同情心の上に倫理哲学を打ち立てた**アダム・スミスのはるかなる先駆者であるといえる。

　ある国の武人の名誉の掟が、他国のものといかに似通っていることか、まことに不思議なものがある。東洋の**道徳観念**はさんざん貶められているが、それとそっくり同じものが、ヨーロッパ文学に表されたもっとも高貴な格言にも存在するのである。詩人ウェルギリウスがローマに呼びかける、有名な一節をひいておこう。

　　これこそが汝の征服の道、和睦の条件をあたえ、
　　卑しき者をいたわり、奢れる者をひきずりおろす。

　これを日本の武士が見れば、我が国の詩文よりの剽窃（ひょうせつ）であると、マントヴァの詩聖ウェルギリウスを責めるであろう。**弱き者、虐げられし者、敗れた者への慈悲**は、いかにも武士にふさわしい徳であるとされてきた。日本画の愛好家におなじみの一つの図柄がある。**一人の僧が牛の背にうしろ向きに座っている**。この僧とは、かつて泣く子も黙るといわれた、勇猛果敢な武将熊谷直実のことである。歴史に残る決戦として名高い須磨の浦の合戦（紀元一一八四年）で、逃げる敵に追いすがり、**一騎討**

mindful of those who are suffering and in distress." Thus did Mencius long anticipate Adam Smith who **founds his ethical philosophy on Sympathy**.

It is indeed striking how closely the code of knightly honor of one country coincides with that of others; in other words, how the much abused oriental **ideas of morals** find their counterparts in the noblest maxims of European literature. If the well-known lines,

> Hae tibi erunt artes—pacisque imponere morem,
> Parcere subjectis, et debellare superbos,

were shown a Japanese gentleman, he might readily accuse the Mantuan bard of plagiarizing from the literature of his own country. **Benevolence to the weak, the downtrodden or the vanquished**, was ever extolled as peculiarly becoming to a samurai. Lovers of Japanese art must be familiar with the representation of **a priest riding backwards on a cow**. The rider was once a warrior who in his day made his name a byword of terror. In that terrible battle of Sumano-ura, (1184 A.D.), which was one of the most decisive in our history, he overtook an enemy and in **single**

ちのすえに松の幹のようなその腕で敵を組み伏せた。こ
のような場合、相手が将士か、同等の力量の者でないか
ぎり、血を流さぬというのが**いくさの掟**であった。馬の
りになった直実は、名を名乗れとせまるが、相手があく
まで拒むので兜を引きむしった。すると色白で髭もはえ
ぬ童顔が出てきた。思わず直実の手がゆるむ。直実は相
手を抱き起こし、**父親のようにやさしく**「若殿、母のも
とに帰るのだ！熊谷の刀をそなたの血で汚すわけにはゆ
かぬ。さあ、敵にみつかる前に、あの道をつたって逃げ
るのだ！」と諭した。ところが貴公子は逃げようとせ
ず、お互いの名誉のため、どうかこの場で首をはねてく
れと懇願した。直実の振りかざした刃が、白髪の頭の上
で冷たくきらめく。これまで幾度となく敵の玉の緒を情
け容赦なく断ちきってきた刃だったが、このとき、武者
の分厚い胸は憐れみにうち震えた。けさもけさ、勇んで
初陣へと駆け出していったわが子の姿が目の前に浮か
ぶ。太い手が小刻みにゆれた。熊谷はもう一度、逃げて
命を全くしてくれるよう哀願したが、いかに説いても相

combat had him in the clutch of his gigantic arms. Now the **etiquette of war** required that on such occasions no blood should be spilt, unless the weaker party proved to be a man of rank or ability equal to that of the stronger. The grim combatant would have the name of the man under him; but he refusing to make it known, his helmet was ruthlessly torn off, when the sight of a juvenile face, fair and beardless, made the astonished knight relax his hold. Helping the youth to his feet, **in paternal tones** he bade the stripling go: "Off, young prince, to thy mother's side! The sword of Kumagaye shall never be tarnished by a drop of thy blood. Haste and flee o'er yon pass before thy enemies come in sight!" The young warrior refused to go and begged Kumagaye, for the honor of both, to despatch him on the spot. Above the hoary head of the veteran gleams the cold blade, which many a time before has sundered the chords of life, but his stout heart quails; there flashes athwart his mental eye the vision of his own boy, who this self-same day marched to the sound of bugle to try his maiden arms; the strong hand of the warrior quivers; again he begs his victim to flee for his life. Finding all his entreaties vain and

手は聞く耳を持たない。同軍の者たちの近づく足音が聞こえる。やむなく、「名もなき者の手にかかるのは不憫じゃ。後のご供養はこの直実がつかまつる！」という言葉とともに、白い刃が空に一閃し、落ちてきたときには幼い武者の赤い血に染まっていた。いくさが終わり、直実は凱旋したものの、もはや手柄にも武名にも心は動かなかった。**頭をまるめて出家し、身を墨染の衣にくるんで巡礼の旅に明け暮れる日々となった。**その後は日の沈む先にある、西方浄土に背を向けることがなかった。

　この話には問題がある、倫理的に正しくないという批判がある。だが、そんなことはどうでもよい。武士道では、いかに血にまみれた武功でさえ、情愛、憐憫、慈しみがつきものであるということを、この逸話は教えてくれているのである。「窮鳥懐に入れば猟師も殺さず」という古いことわざもある。このように考えると、**キリスト教精神の典型といわれる赤十字の運動**が、なぜかくも容易に日本の地に根付いたのかがよく分かる。我が国最高の作家である滝沢馬琴は**ジュネーブ条約**のことなど知る由もなかったが、日本にそれが知識として入ってくる

hearing the approaching steps of his comrades, he exclaims: "If thou art overtaken, thou mayest fall at a more ignoble hand than mine. O, thou Infinite! receive his soul!" In an instant the sword flashes in the air, and when it falls it is red with adolescent blood. When the war is ended, we find our soldier returning in triumph, but little cares he now for honor or fame; **he renounces his warlike career, shaves his head, dons a priestly garb**, devotes the rest of his days to **holy pilgrimage**, never turning his back to the West, where lies the Paradise whence salvation comes and whither the sun hastes daily for his rest.

Critics may point out flaws in this story, which is casuistically vulnerable. Let it be: all the same it shows that Tenderness, Pity and Love, were traits which adorned the most sanguinary exploits of the samurai. It was an old maxim among them that "It becometh not the fowler to slay the bird which takes refuge in his bosom." This in a large measure explains why **the Red Cross movement, considered peculiarly Christian**, so readily found a firm footing among us. For decades before we heard of the **Geneva Convention**, Bakin, our greatest novelist, had famil-

数十年前に、人気の物語に、**倒れた敵の手当てをする話**を登場させている。また薩摩の国は**尚武の気風と薫陶**で有名だが、若者が音楽をたしなむ風習がひろく行われている。音楽といっても、「血と死の到来をかまびすしく知らせる前触れ」、すなわち我らを猛虎のふるまいへとかきたてる、勇壮なラッパや太鼓のたぐいではない。哀調ある琵琶 [9] のやさしい音色が、血気さかんな心を温和にし、血のにおいと、殺戮（さつりく）の光景から思いを遠ざけてくれるのである。ポリュビオスが紹介しているアルカディアの法では、三十歳以下のすべての若者は音楽をたしなむべしとされている。音楽という優しい芸術によって、自然のきびしいこの地方の厳格な気風にも耐えやすくしようというのである。そしてアルカディアの山地の中でも、とくにこの地方で人心が穏やかなのは、音楽のおかげだという。

　武家の人々の心に優しさを涵養（かんよう）しようとしたのは、薩摩だけのことではない。白河の藩主、松平定信（楽翁）はつれづれの思いを筆に残したが、その中に次のような一節がある。「静まった夜更けに、そっと枕元をおとず

---

[9] ギターに似た楽器

iarized us with **the medical treatment of a fallen foe**. In the principality of Satsuma, noted for its **martial spirit and education**, the custom prevailed for young men to practice music; not the blast of trumpets or the beat of drums,—"those clamorous harbingers of blood and death"—stirring us to imitate the actions of a tiger, but sad and tender melodies on the *biwa*,[9] soothing our fiery spirits, drawing our thoughts away from scent of blood and scenes of carnage. Polybius tells us of the Constitution of Arcadia, which required all youths under thirty to practice music, in order that this gentle art might alleviate the rigors of that inclement region. It is to its influence that he attributes the absence of cruelty in that part of the Arcadian mountains.

Nor was Satsuma the only place in Japan where **gentleness was inculcated among the warrior class**. A Prince of Shirakawa jots down his **random thoughts**, and among them is the following: "Though they come stealing to your bedside in the silent watches of the

---

[9] A musical instrument, resembling the guitar.

れてくるものを楽しむがよい。すなわち花の香り、遠くの鐘の音、寒夜の虫の声」。さらに「腹をたてず大目に見るのがよいものは、花を散らす風、月を隠す雲、何かと言いがかりをつける者」ともいう。

　詩歌を作ることが奨励されたのはこうした優しい気持ちを表現するにとどまらず、これを訓育しようという意図があったからである。**よって日本の詩歌は、哀しみと優しさがベースになっている。**よく知られた、田舎侍の逸話をここにご紹介しよう。ある侍が俳諧をたしなむよう勧められた。はじめての題が「鶯の音」[10] だった。荒々しい気性はこれに反発し、ぶこつな一句を師匠にむかって投げつけた。

　　　鶯の初音（はつね）をきく耳は別にしておく武士かな

---

[10] 英語では warbler。日本のナイチンゲールとも称される。

night, drive not away, but rather cherish these—the fragrance of flowers, the sound of distant bells, the insect humming of a frosty night." And again, "Though they may wound your feelings, these three you have only to forgive, the breeze that scatters your flowers, the cloud that hides your moon, and the man who tries to pick quarrels with you."

It was ostensibly to express, but actually to cultivate, these gentler emotions that **the writing of verses was encouraged. Our poetry has therefore a strong undercurrent of pathos and tenderness.** A well-known anecdote of a rustic samurai illustrates a case in point. When he was told to learn versification, and "The Warbler's Notes"[10] was given him for the subject of his first attempt, his fiery spirit rebelled and he flung at the feet of his master this uncouth production, which ran

"The brave warrior keeps apart
The ear that might listen
To the warbler's song."

---

[10] The *uguisu* or warbler, sometimes called the nightingale of Japan.

師匠はこんな粗野な心にも動じることなく、根気よく
教えつづけたところ、この侍の魂が美しい音に目覚め、
鶯の美しい声に感応するようになり、

　　　武士の鶯きいて立ちにけり

と詠んだのであった。

　夭折したドイツの詩人ケルナーは、我々が賛嘆してや
まない、一つの雄々しい逸話を残している。この詩人は
戦場で傷を負って倒れながら、「人生への告別」を書い
たのである。しかしこのような例は、我が国のいくさ場
では枚挙にいとまがない。日本の短詩形は、**単純な感情**
をその場でまとめるのに適している。いかなる教育程度
であれ、日本人は――うまい、へたはあるが――みな歌
人である。行軍する将士がふと立ち止まり、帯から矢立
をとりだして詩歌を詠じることは稀ではない。そして、
そのような者がいくさの野に斃れたとき、兜や胸板の中
から書きつけが見つかるのである。

His master, undaunted by the crude sentiment, continued to encourage the youth, until one day the music of his soul was awakened to respond to the sweet notes of the *uguisu*, and he wrote

"Stands the warrior, mailed and strong,
To hear the uguisu's song,
Warbled sweet the trees among."

We admire and enjoy the heroic incident in Körner's short life, when, as he lay wounded on the battle-field, he scribbled his famous *Farewell to Life*. Incidents of a similar kind were not at all unusual in our warfare. Our pithy, epigrammatic poems were particularly well suited to the improvisation of a **single sentiment**. Everybody of any education was either a poet or a poetaster. Not infrequently a marching soldier might be seen to halt, take his writing utensils from his belt, and compose an ode,—and such papers were found afterward in the helmets or the breast-plates, when these were removed from their lifeless wearers.

第 6 章

礼儀正しさ

いくさの恐怖の最中に憐憫の情をうながすのに、ヨーロッパにあってはキリスト教がその役割を負っていたが、日本では音楽と詩文を愛する心によってなされた。優しい感情を教えることで、他者の苦しみへのまなざしが育まれるのである。そして**他者の気持ちをうやまう**ところから、**謙虚で親切な心**が生まれてくる。謙虚で親切な心は、礼儀の根本である。日本人のていねいで垢抜けた礼儀は、海外から訪れる人々がひとしく、日本の際立った特徴として挙げるものである。

礼儀正しさは、はしたなく見えるのが怖いというだけのことなら、つまらない美徳である。本来は、他人の立場に身をおき、その気持ちに配慮しているのが自然と外に現れ出ている、といったものでなければならない。礼儀の感覚には**物事の軽重や正しさを尊重する気持ち**も含まれ、したがって社会的な上下の差は尊重される。ただし元来これは人爵ではなく天爵、すなわち財産によって

CHAPTER 6

POLITENESS

What Christianity has done in Europe toward rousing compassion in the midst of belligerent horrors, love of music and letters has done in Japan. The cultivation of tender feelings breeds considerate regard for the sufferings of others. **Modesty and complaisance**, actuated by **respect for others' feelings**, are at the root of politeness, that courtesy and urbanity of manners which has been noticed by every foreign tourist as a marked Japanese trait.

Politeness is a poor virtue, if it is actuated only by a fear of offending good taste, whereas it should be the outward manifestation of a sympathetic regard for the feelings of others. It also implies **a due regard for the fitness of things**, therefore due respect to social positions; for these latter express no plutocratic distinc-

もたらされる身分の差ではなく、**人となりから、おのずからにじみ出てくる品格**にもとづく階層であった。

　最高の礼儀は「愛」に近づく。聖書の章句の「愛」を「礼儀」にかえて、こういうことができるだろう。すなわち、礼儀は「辛抱強く、親切である。人をうらやまず己をほこらず、慢心しない。みっともない振る舞いはせず、自らを利することを求めず、容易に腹をたてず、悪を眼中に入れない」と。してみれば、ディーン教授が人間性の六要素を挙げたとき、礼儀を高い位置においたことに何の不思議があろうか。それは社交におけるもっとも熟した果実なのであるから。

　ただし、このように礼儀を讃えはするものの、それを最高の美徳とすることは私の意の中にはない。きちんと分析すれば、礼儀は他のもっと重要な美徳と関連しあっていることが分かる。美徳はそれぞれが孤立して存在しているのではない。礼儀は武士の徳として称揚され、その本来の価値よりも尊重されているにもかかわらず――というより、むしろそれが原因で、似て非なるまがい物を生み出すこととなった。孔子の『礼記』でも、楽の音そのものが「礼」の本質ではないのと同じく、外見は礼儀の本質ではないということが、くりかえし述べられている。

　礼儀が尊重され、**社交の必須**とされると、若者に社会での正しいふるまいを教えるために、**複雑な作法の体系**

tions, but were originally **distinctions for actual merit**.

In its highest form, politeness almost approaches love. We may reverently say, politeness "suffereth long, and is kind; envieth not, vaunteth not itself, is not puffed up; doth not behave itself unseemly, seeketh not her own, is not easily provoked, taketh not account of evil." Is it any wonder that Professor Dean, in speaking of the six elements of Humanity, accords to Politeness an exalted position, inasmuch as it is the ripest fruit of social intercourse?

While thus extolling Politeness, far be it from me to put it in the front rank of virtues. If we analyze it, we shall find it correlated with other virtues of a higher order; for what virtue stands alone? While—or rather because—it was exalted as peculiar to the profession of arms, and as such esteemed in a degree higher than its deserts, there came into existence its counterfeits. Confucius himself has repeatedly taught that external appurtenances are as little a part of propriety as sounds are of music.

When propriety was elevated **to the *sine qua non* of social intercourse**, it was only to be expected that **an elaborate system of etiquette** should come into

がはやってくるのは当然のことである。人に話しかける
ときにどのようにお辞儀するか、どのように歩き、座る
のがよいか、念入りしごくに教えられ、学ばれた。食事
の作法は一つの科学になった。茶の湯のもてなしは一つ
の儀式となった。そして言うまでもなく、**教養人**はこう
したことをすべて身につけているものとされた。ヴェブ
レン氏がその興味深い著作[11] の中で、礼儀は「**有閑階
級の生活の産物であり、その形象である**」と述べている
のは、まったく正しい。

　ヨーロッパの人間が日本の念の入った礼儀作法のこと
を、貶すのを耳にしたことがある。日本人はそんな作法
のことばかり考えており、そこまで厳密にこだわろうと
するのは愚の骨頂だという。たしかに日本の**儀式ばった
作法に、不必要な細則があるのは事実**だが、これを愚か
というなら、目まぐるしく変わるファッションに西洋人
がこだわるのとどちらが愚かなのか、私には判断がつき
かねる。ただし、ファッションといえども、私には単に
はすっぱな見栄だとは思えない。むしろ、**つねに美しい
ものを求める人間精神の発現**だと思っている。いわんや
礼儀においてをや、である。凝った儀式はくだらないこ
だわりなどではない。それは、ある一定の結果を得るに

---

[11] *Theory of the Leisure Class*, N.Y. 1899, p. 46.

vogue to train youth in correct social behavior. How one must bow in accosting others, how he must walk and sit, were taught and learned with utmost care. Table manners grew to be a science. Tea serving and drinking were raised to a ceremony. **A man of education** is, of course, expected to be master of all these. Very fitly does Mr. Veblen, in his interesting book,[11] call decorum "a product and an exponent of **the leisure-class life**."

I have heard slighting remarks made by Europeans upon our elaborate discipline of politeness. It has been criticized as absorbing too much of our thought and in so far a folly to observe strict obedience to it. I admit that **there may be unnecessary niceties in ceremonious etiquette**, but whether it partakes as much of folly as the adherence to ever-changing fashions of the West, is a question not very clear to my mind. Even fashions I do not consider solely as freaks of vanity; on the contrary, I look upon these as **a ceaseless search of the human mind for the beautiful**. Much less do I consider elaborate ceremony as altogether trivial; for it denotes the result of long observation as to the most appropriate method of

はどのような方法がもっともふさわしいのか、長年にわたって観察されてきた成果なのである。何事を行うにも、もっとも適した方法が必ずあり、**もっとも適した方法とは、もっとも無駄のない雅なかたちをとるものである**。スペンサー氏は「雅」とは、もっとも無駄のない動きのことであるという。茶の湯では、抹茶椀、さじ、ふきん等々を扱うときの動作の型が決まっている。しろうとには面倒なだけの作法に見える。だが、決められている方法が、けっきょくは時間と手間をもっとも節約する方法であることがすぐに分かる。それが力をもっとも合理的に使う方法なのだから、スペンサーがいうような意味で、もっとも雅な動作だといえよう。

社会的な作法の精神的な意義（カーライルの『衣装哲学』から表現を借りるなら、「作法と儀式を衣装としてまとっている、規律ある精神」ということにでもなろうか）は、その外見から想像されるところより、はるかに重要である。スペンサー氏の例にならって、日本の様々な儀式作法を研究し、その起源と、それを生み出した倫理的な動機を探ってみるのも面白いかもしれないが、それはこの本のテーマではない。私が焦点を当てたいのは、**礼儀作法を厳密に守ることが、人格の陶冶につながるということである**。

achieving a certain result. If there is anything to do, there is certainly a best way to do it, and **the best way is both the most economical and the most graceful**. Mr. Spencer defines grace as the most economical manner of motion. The tea ceremony presents certain definite ways of manipulating a bowl, a spoon, a napkin, etc. To a novice it looks tedious. But one soon discovers that the way prescribed is, after all, the most saving of time and labor; in other words, the most economical use of force,—hence, according to Spencer's dictum, the most graceful.

The spiritual significance of social decorum,—or, I might say, to borrow from the vocabulary of the *Philosophy of Clothes*, the spiritual discipline of which etiquette and ceremony are mere outward garments,—is out of all proportion to what their appearance warrants us in believing. I might follow the example of Mr. Spencer and trace in our ceremonial institutions their origins and the moral motives that gave rise to them; but that is not what I shall endeavor to do in this book. It is **the moral training involved in strict observance of propriety**, that I wish to emphasize.

日本の作法は限りなく洗練され、きわめて細かい規則ができていると述べた。様々な流派が誕生して、様々な流儀を教えているというのが現状である。しかし、すべてに共通する、**究極の本質**がある。もっとも有名な流派である小笠原流の代表者は、こう述べている。「礼儀作法の目的は、たとえ静かに座っていても、いかなる狼藉者も襲うすきがないというところまで、**心を鍛えることだ**」と。言い換えれば、**正しい作法をつねに鍛錬することで**、肉体のすべての部分と能力が完全に意のままに従い、完璧に肉体や環境と調和するので、そこに**精神が肉体を支配していることが形に現れる**のである。こう考えると、フランス語の「ビアンセアンス」[12] という単語が、ここに新たに深い意味を得たことになると言えるだろう！

「雅」が力の節約を意味するという仮定が真だとするなら、その論理的帰結として、**雅な振る舞い**を常におこなうことで、**力が蓄積し、充満する**ことになる。したがっ

---

[12] 語源的には「きちんと座っていること」を意味する

I have said that etiquette was elaborated into the finest niceties, so much so that different schools advocating different systems, came into existence. But they all united in **the ultimate essential**, and this was put by a great exponent of the best known school of etiquette, the Ogasawara, in the following terms: "The end of all etiquette is to so **cultivate your mind** that even when you are quietly seated, not the roughest ruffian can dare make onset on your person." It means, in other words, that by **constant exercise in correct manners**, one brings all the parts and faculties of his body into perfect order and into such harmony with itself and its environment as to **express the mastery of spirit over the flesh**. What a new and deep significance the French word *bienséance*[12] comes thus to contain!

If the premise is true that gracefulness means economy of force, then it follows as a logical sequence that a constant practice of **graceful deportment** must bring with it **a reserve and storage of force**. Fine manners,

_____

[12] Etymologically *well-seatedness*.

て、美しい作法は**力の漲った静止**を意味する。ガリアの
蛮人がローマを襲ったとき、元老院になだれ込み、尊敬
すべき長老たちの髭を引っ張ったというが、こんなこと
になったのは、長老たちが、威厳ある、力の漲った作法
を欠いていたからである。作法の鍛錬により、精神の高
みに達することはできるだろうか？ そんなことは言う
までもない。すべての道はローマに通ずる、と言うでは
ないか！

　**単純きわまりない事柄が芸術にまで高められ、やがて
精神文化の一部となる**例として、茶の湯、すなわち飲茶
の儀式を挙げておきたい。**茶を飲むことが芸術**だという
と驚くかもしれないが、考えてみるがよい。太古の人間
が岩の上に絵を刻み、砂の上に子どもが絵を描く。そこ
から後のラファエルやミケランジェロが誕生してきた。
茶を飲むという行為は、もっと大きな可能性を秘めてい
る。最初はヒンドゥー教の道士が瞑想の具としてはじめ
たものが、宗教と道徳に付随するものへと育っていくの
は当然のことであった。**乱れぬ思い、波だたぬ心、物静
かで冷静なふるまい**は茶の湯の基本中の基本だが、これ
こそが**正しい思考、正しい心の持ち方への第一条件**であ
る。ささやかで清浄な茶室にこもれば、狂騒的な世間の
人の姿が見えず、声も聞こえない。そこにいるだけで

therefore, mean **power in repose**. When the barbarian Gauls, during the sack of Rome, burst into the assembled Senate and dared pull the beards of the venerable Fathers, we think the old gentlemen were to blame, inasmuch as they lacked dignity and strength of manners. Is lofty spiritual attainment really possible through etiquette? Why not?—All roads lead to Rome!

As an example of how **the simplest thing can be made into an art and then become spiritual culture**, I may take *Cha-no-yu*, the tea ceremony. **Tea-sipping as a fine art!** Why should it not be? In the children drawing pictures on the sand, or in the savage carving on a rock, was the promise of a Raphael or a Michael Angelo. How much more is the drinking of a beverage, which began with the transcendental contemplation of a Hindoo anchorite, entitled to develop into a handmaid of Religion and Morality? That **calmness of mind**, that **serenity of temper**, that **composure and quietness of demeanor**, which are the first essentials of *Cha-no-yu* are without doubt **the first conditions of right thinking and right feeling**. The scrupulous cleanliness of the little room, shut off from sight and sound of the

心が俗世から遠ざかっていく。西洋の客間には絵や骨董のたぐいが所狭しと飾られているものだが、茶室には家具もおかないので、心が乱れることもない。掛け物 [13] は色彩よりも**形の妙**に人の思いをいざなう。**趣味を究極まで洗練させること**、それこそが狙いである。派手なものは徹底的に忌み嫌われ、追放される。戦乱やいくさの噂が絶えなかった時代に、瞑想をこととする隠者によって創（はじ）められたという事実からも、茶の湯という伝統が、ただの**暇つぶし**ではないことが分かる。静かな茶室という空間に入っていくに際して、集まった一同は刀をおき、それとともにいくさ場の荒れた気分や、政（まつりごと）の苦労をそこにおろして、安らかな心のもとに一期一会を楽しむのである。

　茶の湯は一つの儀式にはとどまらず、芸術である。詩である。その韻律はしぐさに表現されている。それは「魂を鍛え、整えるための手段」である。この表現にこそ、そのもっとも大きな意味合いが、表されている。茶の湯に親しむ人々は、その効用として別の言葉を思い浮

---

[13] 掛け軸のこと。装飾として壁につるす書や画のこと。

madding crowd, is in itself **conducive to direct one's thoughts from the world**. The bare interior does not engross one's attention like the innumerable pictures and bric-a-brac of a Western parlor; the presence of *kakemono*[13] calls our attention more to **grace of design** than to beauty of color. **The utmost refinement of taste** is the object aimed at; whereas anything like display is banished with religious horror. The very fact that it was invented by a contemplative recluse, in a time when wars and the rumors of wars were incessant, is well calculated to show that this institution was more than **a pastime**. Before entering the quiet precincts of the tea-room, the company assembling to partake of the ceremony laid aside, together with their swords, the ferocity of the battle-field or the cares of government, there to find peace and friendship.

Cha-no-yu **is more than a ceremony—it is a fine art**; it is poetry, with articulate gestures for rhythm: it is a *modus operandi* of soul discipline. Its greatest value lies in this last phase. Not infrequently the other phases

---

[13] Hanging scrolls, which may be either paintings or ideograms, used for decorative purposes.

かべることも少なくないが、精神的な意味合いこそがその本質であることにかわりはない。

　礼儀作法は**立ち居ふるまいを美しくしてくれる**というだけでも、**身につける価値があるが**、その役割はそれだけには終わらない。礼儀は、他への親切心と、自らをつつしむ謙譲の心に発し、他人(ひと)の気持ちを思いやる優しい感情によってもたらされるものであるがゆえに、それは**常に心の共感を美しく表現するもの**となる。泣く人とともに泣き、喜ぶ人とともに喜ぶことのできる心でなければならない。このような要請は、日々の人生のささやかな出来事の中では、ほとんど目にもとまらない、小さな行為として現れる。たとえ目にとまったとしても、二十年来日本に住んでいる宣教師の夫人にとっては、「とっても滑稽」なものだったと、彼女は私に話した。彼女は日の照りつける真っ昼間に、日傘も帽子もなく外にいた。一人の日本人の知り合いが通りかかったので、挨拶をすると、相手はただちに帽子を脱いだ。これはまあ、ごく自然なしぐさだが、「とっても滑稽」だったというのは、話をしているあいだ、相手はずっと日傘を下げたままで、自らも日に照りつけられて立っていたのである。「ほんとうにお馬鹿なこと！」と言いたくなるかもしれない。まさにその通りなのだが、この人の気持ちを聞いたらそうは言えないだろう。すなわち「あなたは日

preponderated in the mind of its votaries, but that does not prove that its essence was not of a spiritual nature.

Politeness will **be a great acquisition**, if it does no more than **impart grace to manners**; but its function does not stop here. For propriety, springing as it does from motives of benevolence and modesty, and actuated by tender feelings toward the sensibilities of others, is ever **a graceful expression of sympathy**. Its requirement is that we should weep with those that weep and rejoice with those that rejoice. Such didactic requirement, when reduced into small every-day details of life, expresses itself in little acts scarcely noticeable, or, if noticed, is, as one missionary lady of twenty years' residence once said to me, "awfully funny." You are out in the hot glaring sun with no shade over you; a Japanese acquaintance passes by; you accost him, and instantly his hat is off—well, that is perfectly natural, but the "awfully funny" performance is, that all the while he talks with you his parasol is down and he stands in the glaring sun also. How foolish!— Yes, exactly so, provided the motive were less than this: "You are in the sun; I sympathize with

向にいる。私は気の毒に感じている。傘がもっと大きかったら、あるいはもっと親しい間柄だったら、傘に入れてあげたいところだが、それができないので、あなたの不愉快を私も味わうことにしよう」という気持ちなのである。これと同じくらい滑稽、あるいはさらにもっと滑稽かもしれない些細な行為が日常的に行われるが、これをうわべだけのしぐさ、**お決まりの動作**だと片づけてはいけない。そこには**他人の気持ちを思いやる、思慮あふれる感情**が表れているのである。

　もう一つ、日本の礼儀のしきたりから出てくる、「とっても滑稽」な習慣がある。日本について書いている上っ面しか見ない者たちは、**この国では何もかもあべこべだと言って片づける**が、これを経験したことのある外国人は一様に、どう応えればよいのか戸惑ったと打ち明ける。すなわち、プレゼントをするとき、アメリカではプレゼントする相手に向かって、これは実にすばらしい品物だと謳い上げるが、**日本は逆で、謙遜したりけなしたりする**のである。アメリカ人の考えはこうだ。「これはすばらしいプレゼントです。すばらしくなければ、あなたに差し上げるなんて勇気はありません。すばらしくないものを差し上げるなんて、侮辱じゃないですか」。対する日本人の論理はこうだ。「あなたはすてきな人です。**どんなにすてきなプレゼントでも、あなたにふさわしい**

you; I would willingly take you under my parasol if it were large enough, or if we were familiarly acquainted; as I cannot shade you, I will share your discomforts." Little acts of this kind, equally or more amusing, are not mere gestures or **conventionalities**. They are the "bodying forth" of **thoughtful feelings for the comfort of others**.

Another "awfully funny" custom is dictated by our canons of Politeness; but many superficial writers on Japan, have dismissed it by **simply attributing it to the general topsy-turvyness of the nation**. Every foreigner who has observed it will confess the awkwardness he felt in making proper reply upon the occasion. In America, when you make a gift, you sing its praises to the recipient; **in Japan we depreciate or slander it**. The underlying idea with you is, "This is a nice gift: if it were not nice I would not dare give it to you; for it will be an insult to give you anything but what is nice." In contrast to this, our logic runs: "You are a nice person, and **no gift is nice enough for you**.

ものなどあるはずがありません。私があなたの足下に捧げるものは、どうか、もっぱらわたしの好意のしるしとしてお受け取りください。この品のそのものの価値のためではなく、それが表す意味合いを汲んでお受け取りください。どんなにすばらしい品物でも、あなたにふさわしい価値があるなどと言うのは、あなたへの侮辱でしかありません」。この二つの考え方を並べてみよう。究極の考えはまったく同一である。どちらも「とっても滑稽」どころではない。アメリカ人はプレゼントを構成しているモノについて語っている。日本人はプレゼントを差し上げる精神を語っているのだ。

　どんな小さなふるまいにも日本人の礼儀感覚が現れるものだが、だからといって、もっとも瑣末なものを取り上げ、それを典型として、礼儀作法そのものに断を下すのは、理屈としていかがなものであろうか。食べることと、食事の作法を守ることのどちらが重要であろうか。この質問に、ある中国の思想家が答えている。「食べることはきわめて重要で、作法を守ることはさほど重要ではないと一般に言えるとして、この二つを比較したときに、単純に食べることのほうが重要だと言えるだろうか?」「金属は羽毛よりも重い」といえるが、だからといって、一にぎりの金属と、荷車にぎっしり積んだ羽毛についてもそう言えるだろうか? 三十センチの厚みの

You will not accept anything I can lay at your feet except **as a token of my good will; so accept this, not for its intrinsic value, but as a token**. It will be an insult to your worth to call the best gift good enough for you." Place the two ideas side by side; and we see that the ultimate idea is one and the same. Neither is "awfully funny." The American speaks of the material which makes the gift; the Japanese speaks of the spirit which prompts the gift.

It is perverse reasoning to conclude, because our sense of propriety shows itself in all the smallest ramifications of our deportment, to take the least important of them and uphold it as the type, and pass judgment upon the principle itself. Which is more important, to eat or to observe rules of propriety about eating? A Chinese sage answers, "If you take a case where the eating is all-important, and the observing the rules of propriety is of little importance, and compare them together, why merely say that the eating is of the more importance?" "Metal is heavier than feathers," but does that saying have reference to a single clasp of metal and a wagon-load of feathers? Take a piece of wood a foot thick and raise it above

ある木片を持って、寺院の塔の上にのせたからといって、寺院より木のほうが背が高いとは言わないだろう。「真実を話すのと、礼儀をわきまえて話すことのどちらが大事か」と聞かれたら、日本人はアメリカ人と正反対の答えをすると言われている。しかし、私がどう思うかを述べる前に、まず「正直、すなわち嘘をつかないこと」について、語らなければならない。**誠**すなわち真心がなければ、礼儀作法は茶番であり、ただの見せかけとなる。

the pinnacle of a temple, none would call it taller than the temple. To the question, "Which is the more important, to tell the truth or to be polite?" the Japanese are said to give an answer diametrically opposite to what the American will say,—but I forbear any comment until I come to speak of **veracity** or truthfulness, without which Politeness is a farce and a show.

第7章

誠（正直）、
すなわち嘘をつかないこと

「矩を超えた礼儀は嘘となる」とは伊達政宗の言である。ある古代の詩人が、ポローニアス顔負けの助言をしてくれる。「**汝自身に正直であれ**。汝の心が真実より逸れることがなくば、祈らずとも、神は汝をまったく保ちたもう」と。「誠」は子思の『中庸』で神格化されている。それは**超越的な力**をもつとされ、ほとんど「神」と同義に扱われている。すなわち「誠は万物の終わりにして、始まりでもある。**誠**がなければ何ものも存在し得ない」という。ついで、それはあまねく、永続的に存在するという性質をもち、動かずとも変化をもたらし、それがあるだけで努力せずとも目的を達する力があるという。漢字の「誠」は「言」と「成」（完成の意）から成り立

CHAPTER 7

VERACITY OR
TRUTHFULNESS

"Propriety carried beyond right bounds," says Masamuné, "becomes a lie." An ancient poet has outdone Polonius in the advice he gives: "**To thyself be faithful**: if in thy heart thou strayest not from truth, without prayer of thine the Gods will keep thee whole." The apotheosis of Sincerity to which Tsu-tsu gives expression in the *Doctrine of the Mean*, attributes to it **transcendental powers**, almost identifying them with the Divine. "Sincerity is the end and the beginning of all things; without **Sincerity** there would be nothing." He then dwells with eloquence on its far-reaching and long enduring nature, its power to produce changes without movement and by its mere presence to accomplish its purpose without effort. From the Chinese ideogram for Sincerity, which is a combination of "Word" and "Perfect," one is

っている。「誠」はネオプラトニズムの「ロゴス」の説に比すべきものだと言いたくなる。『中庸』にしては珍しく、子思は神秘的な思索へと羽をひろげ、そのような高みへと舞い昇っているのである。

　嘘や言い逃れは、ひとしく卑怯なものだと考えられている。武士は高い社会的地位ゆえに、自分たちには商人や農民よりも、高い「誠」の基準が求められていると思っている。「武士の一言」という言葉がある。すなわち「武士の言葉」という意味で、ドイツ語に逐語訳すれば「リッターヴォルト」となるが、「武士の一言である」といえば、それだけで、述べられたことが真実であることの保証となる。武士の言葉にはたいそう重みがあり、約束は証文なしに交わされ、実行される。証文を書くなどというのは下の下なのである。「二言」すなわち「二枚舌」を死でつぐなった者の緊迫した事例は枚挙にいとまがない。

　キリスト教では一般に、「神に誓ってはいけない」と教えられるが、この戒めは守られたためしがない。武士道では「誠」であることは名誉の問題なので、まともな武士は、ことさらに「誓って真実だ」などと述べることは、むしろ名誉を汚す行為であると感じる。武士も「天地神明に誓って」とか「この刀にかけて」などという言葉を口にすることはあるが、このような言葉が空疎な言

tempted to draw a parallel between it and **the Neo-Platonic doctrine of *Logos***—to such height does the sage soar in his unwonted mystic flight.

Lying or **equivocation** were deemed equally cowardly. The bushi held that his high social position demanded a loftier standard of veracity than that of the tradesman and peasant. *Bushi no ichi-gon*—the word of a samurai or in exact German equivalent *ein Ritter-wort*—was sufficient guaranty of the truthfulness of an assertion. His word carried such weight with it that promises were generally made and fulfilled without **a written pledge**, which would have been deemed quite beneath his dignity. Many thrilling anecdotes were told of those who atoned by death for *ni-gon*, a **double tongue**.

The regard for veracity was so high that, unlike the generality of Christians who persistently violate the plain commands of the Teacher not to swear, the best of samurai looked upon an oath as derogatory to their honor. I am well aware that they did **swear by different deities** or upon their swords; but never has

い回しや、はしたない間投詞として用いられることは絶対にない。誠を形に残したいときには、血判状により、**文字通り血で言葉を封じ込める**ことがある。このような行動について説明が必要なら、どうかゲーテの『ファウスト』をご覧いただきたい。

あるアメリカ人が、最近このようなことを述べている。すなわち、普通の日本人に、嘘をつくことと礼儀を欠くことではどちらを選ぶかと尋ねると、迷わず「嘘をつくほうだ」と答える、というのである。ピーリー博士[14]のこの言は正しくもあり誤ってもいる！普通の日本人なら、武士でさえもがこのように答える、というのは正しい。だが、「嘘」がfalsehoodという英語に訳されているが、日本語の「嘘」と英語のfalsehoodでは重みがちがうのである。日本語の「嘘」には、「誠（真実）」もしくは「本当（事実）」と言えない事柄がすべて含まれる。ローウェルによれば、ワーズワースは真実と事実の区別ができなかったとのことだが、普通の日本人も多かれ少なかれそうである。日本人か、もしくは教養あるアメリカ人をつかまえて、「私のことが嫌いですか？」とか、「気分が悪いですか？」などと尋ねてみるがいい。相手はたいして迷いもしないで嘘をつくだろう。「とても好

[14] Peery, *The Gist of Japan*, p. 86.

swearing degenerated into wanton form and irreverent interjection. To emphasize our words a practice of **literally sealing with blood** was sometimes resorted to. For the explanation of such a practice, I need only refer my readers to Goethe's *Faust*.

A recent American writer is responsible for this statement, that if you ask an ordinary Japanese which is better, to tell a falsehood or be impolite, he will not hesitate to answer "to tell a falsehood!" Dr. Peery[14] is partly right and partly wrong; right in that an ordinary Japanese, even a samurai, may answer in the way ascribed to him, but wrong in attributing too much weight to the term he translates "falsehood." This word (in Japanese *uso*) is employed to denote anything which is not a truth (*makoto*) or fact (*honto*). Lowell tells us that Wordsworth could not distinguish between truth and fact, and an ordinary Japanese is in this respect as good as Wordsworth. Ask a Japanese, or even an American of any refinement, to tell you whether he dislikes you or whether he is sick at his stomach, and he will not hesitate long to tell falsehoods and answer, "I like you much," or, "I am

きですよ」とか、「いいえ、大丈夫です」と答えるに決まっている。ただし、**ただの体裁のために嘘をつくのは**「虚礼」、「巧言令色」であり、決して許されることではない。

この一節のテーマは、武士道における「誠」がいかなるものかということだが、**日本の商人の「正直さ」**について数言を費やしても悪くはないだろう。海外の書物や雑誌で、さんざん叩かれているのを見聞きしているからだ。日本の**商道徳**がいいかげんだということで、我が国の評価が著しく損なわれていることは事実だ。しかし悪口をいったり、安直に日本人の民族性を糾弾する前に、冷静に分析すれば、将来の改善を期して慰められるだろう。

主要な生業（ないわい）を考えてみた場合、武人と商人ほどかけ離れたものはない。商人はあらゆる職の中でもっとも低い位置に置かれている。すなわち「士農工商」である。武士は土地から収入を得ていて、その気になればしろうとの手すさびに土を耕すこともあろうが、**帳場とそろばん**、すなわち商売は忌み嫌われていた。このような社会の構成には深い叡智が感じられる。上層階級を商業活動から排除するのは社会政策として優れている、権力を持

quite well, thank you." To **sacrifice truth merely for the sake of politeness** was regarded as an "empty form" (*kyorei*) and "deception by sweet words," and was never justified.

I own I am speaking now of the Bushido idea of veracity; but it may not be amiss to devote a few words to **our commercial integrity**, of which I have heard much complaint in foreign books and journals. A loose **business morality** has indeed been the worst blot on our national reputation; but before abusing it or hastily condemning the whole race for it, let us calmly study it and we shall be rewarded with consolation for the future.

Of all the great occupations of life, none was farther removed from the profession of arms than commerce. The merchant was placed lowest in the category of vocations,—the knight, the tiller of the soil, the mechanic, the merchant. The samurai derived his income from land and could even indulge, if he had a mind to, in amateur farming; but **the counter and abacus** were abhorred. We knew the wisdom of this social arrangement. Montesquieu has made it clear that the debarring of the nobility from mercantile pursuits was an admirable social policy, in that it prevented wealth

った者への富の集中をふせぐからだ、と述べたのはモンテスキューである。**権力と富を分離**することで、富がより均等に分配される。『西ローマ帝国の最後の百年におけるローマ社会』を著したディル教授は、ローマ帝国の衰退は、もっぱら貴族に商業活動を許したことに起因すると述べている。それによって、富と権力が元老院貴族の少数の権門に独占されることになったのが禍のもとであった、というのである。

したがって封建日本では、商業はさほど発展しなかった。それを可能にする自由な状況を欠いていたからである。商売には悪口がつきもので、「なりふりかまわぬ」などと言われたのは当然のことであった。「**人は泥棒と呼ばれたら盗みをはじめる**」という言葉がある。ある職業に烙印をおすと、その職に従う者は自らの行動規範をそれに合わせるものだ。ヒュー・ブラックが述べるように、「普通の人の良心は要求があってはじめて目覚めるが、予測されている最低のレベルにまでいとも簡単に堕ちるもの」である。商売であろうと何であろうと、人間の活動には**行動の規範**なしではすまされない。封建時代の日本の商人たちにももちろんそれはあった。それがあ

from accumulating in the hands of the powerful. **The separation of power and riches** kept the distribution of the latter more nearly equable. Professor Dill, the author of *Roman Society in the Last Century of the Western Empire*, has brought afresh to our mind that one cause of the decadence of the Roman Empire, was the permission given to the nobility to engage in trade, and the consequent monopoly of wealth and power by a minority of the senatorial families.

Commerce, therefore, in feudal Japan did not reach that degree of development which it would have attained under freer conditions. The obloquy attached to the calling naturally brought within its pale such as cared little for social repute. **"Call one a thief and he will steal:"** put a **stigma** on a calling and its followers adjust their morals to it, for it is natural that "the normal conscience," as Hugh Black says, "rises to the demands made on it, and easily falls to the limit of the standard expected from it." It is unnecessary to add that no business, commercial or otherwise, can be transacted without a **code of morals**. Our merchants of the feudal period had one among themselves, without which they could never have developed, as they

ったからこそ、我が国でも**組合、銀行、株式取引所、保険、小切手、為替手形など基本的な商業制度**が発展してきたのである。しかし、商業の外の人間との関係においては、商人は彼らのかんばしくない世評を裏切ることなくふるまっていたのだ。

このようなありさまだったので、**開国とともに商業が海外に開かれたとき**、港に集まってきたのは、もっとも山っけがあり、なりふりかまわぬ商人ばかりで、まともな商家は、支店を出すことをしきりに政府から求められたにもかかわらず、しばらく見合わせていたのであった。武士道は、時流にのった商人たちのみっともない商売道が広がるのを、とどめることが出来なかったのだろうか？

日本の歴史をご存知の方にはご記憶があろうかと思うが、いくつかの指定の港が外国に開かれてからわずか数年後に、**封建体制が瓦解した**。またそれとともに**武士が家禄を取り上げられた**。その代わりに**公債**が与えられ、これを元手にして商売を始めるのも自由であった。ここで、読者諸氏は「なぜ彼らはご自慢の『誠』を新たな商業の活動に持ち込んで、従来の陋習をあらためようとしなかったのか」と、疑問に思うかもしれない。しかし、**聞くも涙、語るも涙の物語**だが、高潔な武士たちの多くが、新たにとりくんだ不慣れな商売の道でもののみごと

did, **such fundamental mercantile institutions as the guild, the bank, the bourse, insurance, checks, bills of exchange, etc.**; but in their relations with people outside their vocation, the tradesmen lived too true to the reputation of their order.

This being the case, **when the country was opened to foreign trade**, only the most adventurous and unscrupulous rushed to the ports, while the respectable business houses declined for some time the repeated requests of the authorities to establish branch houses. Was Bushido powerless to stay the current of commercial dishonor? Let us see.

Those who are well acquainted with our history will remember that only a few years after our treaty ports were opened to foreign trade, **feudalism was abolished**, and when with it **the samurai's fiefs were taken** and **bonds** issued to them in compensation, they were given liberty to invest them in mercantile transactions. Now you may ask, "Why could they not bring their much boasted veracity into their new business relations and so reform the old abuses?" **Those who had eyes to see could not weep enough, those who had hearts to feel could not sympathize**

に失敗し、あえなく退場となってしまった。平民出身の手練手管のライバルたちと渡り合えるほど、目端のきくものはいなかったのである。アメリカのような産業の発達した国でさえ、八〇パーセントの会社が破綻することを考えると、商売をはじめた武士の中で、成功した者が百人に一人にも満たなかったというのは何ら驚くべきことではない。武士道の倫理を商いの道でも用いようとして、どれほどの人が破産したのか、正確に認識するにはまだまだ時間がかかるだろうが、**富を築く道は名誉の道とはまた別のものである**ということが、物事を見る目のある人にとってはすぐに明らかとなった。では、この二つの道はどのような点で違っているのであろうか?

人を「誠」へと向かわせる動機として、レッキーは三つのカテゴリーを挙げている。すなわち商業的、政治的、哲学的の三つである。このうち第一の商業的動機は武士道とは縁遠い。第二の政治的動機は、封建制度下の政治の世界ではほとんど育つ可能性はない。武士道において、様々な美徳のうち「誠」が高い地位を得ているのは、その哲学的にして、(レッキー述べるところの)もっとも高尚な側面に係わっている。アングロサクソン民族は、商取引では無類に正直であり、そのことについて私は心より敬意を表するものであるが、究極的になぜそうなのかと、その根拠を尋ねると、**「正直は最善の策」**

enough, with the fate of many a noble and honest samurai who signally and irrevocably failed in his new and unfamiliar field of trade and industry, through sheer lack of shrewdness in coping with his artful plebeian rival. When we know that eighty per cent. of the business houses fail in so industrial a country as America, is it any wonder that scarcely one among a hundred samurai who went into trade could succeed in his new vocation? It will be long before it will be recognized how many fortunes were wrecked in the attempt to apply Bushido ethics to business methods; but it was soon patent to every observing mind that **the ways of wealth were not the ways of honor**. In what respects, then, were they different?

Of the three **incentives to Veracity** that Lecky enumerates, viz: the industrial, the political, and the philosophical, the first was altogether lacking in Bushido. As to the second, it could develop little in a political community under a feudal system. It is in its philosophical, and as Lecky says, in its highest aspect, that Honesty attained elevated rank in our catalogue of virtues. With all my sincere regard for the high commercial integrity of the Anglo-Saxon race, when I

であり、正直であれば決して損をしないからだ、という答えが返ってくる。すなわち、正直はそれ自体が報酬だから、というわけではないのである。嘘をつくよりも、正直なほうが実入りが大きいから正直でいるのだ、ということになる。こんなことなら、武士は嘘のほうがましだと考えるであろう！

武士道は「みかえり」の論理を峻烈に拒否するが、これとは対照的に、目ざとい商人はもろ手をひろげてこれを歓迎する。レッキーは、正直の徳が重要なものとされるようになったのは商工業に拠るところが大きいという。ニーチェ流にいうなら「正直はもっとも若い美徳」である。その心は、この徳は産業の――といっても近代産業の申し子にして、養い子なのである。近代産業という母がいなければ、正直は生白い孤児となり、精神修養を積んだ高尚な人間のみが包容し、育てることになるであろう。そのような人間は武士としてはごくありふれているが、この徳が大きく育つには、大衆的で功利的な育ての親が必要なのである。産業が大きく発展するとともに、正直はお手軽な美徳――いや、利を生み出す美徳であることが認識されるようになった。ドイツでは一八八〇年十一月になっても、宰相のビスマルクがドイツ帝国の領事専門官たちに回状を送って、「とりわけドイツの船荷について信頼性の欠如が見られ、嘆かわしきかぎりである。

ask for the ultimate ground, I am told that **"Honesty is the best policy,"** that it pays to be honest. Is not this virtue, then, its own reward? If it is followed because it brings in more cash than falsehood, I am afraid Bushido would rather indulge in lies!

If **Bushido rejects a doctrine of *quid pro quo* rewards**, the shrewder tradesman will readily accept it. Lecky has very truly remarked that Veracity owes its growth largely to commerce and manufacture; as Nietzsche puts it, "Honesty is the youngest of virtues"—in other words, it is **the foster-child of industry**, of modern industry. Without this mother, **Veracity** was like a blue-blood orphan whom only the most cultivated mind could adopt and nourish. Such minds were general among the samurai, but, for want of **a more democratic and utilitarian foster-mother**, the tender child failed to thrive. Industries advancing, Veracity will prove an easy, nay, a profitable, virtue to practice. Just think, as late as November 1880, Bismarck sent a circular to the professional consuls of the German Empire, warning them of "a lamentable lack of reliability with regard to German shipments

質・量のいずれにおいてもそうである」と警告しなければならなかった。ところが今日では、ドイツ人の商取引がとりわけ不注意だとか不正直であるというような世評は、当時と比べれば無にひとしい。二十年の間に、結局は**正直が得**だということを、ドイツ商人は学んだのである。このことはすでに、我が国の商人たちにも分かりはじめている。これ以上のことについては、近年の二冊の著述を紹介しておくので参照されたい。バランスのとれた評価がなされている、よい本である[15]。最後にこのことと関連して、実は、**「正直」と「信用」は何よりも確かな保証である**、ということに注目しておきたい。商人は金を借りるときに**証文**を交わすが、よく考えればこれはまさに、正直と信用が形となったものである。証文には、「借用した金子の支払い不履行の折りは、公衆の面前で恥をかかされるも文句はなく候」とか、「万が一返却せざるときは、馬鹿と呼んでいただくも可なり」などの文言が含まれるのは、ごく普通のことであった。

　武士道で「誠」を貫くのに、「勇気」以上の動機があるのだろうかと、よく思うことがある。嘘の証言をしてはならないなどと、どこにも大書されているわけではない。武士道では、嘘をつくことは罪というより、弱さを露呈する行為であり、それがゆえにはなはだしく不名誉なものなのである。

inter alia, apparent both as to quality and quantity;" now-a-days we hear comparatively little of German carelessness and dishonesty in trade. In twenty years her merchants learned that in the end **honesty pays**. Already our merchants are finding that out. For the rest I recommend the reader to two recent writers for well-weighed judgment on this point.[15] It is interesting to remark in this connection that **integrity and honor were the surest guaranties** which even a merchant debtor could present in the form of **promissory notes**. It was quite a usual thing to insert such clauses as these: "In default of the repayment of the sum lent to me, I shall say nothing against being ridiculed in public;" or, "In case I fail to pay you back, you may call me a fool," and the like.

Often have I wondered whether the Veracity of Bushido had any motive higher than courage. In the absence of any positive commandment against bearing false witness, lying was not condemned as sin, but simply denounced as weakness, and, as such, highly dishonorable.

---

[15] Knapp, *Feudal and Modern Japan*, Vol. I, Ch. IV. Ransome, *Japan in Transition*, Ch. VIII.

第 8 章

名誉

　実のところ「誠」（honesty）の概念は「名誉」（honor）
と深く絡み合っている。ラテン語とドイツ語では、もと
は同一の語であった。よって、このあたりでしばし目を
転じ、騎士道の特徴をなす「名誉」、すなわち「名の誉れ」
という徳目について考えておくのがよいだろう。

　**名誉の感覚には、自らが威厳ある、価値の高い人間で
あるという鮮明な意識**がともなう。武士は身分にともな
う責務と特権のもとに生まれ、それを大事にするように
育てられるのであるから、武士の人格と名誉の感覚は切
っても切れない関係にある。現在、英語の honor の訳と
してふつうに充てられる「名誉」という語は、かつては
さほど一般的ではなく、その意を伝えるのに「名」、「面
目」、「外聞」などの語が用いられた。それぞれ、『聖書』
で用いられている「名前」という語、ギリシャ劇の「マ
スク」（ペルソナ）から生じてきた「人格（パーソナリ
ティ）」という語、そして英語の「評判」という語と対

CHAPTER 8

HONOR

As a matter of fact, the idea of honesty is so intimately blended, and its Latin and its German etymology so identified with honor, that it is high time I should pause a few moments for the consideration of this feature of the Precepts of Knighthood.

The sense of honor, implying **a vivid consciousness of personal dignity and worth**, could not fail to characterize the samurai, born and bred to value the duties and privileges of their profession. Though the word ordinarily given now-a-days as the translation of Honor was not used freely, yet the idea was conveyed by such terms as *na* (name), *menmoku* (countenance), *guaibun* (outside hearing), reminding us respectively of the biblical use of "name," of the evolution of the term "personality" from the Greek mask, and of

応している。「よき名」──すなわち、**名声とは人の本性から獣的な部分を取り去った、人格の根本**であるという考え方からすると、当然のことながら、**名を損なうことは恥である**、ということになる。そしてこの恥の感覚（廉恥心）は、教育のもっとも初期のころから幼児の心に刻みつけられる。子どもがぶざまなことをしようものなら、「人に笑われますよ」、「そんなことをすると恥ですよ」、「恥ずかしくないの？」というのが、諫める際の決め文句である。このように言われると、子どもはもっとも痛いところを衝かれた気になる。まるで母親の腹の中にいたときから、「名誉」に養われていたかのようである。そして生まれてくる前から名誉に縁があるというのは、文字通りの意味である。なぜなら、それは**強い家の意識と密接に結びついている**からである。「家の制度がゆるんで、モンテスキューが『名誉』と名付けた、社会の土台が失われた」とバルザックが述べている。恥の感覚は、日本人が倫理的な意識に目覚めて、もっとも早く現れてくるものである。「禁断の果実」を食べたことで人類に真っ先にもたらされた最悪の罰は、出産の悲しみでも、人生の苦しみでもなく、**恥の感覚に目覚めたことだ**と、私は思う。げんなりしたアダムに摘んでもらっ

"fame." A good name—**one's reputation, the immortal part of one's self, what remains being bestial**—assumed as a matter of course, **any infringement upon its integrity was felt as shame**, and the sense of shame (*Renchishin*) was one of the earliest to be cherished in juvenile education. "You will be laughed at," "It will disgrace you," "Are you not ashamed?" were the last appeal to correct behavior on the part of a youthful delinquent. Such a recourse to his honor touched the most sensitive spot in the child's heart, as though it had been nursed on honor while it was in its mother's womb; for most truly is honor a prenatal influence, being **closely bound up with strong family consciousness**. "In losing the solidarity of families," says Balzac, "society has lost the fundamental force which Montesquieu named Honor." Indeed, the sense of shame seems to me to be the earliest indication of the moral consciousness of our race. The first and worst punishment which befell humanity in consequence of tasting "the fruit of that forbidden tree" was, to my mind, not the sorrow of childbirth, nor the thorns and thistles, but **the awakening of the sense of shame**. Few incidents in history excel in pa-

た数枚のいちじくの葉を、イブがそまつな針を手に、胸をときめかせながら震える指で縫い合わせたが、これほど悲しい出来事が人類の歴史にあっただろうか。この**神に背いた最初の果実**が、何ものにもましてしつこく、現在の我々にもつきまとっている。人類は裁縫の腕の限りをつくしても、恥の感覚を覆い隠してくれる前掛けを縫うことがいまだにできない。武士はたとえ幼いときでも、些細なことにせよ、恥ずかしいことをして名を汚すことを潔しとしなかったものだが、それは正しいことなのである。「恥は木に刻まれた傷と同じで、時間とともに消えるどころか、ますます目立ってくる」からだ。

　近代になってカーライルが述べたことを、何世紀も前に孟子は、ほとんど同じ表現で述べている。すなわち、**「恥はあらゆる美徳、よき礼儀、よき道徳を育てる土である」**。

　武士の**恥を恐れる感覚**はきわめて強い。我が国の文学には、シェイクスピアがノーフォーク公に語らせたような**名調子**は存在しないものの、武士たるものは常住坐臥、ダモクレスの剣が頭上に掛かっているような思いで日々をすごし、いきおい余って、それが病的な様相をおびることもある。**体面にかかわる**といって、武士の風上にもおけない行為がおこなわれる。威張り散らした短気者が、ほんのささいな無礼に怒り、ときには根も葉もな

thos the scene of the first mother plying with heaving breast and tremulous fingers, her crude needle on the few fig leaves which her dejected husband plucked for her. This **first fruit of disobedience** clings to us with a tenacity that nothing else does. All the sartorial ingenuity of mankind has not yet succeeded in sewing an apron that will efficaciously hide our sense of shame. That samurai was right who refused to compromise his character by a slight humiliation in his youth; "because," he said, "dishonor is like a scar on a tree, which time, instead of effacing, only helps to enlarge."

Mencius had taught centuries before, in almost the identical phrase, what Carlyle has latterly expressed,—namely, that **"Shame is the soil of all Virtue, of good manners and good morals."**

The fear of disgrace was so great that if our literature lacks such **eloquence** as Shakespeare puts into the mouth of Norfolk, it nevertheless hung like Damocles' sword over the head of every samurai and often assumed a morbid character. **In the name of Honor**, deeds were perpetrated which can find no justification in the code of Bushido. At the slightest, nay, imaginary insult, the quick-tempered braggart took offense, re-

い思い込みでいきり立って刃傷沙汰となり、いたずらに争いがおきたり、無辜の命が失われたりする。市井でまことしやかに囁かれた、こんな小話がある。あなたの背中でノミがはねましたよと、武士に教えてやった人がいた。善意で言ったのに、一刀のもとにたたき斬られた。なんと、ノミは獣に寄生するもので、獣と武士を同列に並べるとは許せん、というのが理由であった。なんと単細胞で、没義道な言い草であろうか。こんなくだらない話はまじめに信じるに足りないが、こうした話が流布しているということから、三つのことが言える。すなわち、(1) 庶民を脅すためにこんな与太話が作られた、(2) 侍の身分をよいことに、許されざることが実際に行われていた、(3) きわめて強い恥の感覚が、侍の階級に発達していた、ということである。異常な武士の例を挙げて、武士道そのものを弾劾することは明らかに当を得ない。これは異端審問や偽善などといった狂信や行き過ぎを生み出すからといって、キリストの教えそのものを非難してはならないのと同じことである。偏執的な宗教の例と同じく、侍の恥の感覚には**高貴な薫り**がただよっている。酒浸りの人間の目に生じる幻覚とは違うのである。したがって、侍が極端なまでに名にこだわる底には、**真の美徳**が隠されているのではないだろうか？

sorted to the use of the sword, and many an unnecessary strife was raised and many an innocent life lost. The story of a well-meaning citizen who called the attention of a bushi to a flea jumping on his back, and who was forthwith cut in two, for the simple and questionable reason that inasmuch as fleas are parasites which feed on animals, it was an unpardonable insult to identify a noble warrior with a beast—I say, stories like these are too frivolous to believe. Yet, the circulation of such stories implies three things; (1) that they were invented to overawe common people; (2) that abuses were really made of the samurai's profession of honor; and (3) that a very strong sense of shame was developed among them. It is plainly unfair to take an abnormal case to cast blame upon the Precepts, any more than to judge of the true teaching of Christ from the fruits of religious fanaticism and extravagance—inquisitions and hypocrisy. But, as in religious monomania **there is something touchingly noble**, as compared with the delirium tremens of a drunkard, so in that extreme sensitiveness of the samurai about their honor do we not recognize the substratum of **a genuine virtue**?

名へのこだわりは繊細にすぎて、ときに病的に陥るほどだが、それをほどよく中和するものとして、**鷹揚さと忍耐心**の勧めがある。ささいなことで腹を立てるのは「短気」だと笑われる。「耐え難いと思うことに耐えるのが、ほんとうに耐えること」という俗諺もある。徳川家康は子孫のために**家訓**を残しているが、その中に「人の一生は重荷を背負て遠き道をゆくがごとし、いそぐべからず。（中略）おのれを責めて人を責むるな。及ばざるは過ぎたるよりまされり。（中略）堪忍は無事長久の墓」というものがある。**家康はこの教えの正しさを、自らの人生で証明した。歴史上の三人の有名人物**にことよせて、それぞれの性格を巧みに描き出した狂歌がある。「鳴かぬなら殺してしまえホトトギス」が織田信長、「鳴かぬなら鳴かせてみせようホトトギス」が豊臣秀吉であるのにたいして、徳川家康は「鳴かぬなら鳴くまでまとうホトトギス」であった。

　忍耐と**我慢**は、孟子が強く勧めるところでもある。ある一節で次のような趣旨のことを述べている。「あなたが素っ裸になってわたしを侮辱しても、わたしは痛痒を感じない。あなたがいかなる無礼をなそうとも、わたしの魂を汚すことはできない」と。また、「**大人はささい**

The morbid excess into which the delicate code of honor was inclined to run was strongly counterbalanced by preaching **magnanimity and patience**. To take offense at slight provocation was ridiculed as "short-tempered." The popular adage said: "To bear what you think you cannot bear is really to bear." The great Iyéyasu left to posterity a few **maxims**, among which are the following:—"The life of man is like going a long distance with a heavy load upon the shoulders. Haste not... Reproach none, but be forever watchful of thine own short-comings... Forbearance is the basis of length of days." **He proved in his life what he preached.** A literary wit put a characteristic epigram into the mouths of **three well-known personages in our history**: to Nobunaga he attributed, "I will kill her, if the nightingale sings not in time;" to Hidéyoshi, "I will force her to sing for me;" and to Iyéyasu, "I will wait till she opens her lips."

Patience and **long suffering** were also highly commended by Mencius. In one place he writes to this effect: "Though you denude yourself and insult me, what is that to me? You cannot defile my soul by your outrage." Elsewhere he teaches that **anger at a petty**

なことへの怒りには無縁だが、**大事のために憤るのは正義の怒りである**」ともいう。

　秀でた武士は武に訴えることもなく、流れる水のごとく従容としていられるものである。そのような高みに上るとは、どういうことだろうか。何人かの侍の言葉から考えてみよう。例えば小河立所はこのように述べている。「他人に悪口を言われても、邪に邪を返してはならない。むしろ、自分のほうで誠意を欠き、なすべきことをなさなかったのかと疑うべきである」と。また熊沢蕃山の言はこうだ。「他人汝を責めても、汝責め返すなかれ。他人怒っても、汝怒るなかれ。情と欲が去ってのち、喜び自ずから至る」と。もう一つ、西郷隆盛の言葉をひいておいてもよいだろう。西郷は、その太い眉の上に「恥も座するを恥じる」と言われたほどの人物である。「道は天地の道である。それの導くところに進むのが人たる者の定めである。よって、**天を敬うことを生きる目的とせよ**。天は己も他人もひとしく愛する。よって、己を愛するがごとく他人を愛し、人ではなく天を自らの伴侶とすべし。他人を責めず、己が理想に足らざることのなきよう努めるべし」。このような言葉には、**キリスト教の教え**に近いものを感じさせられる。実生活上の道徳を教える点では、自然の宗教は、預言者によって

offense is unworthy a superior man, but **indignation for a great cause** is **righteous wrath**.

To what height of unmartial and unresisting meekness Bushido could reach in some of its votaries, may be seen in their utterances. Take, for instance, this saying of Ogawa: "When others speak all manner of evil things against thee, return not evil for evil, but rather reflect that thou wast not more faithful in the discharge of thy duties." Take another of Kumazawa:—"When others blame thee, blame them not; when others are angry at thee, return not anger. Joy cometh only as Passion and Desire part." Still another instance I may cite from Saigo, upon whose overhanging brows "shame is ashamed to sit;"—"The Way is the way of Heaven and Earth: Man's place is to follow it: therefore **make it the object of thy life to reverence Heaven**. Heaven loves me and others with equal love; therefore with the love wherewith thou lovest thyself, love others. Make not Man thy partner but Heaven, and making Heaven thy partner do thy best. Never condemn others; but see to it that thou comest not short of thine own mark." Some of those sayings remind us of **Christian expostulations** and

開かれた宗教に接近することが分かる。こうした名言は単に言葉として残っているだけではなく、現実世界に行動として表現されたものなのである。

　なんと鷹揚にして忍耐強く、寛容なことか。これほどの高みに達する秀でた侍が稀であることは、遺憾ながら認めざるをえない。「名誉」とは何か、一つの概念としてはっきりと説明する言葉が残されていないのは、まことに残念である。ほんの一にぎりの者のみが悟りをえて、名誉とは「それが生じるための条件は何もなく」、**各々が自分の役割をきちんと果たすところに存する**ということが分かっている。若者は何かの行動に熱中すると、書斎で心静かに孟子から学んだことを、いとも容易に忘れてしまうものだ。孟子いわく「名誉を愛する気持ちは誰の心にもあるが、**真の名誉は他ではなく、自分自身の中にこそある**とは夢にも思わない。他人から与えられる名誉は、たいした名誉ではない。趙孟が貴くする者は、趙孟が賤しくもできるのだ」。ほとんどの人間にとって、無礼な目にあうとそのとたんにいきり立ち、時に相手を殺してしまうこともあったが（後ほどそんな例をご覧いただこう）、そのいっぽうで、名誉——といってもたいていの場合は、たかだか**派手な地位**やあだな**世評**にすぎないのだが、ともかく「名誉」こそがこの世の生の**「至高の善」**であるとして、皆手に入れたがった。

show us how far in practical morality natural religion can approach the revealed. Not only did these sayings remain as utterances, but they were really embodied in acts.

It must be admitted that very few attained this sublime height of magnanimity, patience and forgiveness. It was a great pity that nothing clear and general was expressed as to what constitutes Honor, only a few enlightened minds being aware that it "from no condition rises," but that **it lies in each acting well his part**: for nothing was easier than for youths to forget in the heat of action what they had learned in Mencius in their calmer moments. Said this sage, "'Tis in every man's mind to love honor: but little doth he dream that **what is truly honorable lies within himself and not anywhere else**. The honor which men confer is not good honor. Those whom Châo the Great ennobles, he can make mean again." For the most part, an insult was quickly resented and repaid by death, as we shall see later, while Honor—too often nothing higher than **vain glory** or **worldly approbation**—was prized as the *summum bonum* of earthly existence.

若者が求めようとしたのは、富や学問ではなく、名声であった。武家の子は、**名をあげる**までは二度と家の敷居をまたぐまいという決意を胸に秘めて、世に出ていったものだ。また、母は母で、子どもが「**故郷に錦を飾る**」までは顔を見ないと言ったものである。名を汚さぬため、あるいは名を上げるために、侍の子はどんな窮乏にもたえ、どんなに苦しい肉体、精神の試練にも立ち向かおうとした。**若くして得た名は、歳とともに輝きを増す**ことを知っていたからである。有名な大坂の夏の陣で、家康の若い息子が**前衛**に配されることを願いながら、**後方の陣**に置かれた。城が落ちたとき、悔し涙にくれたので、お付きの老侍がなんとか慰めようとして「殿、そんなに悲しみなさいますな。まだまだこれからではございませんか。長い人生の間には、きっと名を上げる機会がたんとございましょう」と言った。すると若者はきっと睨みつけてこう言った。「たわけたことをぬかすな！十四歳の時は二度とめぐってこぬではないか」と。

Fame, and not wealth or knowledge, was the goal toward which youths had to strive. Many a lad swore within himself as he crossed the threshold of his paternal home, that he would not recross it until **he had made a name in the world**: and many an ambitious mother refused to see her sons again unless they could "return home," as the expression is, **"caparisoned in brocade."** To shun shame or win a name, samurai boys would submit to any privations and undergo severest ordeals of bodily or mental suffering. They knew that **honor won in youth grows with age**. In the memorable siege of Osaka, a young son of Iyéyasu, in spite of his earnest entreaties to be put in the **vanguard**, was placed at the **rear of the army**. When the castle fell, he was so chagrined and wept so bitterly that an old councillor tried to console him with all the resources at his command. "Take comfort, Sire," said he, "at thought of the long future before you. In the many years that you may live, there will come divers occasions to distinguish yourself." The boy fixed his indignant gaze upon the man and said—"How foolishly you talk! Can ever my fourteenth year come round again?"

名誉と名声が得られるなら、命ですら惜しいとは思わなかった。だから、一命を捧げる価値があると思われる大義名分が生じたなら、いとも平然として、惜しげもなく身を捧げたのである。

Life itself was thought cheap if honor and fame could be attained therewith: hence, whenever a cause presented itself which was considered dearer than life, with utmost serenity and celerity was life laid down.

第9章

忠義

　一命を捧げても惜しくないと思われる**大義名分**の中でも、「忠義」、すなわち主君への忠誠はいわば要石_{かなめいし}のようなもので、これを中心として様々の**封建的な美徳**がきれいに左右対称に配置されている。**封建制度下の徳目**は、他の制度下での倫理体系や、他の階級の人々の道徳と共通するものも多いが、忠義——すなわち**長上_{めうえ}の者への崇敬と忠誠**——は、封建制度ならではのものである。誰かに忠誠を尽くすというのは、あらゆる種類の人間、あらゆる身分の人間に共通する徳目ではある。スリの一団ですら、フェイギンへの強烈な忠誠心をもっている。だが、「忠義」という徳目に**何よりも重い価値**が付与されているのは、武士道の名誉のおきてのみである。

　封建制度での臣下の者たちの忠誠心は、**個人への義務**であり、社会を対象とするものではないので、まったく**理不尽な原理**[16] に基づいた紐帯_{きずな}だと、ヘーゲルが批判

CHAPTER 9

THE DUTY OF
LOYALTY

Of the **causes** in comparison with which no life was
too dear to sacrifice, was the duty of loyalty which
was the key-stone making **feudal virtues** a symmetri-
cal arch. Other virtues **feudal morality** shares in
common with other systems of ethics, with other
classes of people, but this virtue—**homage and fealty
to a superior**—is its distinctive feature. I am aware
that personal fidelity is a moral adhesion existing
among all sorts and conditions of men,—a gang of
pickpockets owe allegiance to a Fagin; but it is only in
the code of chivalrous honor that Loyalty assumes
paramount importance.

In spite of Hegel's criticism that the fidelity of feudal vassals, being **an obligation to an individual** and
not to a Commonwealth, is a bond established on to-
tally **unjust principles**,[16] a great compatriot of his

した。しかし同じドイツ人でも、ビスマルクは**個人への忠誠**はゲルマン民族の美徳であると誇らしげに語っている。それも故なしとしない。ビスマルクの誇る「忠誠心（Treue）」が彼の祖国、どこかの一つの国や一つの民族の**独占物**だからというわけではなく、騎士道の申し子ともいうべきこの徳目は、封建制度がもっとも長く続いた民族のもとで最後まで残っていたからである。アメリカのように**「万人が同じ価値をもって」**おり、それに加えて、かのアイルランド人の言うように「誰もが自分は他人よりすばらしい」とすら思っている国では、我が国の者が主君に感じるようなかたちで忠誠心を理想化するのは、「ある程度まではけっこう」だが、日本のように過度に奨励されるのは愚かしいことだ、と考えられるかもしれない。ピレネー山脈のこちら側とあちら側では正邪が逆だとモンテスキューが喝破（かっぱ）したのは大昔のことだが、フランスの正義を隔てるのがピレネー山脈だけかどうかを別にすれば、この言葉が今でも真実であることをドレフュス事件が証明した。同様に、日本の「忠義」は他国ではほとんど分かってもらえないが、これは、その考え方が誤っているからではなく、その価値が他国（よそ）で忘れられてしまったからにほかならず、かつ、日本はどこ

---

[16] *Philosophy of History* (Eng. trans. by Sibree), Pt. IV, Sec. II, Ch. I.

made it his boast that **personal loyalty** was a German virtue. Bismarck had good reason to do so, not because the *Treue* he boasts of was the **monopoly** of his Fatherland or of any single nation or race, but because this favored fruit of chivalry lingers latest among the people where feudalism has lasted longest. In America where **"everybody is as good as anybody else,"** and, as the Irishman added, "better too," such exalted ideas of loyalty as we feel for our sovereign may be deemed "excellent within certain bounds," but preposterous as encouraged among us. Montesquieu complained long ago that right on one side of the Pyrenees was wrong on the other, and the recent Dreyfus trial proved the truth of his remark, save that the Pyrenees were not the sole boundary beyond which French justice finds no accord. Similarly, Loyalty as we conceive it may find few admirers elsewhere, not because our conception is wrong, but because it is, I am afraid, forgotten, and also because we carry it to a degree not reached in any other country.

の国よりも徹底しているからである。中国では、**儒教倫理**によって**親への服従**が人間にとってもっとも重要な義務であるとされるのにたいして、日本では、主君への服従が優先するとグリフィス[17]が述べているが、これはまったく正しい。読者諸氏を驚愕させるのは本意ではないが、ここで、シェイクスピアが言うところの「零落した主にどこまでもついて行き」、「それがゆえに語りぐさとなった」ある一人の人物のことをご紹介しておこう。

　それは日本の歴史でもっとも純な心の持ち主とされる、菅原道真にまつわる話である。道真は**嫉妬と中傷**のために、流謫（るたく）の身をかこった。敵はこれに飽き足らず、一族を根絶やしにしようとした。元服もしていない息子の行方がきびしく詮議（せんぎ）され、道真の旧臣、武部源蔵が鄙（ひな）でひらいている**寺子屋**にかくまわれていることが判明した。何時（いつ）いつまでに幼子の首級（くび）を差し出すようにと、源蔵に達しがいった。源蔵は子どもの**すり替え**を思いつく。寺子屋の子どもたちの名を思い浮かべ、やってきた子どもたちの顔を一人ひとり吟味したが、**土地の子たち**のうち誰一人として、預かっている若殿に容貌の似通っている者はいない。しかし、がっかりしたのも束の間の

[17] *Religions of Japan.*

Griffis[17] was quite right in stating that whereas in China **Confucian ethics** made **obedience to parents** the primary human duty, in Japan precedence was given to Loyalty. At the risk of shocking some of my good readers, I will relate of one "who could endure to follow a fall'n lord" and who thus, as Shakespeare assures, "earned a place i' the story."

The story is of one of the purest characters in our history, Michizané, who, falling a victim to **jealousy and calumny**, is exiled from the capital. Not content with this, his unrelenting enemies are now bent upon the extinction of his family. Strict search for his son—not yet grown—reveals the fact of his being secreted in a **village school** kept by one Genzo, a former vassal of Michizané. When orders are dispatched to the schoolmaster to deliver the head of the juvenile offender on a certain day, his first idea is to find a **suitable substitute** for it. He ponders over his school-list, scrutinizes with careful eyes all the boys, as they stroll into the class-room, but none among the **children born of the soil** bears the least resemblance to his protégé. His despair, however, is but for a moment;

こと、そこに新たな子どもが入ってきた。主君の子息と同い年の、端正な容貌の少年が、これも高貴な面立ちの母親に付き添われている。幼い主君と幼い家来の容貌が似ていることには、母親も、子ども自身も気づいていた。家に帰って二人きりになると、母と子はともに神前に供物を捧げた。子は玉の緒を、母は張り裂ける胸を差し出した。しかし、そのことを二人のほかは誰も知らない。そのような事情とはつゆしらず、源蔵からそうしてほしいという願いがとどいた。

　そして、そこにはすでに**生贄**があった！──このあとの話はかんたんにすませよう。──指定された日に、若殿の首級を検分し、受け取る役を申しつかった役人がやってきた。すりかえた首級に騙されるだろうか？ 気の毒な源蔵の手は**刀の柄**の上にある。首実検で**たくらみ**が見破られたら、即座に役人を斬りすてようか、それとも自害して果てようか。役人はその凄惨な物を目の前にかかげ、目鼻の一々を静かに調べていたかと思うと、やがて冷静な口調で、一語一語かみしめるように「まちがい御座らん」と言った……。先日寺子屋をおとずれた母親は、その夜、ひとり家で待っている。母はわが子の運命を知っているのだろうか？ だが、枝折戸の開くのを待ちわびていたのは、子の帰ってくるのを期待していたか

for, behold, a new scholar is announced—a comely boy of the same age as his master's son, escorted by a mother of noble mien. No less conscious of the resemblance between infant lord and infant retainer, were the mother and the boy himself. In the privacy of home both had laid themselves upon the altar; the one his life,—the other her heart, yet without sign to the outer world. Unwitting of what had passed between them, it is the teacher from whom comes the suggestion.

Here, then, is the **scape-goat**!—The rest of the narrative may be briefly told.—On the day appointed, arrives the officer commissioned to identify and receive the head of the youth. Will he be deceived by the false head? The poor Genzo's hand is on the **hilt of the sword**, ready to strike a blow either at the man or at himself, should the examination defeat his **scheme**. The officer takes up the gruesome object before him, goes calmly over each feature, and in a deliberate, business-like tone, pronounces it genuine.—That evening in a lonely home awaits the mother we saw in the school. Does she know the fate of her child? It is not for his return that she watches with eagerness for

らではなかった。彼女の義父は長年道真の恩義をこうむっていたが、道真が左遷されてこの方、夫はこれまで禄を食んだ主家の敵に仕えることを余儀なくされた。**夫みずからは無情な主君の命にそむくわけにはいかない。**だが、**その息子は祖父のために筋を通すことができる。**流謫の身となった菅家の知己ということで、夫は若君の首を検分する役目をおおせつかった。そしていま、この日の仕事、いや生涯の難事を果たした夫が帰ってきた。敷居をまたぐのももどかしく、夫は妻に言った。「喜ぶがよい。息子はりっぱにご主君のために勤めを果たしたぞ！」と。

　私の耳には「なんとおぞましい話であることよ！」という読者諸氏の声が聞こえる。「**腹をいためた親が、他人の子を救うために、何の罪もないわが子の生命をよろこんで犠牲にする**などとんでもない」と。だが、子ども自身が考え、望んだことでもあるのだ。これは**身代わりの死の物語**であり、アブラハムがイサクを生贄に捧げようとした物語と同趣旨にして、どちらがよりおぞましいなどというようなものではない。重要なのは、**義務の求めるところに従ったということ**である。天からの声の命じるところには、無条件に従うのである。目に見える天の使いが訪れるかどうか、内なる声か、外から聞こえてくる声か、そんなことはどうでもよい……。が、牧師ま

the opening of the wicket. Her father-in-law has been for a long time a recipient of Michizané's bounties, but since his banishment circumstances have forced her husband to follow the service of the enemy of his family's benefactor. **He himself could not be untrue to his own cruel master**; but **his son could serve the cause of the grandsire's lord**. As one acquainted with the exile's family, it was he who had been entrusted with the task of identifying the boy's head. Now the day's—yea, the life's—hard work is done, here turns home and as he crosses its threshold, he accosts his wife, saying: "Rejoice, my wife, our darling son has proved of service to his lord!"

"What an atrocious story!" I hear my readers exclaim,—**"Parents deliberately sacrificing their own innocent child to save the life of another man's."** But this child was a conscious and willing victim: it is a story of **vicarious death**—as significant as, and not more revolting than, the story of Abraham's intended sacrifice of Isaac. In both cases it was **obedience to the call of duty**, utter submission to the command of a higher voice, whether given by a visible or an invisible angel, or heard by an outward or an inward ear;—

がいの口上はこのへんで切り上げよう。

西洋は個人主義で、父と子、夫と妻の利害は別であると考えるので、それぞれが他に対して負う義務に注目がいくのは当然のことである。これに対し、主家とその一家の者は何があっても守らねばならないと考えるのが武士道である。また家と人は**同一**にして、**不可分**である。このような気持ちは、自然で本能的で抗しがたい愛情に裏打ちされている。自然な愛情をそそぐ（動物の本性として愛する）者のために死ぬとしても、それがなんであろうか？「汝を愛する人を愛するなら、いかなる見返りを求めるであろうか？　収税吏ですら求めないであろう」。

頼山陽の『日本外史』では、父親が犯した主君への裏切りに窮して、「忠ならんと欲すれば孝ならず、孝ならんと欲すれば忠ならず」と悩んだ重盛の**心の葛藤**が、感動的な筆致で語られている。なんと気の毒なことであろうか！その後、重盛は自らの上に死の来たらんことを念願した。**義と誠の住みがたいこの世**から解き放たれることを希ってのことである。

重盛のように、**忠義と愛情の板挟みに胸の張り裂ける思いをする者**は少なくない。シェイクスピアにも『旧約

but I abstain from preaching.

The individualism of the West, which recognizes separate interests for father and son, husband and wife, necessarily brings into strong relief the duties owed by one to the other; but Bushido held that the interest of the family and of the members thereof is intact,—**one and inseparable**. This interest it bound up with affection—natural, instinctive, irresistible; hence, if we die for one we love with natural love (which animals themselves possess), what is that? "For if ye love them that love you, what reward have ye? Do not even the publicans the same?"

In his great history, Sanyo relates in touching language the **heart struggle** of Shigemori concerning his father's rebellious conduct. "If I be loyal, my father must be undone; if I obey my father, my duty to my sovereign must go amiss." Poor Shigemori! We see him afterward praying with all his soul that kind Heaven may visit him with death, that he may be released from **this world where it is hard for purity and righteousness to dwell**.

Many a Shigemori has **his heart torn by the conflict between duty and affection**. Indeed neither

聖書』にも、孝、すなわち**子の親を思う情**は適格に描かれてはいないが、このような葛藤にあって**武士道では忠を選ぶことになんのためらいもない**。母親も、主のためにすべてを犠牲にすることを子に求める。気丈な母親といえば、有名なウィンダム卿の未亡人の例が思い浮かぶが、侍の妻たちも自らの息子を主君への忠義のために死なせる覚悟が常にできていたのである。

　武士道では、アリストテレスや、一部の現代の社会思想家と同じように、**個人よりも国家が先にある**──個人は国家の一部として生まれてくると考えられていた。したがって個人は、国家のため、あるいはその**正統な権威の求める義務**として、死ななければならないのである。ここで読者諸氏の中には、プラトンの著書『クリトン』で展開されている議論を思い出される向きもあるのではなかろうか。死罪を言い渡されたソクラテスに対して、都市国家（ポリス）の法が逃亡を思いとどまるように説く。とりわけ、法もしくは国家が次のように述べる一節に注目しよう。いわく──「そなたも、そしてそなたの父祖もまた、我らのもとで生まれ、育まれ、教えを受けたのであるから、そなたは 我らの子にして召使ではないなどと、口が裂けても言ってはならぬ」。このような言葉は、我々日本人の耳には何ら奇異なものとは聞こえない。**同じことが昔から武士道で言われてきたからである**。ただ

Shakespeare nor the Old Testament itself contains an adequate rendering of *ko*, our **conception of filial piety**, and yet in such conflicts **Bushido never wavered in its choice of Loyalty**. Women, too, encouraged their offspring to sacrifice all for the king. Ever as resolute as Widow Windham and her illustrious consort, the samurai matron stood ready to give up her boys for the cause of Loyalty.

Since Bushido, like Aristotle and some modern sociologists, conceived **the state as antedating the individual**—the latter being born into the former as part and parcel thereof—he must live and die for it or for the **incumbent of its legitimate authority**. Readers of *Crito* will remember the argument with which Socrates represents the laws of the city as pleading with him on the subject of his escape. Among others he makes them (the laws, or the state)say:—"Since you were begotten and nurtured and educated under us, dare you once to say you are not our offspring and servant, you and your fathers before you!" These are words which do not impress us as anything extraordinary; for **the same thing has long been on the lips of Bushido**, with this modification, that the laws and

し、一つ違いがある。日本人にとっては、法と国家の部分が、一人の個人に置き換えられる。**この政治理論から出てくる倫理的帰結が、忠義という概念である。**

スペンサー氏は政治的な服従すなわち忠義は、単に**一時的に機能するのみ**であると述べている [18]。私もスペンサー氏の考えを知らないわけではないし、実際にその通りかもしれないとは思う。ただしその効力はその日かぎりなのであろう。しかし日本人はそれを喜んで繰り返す。日本人にとっての「その日」とは、長い年月を意味する。すなわち**国歌**に詠われている「**さざれ石の巌となりて苔のむすまで**」という、途方もない時間である。ここで注目しておきたいことが一つある。イギリス人のような民主的な国民でさえ、ブートミー氏が最近記しているように、「かつてゲルマンの先祖が族長に対して感じたような、一人の人間及びその子どもたちへと向かう忠誠心が存在していたが、それが時代とともに形をかえて、**現在の民族や王族の血に対する深い忠誠心へ**とつながっている。**イギリス人の王室好きは尋常ではない**」。

政治的な服従は、**良心の権威への忠誠へ**と変わってい

---

[18] *Principles of Ethics*, Vol. I, Pt. II, Ch. X.

the state were represented with us by a personal being. **Loyalty is an ethical outcome of this political theory.**

I am not entirely ignorant of Mr. Spencer's view according to which political obedience—Loyalty—is accredited with **only a transitional function.**[18] It may be so. Sufficient unto the day is the virtue thereof. We may complacently repeat it, especially as we believe that day to be a long space of time, during which, so our **national anthem** says, **"tiny pebbles grow into mighty rocks draped with moss."** We may remember at this juncture that even among so democratic a people as the English, "the sentiment of personal fidelity to a man and his posterity which their Germanic ancestors felt for their chiefs, has," as Monsieur Boutmy recently said, "only passed more or less into **their profound loyalty to the race and blood of their princes**, as evidenced in **their extraordinary attachment to the dynasty.**"

Political subordination, Mr. Spencer predicts, will give place to **loyalty to the dictates of conscience.**

くと、スペンサー氏は予言している。この予言が現実と
なったあかつきには、忠誠心、及びそこから自然に湧き
出てくる敬意は、永遠に消えてしまうのであろうか？
日本人は忠義にもとることなく、仕える主君を変えるこ
とができる。この世でつかの間の王笏をふるう君王に従
いながらも、これとは別に魂の奥に主を祭り、これに仕
えることができる。数年前のこと、スペンサーの弟子を
標榜する愚か者たちが、日本の**論壇**に混乱をもたらした
ことがあった。この輩は**天皇への唯一無二の忠誠**を主張
　　　　　　やから
するあまり、キリスト教徒は**天の主への忠誠を誓う**がゆ
えに反逆者である、といって非難した。詭弁家ほどの機
　　　　　　　　　　　　　　　　　ソフィスト
転もないのに詭弁をもてあそび、スコラ神学者ほどの緻
密さを持ち合わせないのに、複雑きわまりない神学論争
に及んだのである。**ある意味で**、我ら日本人は「どちら
かを奉じ、他方を蔑ろにするということなく、**二人の主
に仕え**」、「カエサルのものはカエサルへ、主のものは主
へ返す」ことができるのである。ソクラテスは、彼の
　　　　　　　　　　　　　　　　　　　ダイモーン
神霊への忠誠心を捨てることを敢然とこばみながら、忠
誠心を失うことなく、地上における主人、すなわち都市
国家の命に従容として従ったのではなかったか？　**生き**

Suppose his induction is realized—will loyalty and its concomitant instinct of reverence disappear forever? We transfer our allegiance from one master to another, without being unfaithful to either; from being subjects of a ruler that wields the temporal sceptre we become servants of the monarch who sits enthroned in the penetralia of our heart. A few years ago a very stupid controversy, started by the misguided disciples of Spencer, made havoc among the **reading class** of Japan. In their zeal to uphold **the claim of the throne to undivided loyalty**, they charged Christians with treasonable propensities in that they **avow fidelity to their Lord and Master**. They arrayed forth sophistical arguments without the wit of Sophists, and scholastic tortuosities minus the niceties of the Schoolmen. Little did they know that we can, **in a sense**, "**serve two masters** without holding to the one or despising the other," "rendering unto Caesar the things that are Caesar's and unto God the things that are God's." Did not Socrates, all the while he unflinchingly refused to concede one iota of loyalty to his daemon, obey with equal fidelity and equanimity the command of his earthly master, the State? **His**

て良心に従い、死しては祖国に仕えたのではなかった
か？ 嗚呼、国家の権力が強大化し、個人の良心の声ま
で国に奉納させようとする日の永遠に来ざらんことを！

　武士道は、**良心を王や君主の奴隷にする**ことを求めな
い。トマス・モウブレイが、私の言いたいことを述べて
くれている。

　　畏れ多き陛下、我は陛下の足元に平伏し、
　　生き死には陛下の御意なれど、我が恥辱はさにあらず。
　　わが命を捧ぐは義務なれど、わがよき名は、
　　我が身死すといえども、墓碑の上に生きながらえ、
　　黒き汚辱を着せることは、陛下といえども許しませぬ。

　君主の勝手な気まぐれや思いつきのために、良心を屈
服させるのは下であると、武士道では考えられていた。
そのような人物は、恥も外聞もなくおべっかをつかう
「佞臣」、あるいは卑屈に王の言うがままになることで寵
を得る「寵臣」のどちらかで、歯牙にかけるに価しない
と考えられていた。この二つのタイプは、イアーゴーが
述べているタイプとぴったり重なっている。一つはお辞

conscience he followed, alive; his country he served, dying. Alack the day when a state grows so powerful as to demand of its citizens the dictates of their conscience!

Bushido did not require us to **make our conscience the slave of any lord or king**. Thomas Mowbray was a veritable spokesman for us when he said:

> "Myself I throw, dread sovereign, at thy foot.
>   My life thou shalt command, but not my shame.
>   The one my duty owes; but my fair name,
>   Despite of death, that lives upon my grave,
>   To dark dishonor's use, thou shalt not have."

A man who sacrificed his own conscience to the capricious will or freak or fancy of a sovereign was accorded a low place in the estimate of the Precepts. Such a one was despised as *nei-shin*, a cringeling, who makes court by unscrupulous fawning or as *chô-shin*, a favorite who steals his master's affections by means of servile compliance; these two species of subjects corresponding exactly to those which Iago describes,—the one, a duteous and knee-crooking knave,

儀のしすぎで膝の曲がった従順な男、地を舐めるほどの自分の頭の低さに酔いしれ、四六時中主人の尻についてまわるタイプ。もう一つは、まるで忠義の権化のような顔と衣服をまといながらも、心の中では自己の利益ばかり考えているタイプである。家臣が主君と意見をことにすれば、ケント公がリア王に対してそうしたように、何としてでも主君に誤りを悟らせようとするのが忠の道である。それがうまく行かなければ、いさぎよく主の処置にわが身をゆだねる。このような場合、**腹を切って、一点の曇りなき誠を示すことで主の理性と良心に訴えよう**とするのが、**侍の常道**であった。

doting on his own obsequious bondage, wearing out his time much like his master's ass; the other trimm'd in forms and visages of duty, keeping yet his heart attending on himself. When a subject differed from his master, the loyal path for him to pursue was to use every available means to persuade him of his error, as Kent did to King Lear. Failing in this, let the master deal with him as he wills. In cases of this kind, it was **quite a usual course for the samurai** to make the last **appeal to the intelligence and conscience of his lord** by **demonstrating the sincerity of his words with the shedding of his own blood.**

第 10 章

教育、
侍の鍛錬

　命は主に仕えるための手段であり、その理想とするところは名誉であったので、この理想に沿うように、訓育、すなわち侍となるための鍛錬が行われた。

　武士の訓育でもっとも重要なことは、**人格の陶冶**である。それ以外の思慮、知性、弁舌など、細々とした要目はさして注目されなかった。侍の教育の中で、**芸術的な嗜み**が重要な役割をはたしていることはすでに述べた。それは教養人としては不可欠であったが、**侍の教育においては必須というより、装飾のようなもの**であった。知的能力が重んじられたことはいうまでもないが、一般に「知性」を意味する「知」という言葉で意識されたのは**「叡智」**であり、**「知識」**は二の次であった。武士道の骨格は三つの徳から成り立っているといわれる。知・仁・

CHAPTER 10

EDUCATION AND TRAINING OF A SAMURAI

Life being regarded as the means whereby to serve his master, and its ideal being set upon honor, the whole education and training of a samurai were conducted accordingly.

The first point to observe in **knightly pedagogics** was to **build up character**, leaving in the shade the subtler faculties of prudence, intelligence and dialectics. We have seen the important part **aesthetic accomplishments** played in his education. Indispensable as they were to a man of culture, they were **accessories rather than essentials of samurai training**. Intellectual superiority was, of course, esteemed; but the word *Chi*, which was employed to denote intellectuality, meant **wisdom** in the first instance and placed **knowledge** only in a very subordinate place. The tripod that supported the framework of Bushido

勇、すなわち**叡智**、**仁愛**、**勇気**がそれである。侍は基本的に行動する者である。しかるに知識は行動の域外にあった。知識は、武術に関わるかぎりにおいて利用するのみであった。仏の道や神道は僧や神主が修めればよい。侍がそれに関心をもつとすれば、その目的はそれによって**勇気を養う**ということに尽きる。「信仰が人を救うのではない。人が信仰を救うのである」と言ったのはイギリスの詩人だが、これはまさに侍の信条でもあった。**儒学**と**歌道**は武士の**知的鍛錬**の中核を占めているが、それを修めるにしても、真理を得るためではなかった。歌道は**消閑の具**、儒学は**人格の陶冶**に向けて指南を得るための実践的な手引であった。戦あるいは政に関わる疑問を解くための道具でもあったが。

　以上に述べたところから、武士道で修めるべき要目とされたのがおよそ以下のようなものであったことを紹介しても、何ら驚きはないだろう。すなわち**剣術**、**弓術**、**柔術**、**馬術**、**薙刀**、**兵法**、**書道**、**儒学**、**歌道**、**歴史**がそれである。この中で柔術と書道については一言説明が必

was said to be *Chi, Jin, Yu,* respectively **Wisdom, Benevolence**, and **Courage**. A samurai was essentially a man of action. Science was without the pale of his activity. He took advantage of it in so far as it concerned his profession of arms. Religion and theology were relegated to the priests; he concerned himself with them in so far as they helped to **nourish courage**. Like an English poet the samurai believed "'tis not the creed that saves the man; but it is the man that justifies the creed." **Philosophy** and **literature** formed the chief part of his **intellectual training**; but even in the pursuit of these, it was not objective truth that he strove after,—literature was pursued mainly as **a pastime**, and philosophy as a practical aid in **the formation of character**, if not for the exposition of some military or political problem.

From what has been said, it will not be surprising to note that the curriculum of studies, according to the pedagogics of Bushido, consisted mainly of the following,—**fencing, archery, *jiujutsu* or *yawara*, horsemanship, the use of the spear, tactics, caligraphy, ethics, literature** and **history.** Of these, *jiujutsu* and caligraphy may require a few words of explana-

要だろう。日本では美しく書くことが重要視されていた。これは我が国で記される**文字**には、絵の要素が含まれているがゆえに**美術としての価値がある**からだろう。さらに**筆跡は人格を顕す**ものだとされていた。柔術をかんたんに定義するなら、肉体の解剖学的な知識を攻撃や防御に応用するものと言える。レスリングとは違う。**筋力を利用するのではない**からだ。武器を用いないという点で他の武術とも異なっている。柔術の美点は敵の体の急所をつかんだり打ったりすることによって、麻痺させたり、抵抗できなくすることである。その目的は殺すことではなく、**しばらく相手を動けなくする**ことにある。

　数学は軍人教育には必須の要目なので、それが武士道で教えられないのは際立った特徴に見えるかもしれない。しかし、なぜそうなのか、理由を見つけるのは難しくない。封建時代のいくさは科学的に厳密な形で行われたわけではない、というのが一つ。それに加えて、そもそも侍の鍛錬そのものが、数的観念を育むのに適してはいなかったということが挙げられる。

　騎士道は物惜しみとは縁遠く、**清貧をほこりとする**。ウェンティディウスは「野心こそ武人の美徳にして、も

tion. Great stress was laid on good writing, probably because our **logograms**, partaking as they do of the nature of pictures, **possess artistic value**, and also because chirography was accepted as **indicative of one's personal character**. *Jiujutsu* may be briefly defined as an application of anatomical knowledge to the purpose of offense or defense. It differs from wrestling, in that **it does not depend upon muscular strength**. It differs from other forms of attack in that it uses no weapon. Its feat consists in clutching or striking such part of the enemy's body as will make him numb and incapable of resistance. Its object is not to kill, but to **incapacitate one for action for the time being**.

A subject of study which one would expect to find in military education and which is rather conspicuous by its absence in the Bushido course of instruction, is mathematics. This, however, can be readily explained in part by the fact that feudal warfare was not carried on with scientific precision. Not only that, but the whole training of the samurai was unfavorable to fostering numerical notions.

Chivalry is uneconomical; **it boasts of penury.** It says with Ventidius that "ambition, the soldier's vir-

のを得て心を暗くするよりは、失うことを選ぶ」と述べたが、これは武士道そのものである。ドン・キホーテは黄金と領地を恥じ、錆び毀れた槍とやせこけた馬をほこる。侍はこの大仰なラ・マンチャの同志に、満腔の同情をおぼえるであろう。**侍は金を軽蔑する。**金をもうけ、金をたくわえる技術を厭悪する。**利殖は侍にとって不浄のいとなみにほかならない。**世の退廃をなげくのに「民が金を愛し、兵が死を恐れる」という決まり文句があるが、命や黄金を惜しげもなく捨てれば神と讃えられ、捨てるのを惜しめば人にあらずと貶されるのである。「何を惜しむも、金だけは惜しむなかれ。富は明智をくもらす」という。したがって、武家の子は**金のことは心におくな**といって育てられた。金のことを話すのははしたないことであり、銭の見分けもつかないのが**育ちのよさの証拠であった。臣下に碌を分け、兵を集めるには数の算段を知らないではすまないが、**金勘定は下々の者の仕事であった。**多くの藩では、財務は下級武士や僧職の者によってとり行われていた。ものを考える侍なら、いくさでものを言うのは金であることを知らぬ者はなかった

tue, rather makes choice of loss, than gain which darkens him." Don Quixote takes more pride in his rusty spear and skin-and-bone horse than in gold and lands, and a samurai is in hearty sympathy with his exaggerated confrère of La Mancha. **He disdains money itself,**—the art of making or hoarding it. **It is to him veritably filthy lucre.** The hackneyed expression to describe the decadence of an age is "that the civilians loved money and the soldiers feared death." Niggardliness of gold and of life excites as much disapprobation as their lavish use is panegyrized. "Less than all things," says a current precept, "men must grudge money: it is by riches that wisdom is hindered." Hence children were brought up **with utter disregard of economy**. It was considered bad taste to speak of it, and ignorance of the value of different coins was a token of **good breeding**. Knowledge of numbers was indispensable in the mustering of forces as well, as in the distribution of benefices and fiefs; but **the counting of money was left to meaner hands**. In many feudatories, public finance was administered by a lower kind of samurai or by priests. Every thinking bushi knew well enough that money

が、金をありがたがることを美徳とするなど、思いもよらぬことであった。**武士道では倹約が求められたが、**それは理財のためではなく、**自制心を鍛えるためである。**奢侈は人を堕落させるものとされ、侍の身分の者には**極端なまでの質朴**が求められた。奢侈を禁じる法を出している藩も多かった。

ものの本によれば、古代ローマでは、収税吏や財務官吏はしだいに騎士の身分へと引き上げられていったらしい。国家が彼らの仕事を重んじ、金そのものの重要性を示すためであったという。ローマの人びとが贅沢と貪欲にまみれていたというのも、うべなるかなである。武士道の教えはこれとは正反対である。武士道では理財は卑しいものだという考えが一貫していた。それは**人の道を教え、学問を修める職業**などとは一線を画す、卑しい職業であったのだ。

このように金と金銭欲が徹底的に無視されるので、武士道は金がもたらす数かぎりない悪から逃れていることができる。**我が国では長いあいだ、公人が腐敗とは無縁であったことが、**これによって十分に説明がつく。だが

formed the sinews of war; but he did not think of raising the appreciation of money to a virtue. It is true that **thrift was enjoined by Bushido**, but not for economical reasons so much as **for the exercise of abstinence**. Luxury was thought the greatest menace to manhood, and **severest simplicity** was required of the warrior class, sumptuary laws being enforced in many of the clans.

We read that in ancient Rome the farmers of revenue and other financial agents were gradually raised to the rank of knights, the State thereby showing its appreciation of their service and of the importance of money itself. How closely this was connected with the luxury and avarice of the Romans may be imagined. Not so with the Precepts of Knighthood. These persisted in systematically regarding finance as something low—low as compared with **moral and intellectual vocations.**

Money and the love of it being thus diligently ignored, Bushido itself could long remain free from a thousand and one evils of which money is the root. This is sufficient reason for the fact that **our public men have long been free from corruption**; but, alas,

遺憾なことに、我々の時代、この世代になって、またたくまに**金権政治**が横行するようになってしまった！

今日では**頭脳的鍛錬**が数学を学ぶことで行われているが、武士道では**文献の解釈**と、**倫理問題の議論**によってなされていた。若者は抽象的なテーマに心を悩ますことはなかった。教育の第一の目的は、上に述べたように人格の形成である。頭に表層の知識をつめこんだだけの人間は尊敬されなかった。ベーコンは、研究によって知的快楽、知的装飾、知的能力がもたらされると述べたが、武士道は何の迷いもなくこの三番目の知的能力に重きをおいている。それは「**ものごとの判断と現実問題の処理**」に用いられるものであるからだ。公の問題を処理するにせよ、自らを律するにせよ、教育はこのように現実的な目的のためである。孔子が述べているように、「学びて思わざれば則ち罔（くら）し、思いて学ばざれば則ち殆（あやう）し」である。

このように師が教え、育てようとする対象は、知性ではなく人格、頭ではなく魂だったので、人を教えることは神聖な仕事であった。「**私を生んだのは親、人にした**

how fast **plutocracy** is making its way in our time and generation!

The **mental discipline** which would now-a-days be chiefly aided by the study of mathematics, was supplied by **literary exegesis** and **deontological discussions**. Very few abstract subjects troubled the mind of the young, the chief aim of their education being, as I have said, decision of character. People whose minds were simply stored with information found no great admirers. Of the three services of studies that Bacon gives,—for delight, ornament, and ability, —Bushido had decided preference for the last, where their use was **"in judgment and the disposition of business."** Whether it was for the disposition of public business or for the exercise of self-control, it was with a practical end in view that education was conducted. "Learning without thought," said Confucius, "is labor lost: thought without learning is perilous."

When character and not intelligence, when the soul and not the head, is chosen by a teacher for the material to work upon and to develop, his vocation partakes of a sacred character. **"It is the parent who has borne me: it is the teacher who makes me man."**

のは師」という。そんな考え方だったので、師を尊び敬う気持ちにはひとかたならぬものがあった。そして、若者からこれほどの信頼と尊敬をえることのできる人間は、当然のことながら**人格に秀で**、学識も深くなければならなかった。父なき者には父となり、惑える者にはよき助言者であった。日本の格言では「父と母は天と地。師と主は日と月」という。

　どのような奉仕にも値段がつく今日のような制度は、武士道を信奉する者たちにとっては無縁であった。値をつけず、金を払わないからこそ成立する奉仕があるというのが、武士道の考え方である。聖職者や教師による**精神的な奉仕**にたいして、金や銀で報いることはできない。**価値がないからではなく、価値がつけられないほど尊い**ものだからである。この点において、代数的ならざる、本能にもとづく武士道の名誉感覚は、現代の経済学では到達できない真理を衝いている。賃金や給与は、成果が有形で、手に触れ、測定することのできるものでなければ支払うことができない。これに比して、**教育における最高の成果**、すなわち**魂の成長**（これには宗教者による教えも含まれる）は、無形であり、手に触れることも、測定することもできない。測定することができない

With this idea, therefore, the esteem in which one's preceptor was held was very high. A man to evoke such confidence and respect from the young, must necessarily be **endowed with superior personality** without lacking erudition. He was a father to the fatherless, and an adviser to the erring. "Thy father and thy mother"—so runs our maxim—"are like heaven and earth; thy teacher and thy lord are like the sun and moon."

The present system of paying for every sort of service was not in vogue among the adherents of Bushido. It believed in a service which can be rendered only without money and without price. **Spiritual service**, be it of priest or teacher, was not to be repaid in gold or silver, not because **it was valueless** but because **it was invaluable**. Here the non-arithmetical honor-instinct of Bushido taught a truer lesson than modern Political Economy; for wages and salaries can be paid only for services whose results are definite, tangible, and measurable, whereas **the best service done in education**,—namely, in **soul development** (and this includes the services of a pastor), is not definite, tangible or measurable. Being immeasurable, money, the

かぎり、価値を測定するのが役割である金は、まったく役たたずなのである。たしかに、四季の折々に、師のもとに金品の付け届けをする習慣はある。しかし**これは報酬ではなく、贈り物である。**また、受け取る側にしてみれば、ありがたくなくもなかった。師と仰がれるほどの者はたいてい、背骨がまっすぐに通り、清貧をほこる者たちであったので、賃仕事でかせいだり、代価を求めて品位を下げることなど思いもよらないからである。彼らは**どんな逆境にも負けることのない、高い精神性がそのまま人の姿となったような存在**であった。彼らはその生身の姿のまま、自己統御の象徴として皆から仰ぎ見られているのである。そしてこの自己統御こそが、教育の到達すべき最終目的なのであった。自己統御はどの侍にも求められる資質であったからだ。

ostensible measure of value, is of inadequate use. Usage sanctioned that pupils brought to their teachers money or goods at different seasons of the year; but **these were not payments but offerings**, which indeed were welcome to the recipients as they were usually men of stern calibre, boasting of honorable penury, too dignified to work with their hands and too proud to beg. They were **grave personifications of high spirits undaunted by adversity**. They were an embodiment of what was considered as an end of all learning, and were thus a living example of that discipline of disciplines, self-control which was universally required of samurai.

自己統御

その一つの側面は常在戦場の覚悟である。侍はどんな苦境にあっても、**声一つあげずに耐える力**を養わねばならぬ。もう一つの側面は他人への**礼儀**である。自分の悲しみや痛みをあらわにすることで、他人の喜びを曇らせたり、心の平静を乱したりしないことが求められる。この二つの側面が合わさると**禁欲的な性向**を生じ、それがやがて国民性へと固定化して、日本人は一見して**禁欲的**だと言われるようになる。ここで「一見して禁欲的」と言ったのは、真の禁欲主義が、一つの国民の性格とはなりえないと思うからである。また、我が国民の作法や習慣が、外国人の目に**無情**に見えているだけかもしれないからである。実際には、日本人は世界のどの国民と比べても、**優しい感情に心を動かされやすい**という点でひけをとらない

むしろ、日本人はある意味で、他国の民よりももっと感受性が強い――二倍にもそうであるはずだと、私は思

CHAPTER 11

SELF-CONTROL

The **discipline of fortitude** on the one hand, inculcating **endurance without a groan**, and the teaching of **politeness** on the other, requiring us not to mar the pleasure or serenity of another by manifestations of our own sorrow or pain, combined to engender a **stoical turn of mind**, and eventually to confirm it into a national trait of apparent **stoicism**. I say apparent stoicism, because I do not believe that true stoicism can ever become the characteristic of a whole nation, and also because some of our national manners and customs may seem to a foreign observer **hard-hearted**. Yet we are really as **susceptible to tender emotion** as any race under the sky.

I am inclined to think that in one sense we have to feel more than others—yes, doubly more—since the

いたいのである。なぜなら、**自然な感情を抑えようとすること**は、それ自体が心に苦しみを与えるからである。男児が――そして女児でも同じことだが――涙を流してはいけない、苦しいからといって声をあげてはいけない、といって育てられたとする。このような努力が神経を鈍麻するか、より繊細にするかは、心理学の問題である。

侍が**感情を顔に出す**のは「女々しい」と言われた。「**喜びも怒りも顔に出さない**」というのが、精神の強さを言い表す表現であった。もっとも自然な感情が抑制される。父が子を抱くと、権威がそこなわれる。夫はけっして妻にキスをしない。二人だけのときはいざしらず、他人のいるところでは決してそうしない！ある頓知(とんち)の得意な若者がこういった。――「アメリカでは、夫は人前で妻にキスをして、家で妻をぶつ。日本では、夫は人前で妻をぶち、家でキスをする」。たしかにこれは一面の真実をついている。

もの静かなふるまい、平静な心は、いかなる感情にも乱されてはならないのである。それで思い出したことがある。先ごろ中国と戦争をしたときのこと、ある連隊が町から出征した。指揮官と兵士たちを見送りに、大勢の

very **attempt to restrain natural promptings** entails suffering. Imagine boys—and girls too—brought up not to resort to the shedding of a tear or the uttering of a groan for the relief of their feelings,—and there is a physiological problem whether such effort steels their nerves or makes them more sensitive.

It was considered unmanly for a samurai to **betray his emotions on his face. "He shows no sign of joy or anger,"** was a phrase used in describing a strong character. The most natural affections were kept under control. A father could embrace his son only at the expense of his dignity; a husband would not kiss his wife,—no, not in the presence of other people, whatever he might do in private! There may be some truth in the remark of a witty youth when he said, "American husbands kiss their wives in public and beat them in private; Japanese husbands beat theirs in public and kiss them in private."

Calmness of behavior, composure of mind, should not be disturbed by passion of any kind. I remember when, during the late war with China, a regiment left a certain town, a large concourse of people flocked to the station to bid farewell to the general

人が駅に集まった。この場所にアメリカ人の住人が出かけていった。国全体が大いに興奮し、兵士たちの父や母や恋人が来ているのだから、さぞはでやかな見送りの場面となるだろうと期待してのことだった。ところが意外にも失望させられることとなった。笛が鳴って汽車が動き出すと、集まった数千の人は無言のまま帽子をとり、ていねいに頭を下げて見送ったのである。ハンカチを振る者もなければ、言葉を発する者もいない。ただ深い沈黙があたりを領し、耳をすませばほんの数名、**たまらずにすすり泣く声**が聞こえるばかりであった。家庭の中でも同じことである。子どもが病気になり、扉の外で子どもの苦しい息に聞き耳をたてながら幾晩もすごした父親のことを知っている。そのような親としての情にほだされた弱い姿を、人に見られてはならないのである！いまわの際になっても、息子の勉強の妨げになってはといって、息子を呼ぼうとしなかった母親のことも耳にしたことがある。日本の歴史にも、そして日常の場面にも、プルタークのもっとも感動的な物語にも比すべき、**英雄的な女性の例**があふれている。我が国の農村にも、イアン・マクラーレンの描くマーゲット・ハウのような女性が数多く存在するのである。

　日本のキリスト教の教会がなかなか本格的に復活して

and his army. On this occasion an American resident resorted to the place, expecting to witness loud demonstrations, as the nation itself was highly excited and there were fathers, mothers, and sweethearts of the soldiers in the crowd. The American was strangely disappointed; for as the whistle blew and the train began to move, the hats of thousands of people were silently taken off and their heads bowed in reverential farewell; no waving of handkerchiefs, no word uttered, but deep silence in which only an attentive ear could catch a few **broken sobs**. In domestic life, too, I know of a father who spent whole nights listening to the breathing of a sick child, standing behind the door that he might not be caught in such an act of parental weakness! I know of a mother who, in her last moments, refrained from sending for her son, that he might not be disturbed in his studies. Our history and everyday life are replete with **examples of heroic matrons** who can well bear comparison with some of the most touching pages of Plutarch. Among our peasantry an Ian Maclaren would be sure to find many a Marget Howe.

It is the same discipline of self-restraint which is ac-

こないのも、この自己統御の訓練によって説明ができよう。男でも女でも心が動かされるのを感じたとき、本能的に、それが顔に出るのをそっと抑えようとする。稀なできごととして、抗しようのない気持ちによって舌が開放された結果、**何一つ包み隠すことなく、浮かれたように喋ってしまうこと**がある。魂の経験を軽々しく口にすることをうながすのは、「神の名をみだりに唱えてはならない」という**モーセの第三の戒律を破ること**を奨励するに等しい。**もっとも神聖な言葉、もっとも隠しておくべき心の経験**が、相手かまわず語られるのを聞くと、日本人は耳をふさぎたくなる。「優しい思いで魂の土がゆり動かされるのを感じるなら、それは種が芽ぶいているのだ。言葉で妨害してはならない。静かに、密やかに見まもるがよい」と、ある若い侍が日記に記している。

　心の奥の──とくに宗教的な──**思いや気持ちを雄弁に語ること**は、実はそれが深いものではなく、誠から出たものでもないことを、まごうかたなく示しているというのが、日本人の感じ方である。「口開けて 腸 見せる 柘榴 かな」という俗な言い回しがある。

　心が動かされると口をかたく閉じて隠そうとするというのは、必ずしも**東洋人にありがちの不可思議なふるま**

countable for the absence of more frequent revivals in the Christian churches of Japan. When a man or woman feels his or her soul stirred, the first instinct is to quietly suppress any indication of it. In rare instances is the tongue set free by an irresistible spirit, when we have **eloquence of sincerity and fervor**. It is putting a premium upon **a breach of the third commandment** to encourage speaking lightly of spiritual experience. It is truly jarring to Japanese ears to hear **the most sacred words, the most secret heart experiences**, thrown out in promiscuous audiences. "Dost thou feel the soil of thy soul stirred with tender thoughts? It is time for seeds to sprout. Disturb it not with speech; but let it work alone in quietness and secrecy,"—writes a young samurai in his diary.

To give in so many articulate words **one's inmost thoughts and feelings**—notably the religious—is taken among us as an unmistakable sign that they are neither very profound nor very sincere. "Only a pomegranate is he"—so runs a popular saying —"who, when he gapes his mouth, displays the contents of his heart."

It is not altogether **perverseness of oriental minds** that the instant our emotions are moved we try to

いとはいえない。日本人も言葉を発することが多い。話すということは、あるフランス人がいみじくも述べているように「心の思いを隠す手立て」なのだ。

苦悩の淵にある日本の友人を訪ねてみるがよい。その友人は、泣きはらした目、濡れた頬をしていようと、まちがいなく笑ってあなたを迎えるだろう。それを見た人は、相手がヒステリーの状態にあるのかと思うかもしれない。そしてどうしたのかと尋ねると、途切れとぎれに**陳腐な言い回し**が返ってくることだろう。「人生は悲しいですね」、「人は出会っても必ず離別するものです」、「この世に生まれたからには必ず死なねばなりません」、「死んだ子の歳を数えるのは愚かだが、女の情は馬鹿なことをしないではいられません」等々。ホーエンツォレルン侯は気高くも「口に出さずに苦しむことを学べ」と言ったが、そのはるか以前から、日本人の胸はこの格言に共鳴していたのである。

そもそも、**本来の人間の弱さがきびしい試練にさらされた**とき、日本人は笑うことによって耐えようとする。デモクリトスは「笑う哲学者」と称されたが、このデモクリトスに比して、日本人の笑うという戦術にはそれなりの根拠がある。日本人の笑いの下には、不幸な状況によって**波立った心を沈めようとする努力**が隠されているのである。笑いは、**悲しみや怒りの解毒剤**である。

guard our lips in order to hide them. Speech is very often with us, as the Frenchman defined it, "the art of concealing thought."

Call upon a Japanese friend in time of deepest affliction and he will invariably receive you laughing, with red eyes or moist cheeks. At first you may think him hysterical. Press him for explanation and you will get a few broken **commonplaces**—"Human life has sorrow;" "They who meet must part;" "He that is born must die;" "It is foolish to count the years of a child that is gone, but a woman's heart will indulge in follies;" and the like. So the noble words of a noble Hohenzollern—"Lerne zu leiden ohne Klagen"—had found many responsive minds among us, long before they were uttered.

Indeed, the Japanese have recourse to risibility whenever **the frailties of human nature are put to severest test**. I think we possess a better reason than Democritus himself for our Abderian tendency; for laughter with us oftenest veils **an effort to regain balance of temper**, when disturbed by any untoward circumstance. It is a **counterpoise of sorrow or rage**.

このように昔から**感情を抑えること**が求められてきた
一方で、その**はけ口**として詩歌が用いられた。十世紀の
歌人（紀貫之）は、「日本でも唐土でも、人は悲しみに心が
動いたとき、苦悩を詩文にあらわす」と述べている。子を
なくした傷心の母親が、不在の子を詠んだ俳句がある。

　　蜻蛉つり、今日はどこまで行ったやら

いつものように蜻蛉取りに出かけていないのだ、という
見立てである。

　例はこれだけにしておこう。我が国の詩文には、珠玉
の思いが連ねられている。傷ついた胸からしたたり落ち
る血が凝縮し、真珠の首飾りのようにつらなった、世に
二つとない宝物である。その雅な風姿そのままに、異国
の言の葉に移すすべを私は持ち合わせない。しかし、こ
れ以上の例がなくとも、皮相な観察からは見えない**日本
人の心の動きかた**を、それなりに示し得たのではないか
と思う。日本人は**無慈悲**に見えるかもしれない。**同時に
笑い、悲しむヒステリー**な国民とうつり、精神の働きが
正常ではないと言われることもあるが、それが迷妄であ
ることを示しえたと思う。

　さらに、日本人が**苦痛に耐えること**ができ、**死を恐れ
ない**のは、**神経が鈍い**からだとも言われることがある。

The **suppression of feelings** being thus steadily insisted upon, they find their **safety-valve** in poetical aphorism. A poet of the tenth century writes, "In Japan and China as well, humanity, when moved by sorrow, tells its bitter grief in verse." A mother who tries to console her broken heart by fancying her departed child absent on his wonted chase after the dragon-fly, hums,

> "How far to-day in chase, I wonder,
>   Has gone my hunter of the dragon-fly!"

I refrain from quoting other examples, for I know I could do only scant justice to the pearly gems of our literature, were I to render into a foreign tongue the thoughts which were wrung drop by drop from bleeding hearts and threaded into beads of rarest value. I hope I have in a measure shown that **inner working of our minds** which often presents an appearance of **callousness** or of an **hysterical mixture of laughter and dejection**, and whose sanity is sometimes called in question.

It has also been suggested that our **endurance of pain** and **indifference to death** are due to **less sensi-**

表層だけをうかがえばいかにもそのとおりに見える。では、次なる疑問は、なぜ日本人の神経は、他国民ほどぴんと張っていないのか、ということになる。日本の気候がアメリカほど刺激に富んでいないからだろうか。我が国は**天皇制**だが、**共和制**がフランス人を興奮させるほど、わが国民は興奮しないのだろうか。イギリス人ほど、『衣装哲学』を熱心に読まないからだろうか。我が国民ははあまりに興奮しやすく、感受性が強いからこそ、つねに自己統御を意識し、自らに課さねばならないのではないかというのが、私の考えである。どんな説明を試みるにせよ、日本では長年に渡って自己統御の修練がなされるということを考慮しないでは、正しい結論にはいたらないであろう。

自己統御の修練はえてして行き過ぎることがある。魂の明るい素質を、圧し殺すことがある。もともと柔軟な性質なのに、ゆがんだ性格破綻者を作り上げることもある。**狂信**を生み、**偽善**を育て、**愛情**を鈍らせることもある。どんな高貴な徳であれ、本物にもなれば偽物にもなる。どの美徳にもすぐれた面を見出して、その理想に即くべきである。そして自己統御の理想とは、**心を平らに保つこと**、すなわちギリシアの言葉を借りるなら、デモクリトスが至高の善と呼んだ「エウテミア（快活さ）」を達成することである。

tive nerves. This is plausible as far as it goes. The next question is,—Why are our nerves less tightly strung? It may be our climate is not so stimulating as the American. It may be our **monarchical form of government** does not excite us as much as **the Republic** does the Frenchman. It may be that we do not read *Sartor Resartus* as zealously as the Englishman. Personally, I believe it was our very excitability and sensitiveness which made it a necessity to recognize and enforce constant self-repression; but whatever may be the explanation, without taking into account long years of discipline in self-control, none can be correct.

Discipline in self-control can easily go too far. It can well repress **the genial current of the soul**. It can force pliant natures into distortions and monstrosities. It can beget **bigotry**, breed **hypocrisy** or hebetate **affections**. Be a virtue never so noble, it has its counterpart and counterfeit. We must recognize in each virtue its own positive excellence and follow its positive ideal, and the ideal of self-restraint is to **keep our mind level**—as our expression is—or, to borrow a Greek term, attain the state of euthymia, which Democritus called the highest good.

第 12 章

腹切と仇討

　この章では腹切と仇討という二つの制度を紹介するが、これらについてはすでに外国の著者によって、深浅さまざまに論じられている。

　まずは「ハラキリ」について述べるが、ここで扱うのは俗にいう腹切、すなわち切腹もしくは割腹のみであることをお断りしておく。腹切とは、**腹部を切って自殺する儀式**のことである。はじめて聞くと、「腹部を切るだと？　なんと馬鹿げたことよ！」と呆れるかもしれない。異国の人々には途方もないことに見えるかもしれないが、シェイクスピアを知っている人にはそう不自然なことではないはずだ。「おまえ（シーザー）の魂は地上を歩き回り、おれたちを唆して、おのが剣で、おのれの臓腑を掻き取らせる」とブルータスが述べる。『アジアの光』では、現代の英国詩人によって、女王の腸が刺し貫かれるさまが記されているが、まずい英語であるとか、

CHAPTER 12

THE INSTITUTIONS OF SUICIDE AND REDRESS

We shall now bring to view two institutions; namely, the institutions of suicide and redress of which (the former known as *hara-kiri* and the latter as *kataki-uchi*) many foreign writers have treated more or less fully.

To begin with suicide, let me state that I confine my observations only to *seppuku* or *kappuku*, popularly known as *hara-kiri*—which means **self-immolation by disembowelment**. "Ripping the abdomen? How absurd!"—so cry those to whom the name is new. Absurdly odd as it may sound at first to foreign ears, it can not be so very foreign to students of Shakespeare, who puts these words in Brutus' mouth—"Thy (Caesar's) spirit walks abroad and turns our swords into our proper entrails." Listen to a modern English poet, who in his *Light of Asia*, speaks of a sword piercing the

品位に欠けるなどという批判は聞こえてこない。もう一つ例を挙げておこう。ジェノヴァのパラッツォロッソ（赤の宮殿）に飾られている、画家グエルチーノが描いたカトーの自害の場面を見るがよい。アディソンの劇でカトーが話す最後の言葉を読んで、カトーの腹に突き立った剣をあざ笑う者はいないだろう。日本人にとって、このような死に方は、何にもまして**気高いふるまい、感動的な情愛**の場面と結びついており、嫌悪感はいうに及ばず、馬鹿馬鹿しいというような感想など生じる余地はない。あまりに高い精神性、あまりに偉大で優しい行為にはすべてを変えてしまう力があるがゆえに、切腹という**残忍きわまりない死に方が崇高な輝きをおび、新たな生命の象徴**となるのである。さもなくば、コンスタンティヌス帝が見た十字架の徴（しるし）が世界を征服することもないであろう！

　切腹は西欧人の目には愚にもつかないものに見えるかもしれないが、日本人にとってはそうではない。それは、切腹にまつわる諸々の外面的な事柄のみが理由というわけではない。傷つけるのが、とくに腹部であるということには根拠がある。古来、腹こそが**魂と情愛のやどる場所**だと信じられていたのである。モーセがヨセフの「腸（はらわた）が弟を懐かしみ」（創世記 43：30）と述べ、ダヴィデが「わが腸」を忘れぬようにと主に祈り、イザヤ、エ

bowels of a queen:—none blames him for bad English or breach of modesty. Or, to take still another example, look at Guercino's painting of Cato's death, in the Palazzo Rossa in Genoa. Whoever has read the swan-song which Addison makes Cato sing, will not jeer at the sword half-buried in his abdomen. In our minds this mode of death is associated with instances of **noblest deeds** and of most **touching pathos**, so that nothing repugnant, much less ludicrous, mars our conception of it. So wonderful is the transforming power of virtue, of greatness, of tenderness, that **the vilest form of death assumes a sublimity** and becomes **a symbol of new life**, or else—the sign which Constantine beheld would not conquer the world!

Not for extraneous associations only does *seppuku* lose in our mind any taint of absurdity; for the choice of this particular part of the body to operate upon, was based on an old anatomical belief as to **the seat of the soul and of the affections**. When Moses wrote of Joseph's "bowels yearning upon his brother," or David prayed the Lord not to forget his bowels, or when Isaiah, Jeremiah and other inspired men of old spoke

レミアなど古代の預言者によって「腸が音を出す」や「腸の苦しみ」などという表現が用いられているのは、日本人にはおなじみの、**魂は腹に宿っている**という思いと軌を一にしているのである。ユダヤの民は通常、肝臓と腎臓、及びその周囲の脂肪が感情と生命の宿る場所であるとする。「腹」という日本語のほうが、ギリシャ語の「フレン」や「トゥモス」（気概）と比べて意味の範囲が広いが、人間の魂が肉体のこの部分にやどっていると考えていた点では、ギリシャ人も日本人も同じである。そしてこのような考えを持っていたのは、**古代の諸民族**だけではない。有名な哲学者デカルトこそ魂は松果体に宿ると主張したが、フランスでは一般に「ヴァントル（ventre）」という語が、解剖学的には曖昧ではあるものの、生理学的には意味のある語として用いられている。同じことが「アントライユ（entrailles）」についても言える。本来は「内臓」だが、**「愛情、同情」という意味で用いられている**。さらに言っておくなら、このような考え方は、**単なる迷信**ではなく、一般に広まっている心臓が感情の中枢であるという考えより、はるかに科学的根拠がある。「この体のどの醜い部分に、ロメオという名前が宿っているのです？」とロメオは修道士に尋ねたが、日本人であれば、そんなことは尋ねるまでもないのである。現代の神経医学では腹部神経叢や骨盤神経

of the "sounding" or the "troubling" of bowels, they all and each endorsed the belief prevalent among the Japanese that **in the abdomen was enshrined the soul**. The Semites habitually spoke of the liver and kidneys and surrounding fat as the seat of emotion and of life. The term *hara* was more comprehensive than the Greek *phren* or *thumos* and the Japanese and Hellenese alike thought the spirit of man to dwell somewhere in that region. Such a notion is by no means confined to the **peoples of antiquity**. The French, in spite of the theory propounded by one of their most distinguished philosophers, Descartes, that the soul is located in the pineal gland, still insist in using the term *ventre* in a sense, which, if anatomically too vague, is nevertheless physiologically significant. Similarly *entrailles* **stands** in their language **for affection and compassion**. Nor is such belief **mere superstition**, being more scientific than the general idea of making the heart the centre of the feelings. Without asking a friar, the Japanese knew better than Romeo "in what vile part of this anatomy one's name did lodge." Modern neurologists speak of the abdominal and pelvic brains, denoting thereby sympathetic

叢という語が用いられ、それぞれ該当部分の交感神経を意味するが、これは**精神の作用**によって大きく影響されるのである。この神経生理学の見地を受け入れれば、そこから**切腹の論理**はいともかんたんに導き出すことができる。「私の魂の座を開いて、中のありさまをお見せしましょう。けがれているか、それとも清浄か、ご自分の目でとくとご覧あれ」ということである。

　私がここで宗教、もしくは道徳の見地から自殺を正当化しようとしているとは思わないでいただきたい。武士道では名誉がきわめて重んじられていたので、自らの生命を断つ**理由としてじゅうぶん**であると考えられたのである。詩人ガースは次のように詠っている。

　　名誉が失われると、死ぬことが救いだ
　　死ねば不名誉から確実に逃れることができる

これに共感して、自らの魂を忘却に淵に投げ入れた者は、なんと多かったことか！武士道では、**名誉がかかわっている場合**に、自害こそが**複雑な問題を解決する手段**とされていたのである。血気盛んな侍にとって、畳の上でふつうに迎える死はなまぬるく、男児の本懐とするところではなかった。キリスト教徒の中にも、カトー、ブルータス、ペトロニウスなど古代の偉人たちが、**神々し**

nerve-centres in those parts which are strongly affected by any **psychical action**. This view of mental physiology once admitted, **the syllogism of *seppuku*** is easy to construct. "I will open the seat of my soul and show you how it fares with it. See for yourself whether it is polluted or clean."

I do not wish to be understood as asserting religious or even moral justification of suicide, but the high estimate placed upon honor was **ample excuse** with many for taking one's own life. How many acquiesced in the sentiment expressed by Garth,

> "When honor's lost, 'tis a relief to die;
>   Death's but a sure retreat from infamy,"

and have smilingly surrendered their souls to oblivion! Death **when honor was involved**, was accepted in Bushido as **a key to the solution of many complex problems**, so that to an ambitious samurai a natural departure from life seemed a rather tame affair and a consummation not devoutly to be wished for. I dare say that many good Christians, if only they are honest enough, will confess the fascination of, if not positive

いほどの平常心を保ちながらこの地上の生を終えたことを、積極的に褒めたたえることはしないまでも、魅力的に感じることを、正直に白状する人は多いのではなかろうか。そもそも、世界で最初の哲学者ともいうべき人物、すなわちソクラテスが地上の生を終えたのも、ほぼ自殺であったと言えば、言いすぎだろうか？ ソクラテスが**都市国家の命令に従容として服した**ということが、弟子たちによって細やかに伝えられている。この命令は倫理的に誤ったものであることをソクラテスは意識しており、その気になれば逃亡することもできたのである。それにもかかわらず、ドクニンジンの容器を手に取り、死を含んだ液体を神に捧げようとさえした。このようなふるまいに、**自己抹殺**の匂いを嗅ぎつけることはできないだろうか？ 通常の処刑とは違って、ここには何の物理的強制も存在しない。たしかに判事たちの評決は、服さねばならない義務であった。「汝、死すべし。汝自身の手によるものとす」というものであった。自殺の定義が自分自身の手によって死ぬということだけであれば、ソクラテスは明らかに自殺である。しかし、自殺という罪をおかしたといって、ソクラテスを責める者はいない。自殺を嫌悪したプラトンも、師の終焉について決してそのようには言わなかった。

　読者諸氏には、**切腹は単なる自殺ではないこと**を、き

admiration for, **the sublime composure** with which Cato, Brutus, Petronius and a host of other ancient worthies, terminated their own earthly existence. Is it too bold to hint that the death of the first of the philosophers was partly suicidal? When we are told so minutely by his pupils how their master **willingly submitted to the mandate of the state**—which he knew was morally mistaken—in spite of the possibilities of escape, and how he took up the cup of hemlock in his own hand, even offering libation from its deadly contents, do we not discern in his whole proceeding and demeanor, **an act of self-immolation**? No physical compulsion here, as in ordinary cases of execution. True the verdict of the judges was compulsory: it said, "Thou shalt die,— and that by thy own hand." If suicide meant no more than dying by one's own hand, Socrates was a clear case of suicide. But nobody would charge him with the crime; Plato, who was averse to it, would not call his master a suicide.

Now my readers will understand that *seppuku* **was**

ちんと理解していただきたい。それは一つの制度であった。法的制度であり、かつ儀式でもあった。それの起こりは中世にさかのぼり、武士が自分のおかした**罪の償いをし、過ちに対して謝罪し、不名誉をのがれ、同志の者たちを断罪から免れさせ、自らの誠を証明する**ものであった。法的な罰として行われるときには、しかるべき儀式として実行された。きわめて**洗練された自己抹殺の形**であり、**極度なまでの冷静沈着な精神**と、**乱れることのない所作ふるまい**を身につけていなければ完遂することができない。それがゆえに、とくに武士という身分にふさわしいといえる。

　この切腹という、かつての時代の儀式については、歴史的な興味もあり、それがどのようなものであったのかここに記しておきたいところだが、私などより練達の文章家によってすでに書かれたものがあり、それは現在ではあまり読まれることもないので、長文をいとわず引用したい。それはミットフォードによる『古い日本の物語』という本で、珍しい日本の手書きの文書から、切腹を論じた文章を翻訳したあとで、彼自身が目撃した切腹の場面をありありと描いているのである。

　　我々（七人の外国人の代表）は、日本人の検使役のあとについて、その儀式が行われる寺の本堂に入るよ

not a mere suicidal process. It was an institution, legal and ceremonial. An invention of the middle ages, it was a process by which warriors could **expiate their crimes**, **apologize for errors**, **escape from disgrace**, **redeem their friends**, or **prove their sincerity**. When enforced as a legal punishment, it was practiced with due ceremony. It was a **refinement of self-destruction**, and none could perform it without the **utmost coolness of temper** and **composure of demeanor**, and for these reasons it was particularly befitting the profession of bushi.

Antiquarian curiosity, if nothing else, would tempt me to give here a description of this obsolete ceremonial; but seeing that such a description was made by a far abler writer, whose book is not much read now-a-days, I am tempted to make a somewhat lengthy quotation. Mitford, in his *Tales of Old Japan*, after giving a translation of a treatise on *seppuku* from a rare Japanese manuscript, goes on to describe an instance of such an execution of which he was an eye-witness:—

"We (seven foreign representatives) were invited to follow the Japanese witness into the *hondo* or main

ううながされた。そこは自ずと粛然とさせられる舞台であった。黒々とした太い柱の上に高い天井がのっている、大きな広間だ。天井からは、大きな金の灯籠や、仏教寺院に特有の装具がずらりとつるされている。祭壇の前は床に美しい畳が置かれ、周囲より数インチ高くなっている。そして、その上に緋の毛氈がしかれている。きれいに並べられた蠟燭が暗く妖しい光を放ち、儀式のもようがかろうじて見える。畳の左手に七人の日本人が座り、七人の外国人は右側に座る。同席するのはただそれだけである。

　緊張の数分がすぎて、滝善三郎がきりりとした表情で本堂に入ってきた。三十二歳のたくましい人物で、切腹のための衣装、すなわち麻の裃（正式な儀式用の衣装）をまとっている。滝善三郎とともに介錯人と、三人の役人が入ってきた。こちらは陣羽織を着ている。すなわち金糸入りの垂れ襟がついた、いくさ用の上衣である。「介錯人」について一言述べておくと、英語の「死刑執行人」とは異なることに注意が必要だ。これは侍の役どころである。切腹する者の親戚や

hall of the temple, where the ceremony was to be performed. It was an imposing scene. A large hall with a high roof supported by dark pillars of wood. From the ceiling hung a profusion of those huge gilt lamps and ornaments peculiar to Buddhist temples. In front of the high altar, where the floor, covered with beautiful white mats, is raised some three or four inches from the ground, was laid a rug of scarlet felt. Tall candles placed at regular intervals gave out a dim mysterious light, just sufficient to let all the proceedings be seen. The seven Japanese took their places on the left of the raised floor, the seven foreigners on the right. No other person was present.

"After the interval of a few minutes of anxious suspense, Taki Zenzaburo, a stalwart man thirty-two years of age, with a noble air, walked into the hall attired in his dress of ceremony, with the peculiar hempen-cloth wings which are worn on great occasions. He was accompanied by a *kaishaku* and three officers, who wore the *jimbaori* or war surcoat with gold tissue facings. The word *kaishaku*, it should be observed, is one to which our word executioner is no equivalent term. The office is that of a

朋友がつとめることが多い。罪人と処刑人ではなく、決闘の当事者と介添人の関係にひとしい。この場合には、介錯人は滝善三郎の弟子がつとめた。本人の知り合いが協議して、仲間の中から剣の道に秀でた者が選ばれたのである。

滝善三郎は、介錯人を左にしたがえて日本人の立会のほうへと静々と進んでゆき、二人は深々と辞儀をした。ついで外国人の立会のほうへと行き、同じように深々と頭を下げた。こちらのほうがより敬意がこもっているようにも見える。どちらの場合も、立会が礼をかえした。ゆっくりと、そして堂々としたしぐさで滝善三郎は一段高い畳の上にあがり、祭壇に向かって二度額づいてからそれに背をむけ、毛氈の上に正座した [19]。介錯人は左側にしゃがむ。三人の役人のうちの一人が三宝をささげながら進んでくる。その上に紙

---

[19] 敬意を示す座り方で、滝善三郎は死ぬまでこの姿勢を保った。

gentleman: in many cases it is performed by a kinsman or friend of the condemned, and the relation between them is rather that of principal and second than that of victim and executioner. In this instance the *kaishaku* was a pupil of Taki Zenzaburo, and was selected by friends of the latter from among their own number for his skill in swordsmanship.

"With the *kaishaku* on his left hand, Taki Zenzaburo advanced slowly towards the Japanese witnesses, and the two bowed before them, then drawing near to the foreigners they saluted us in the same way, perhaps even with more deference; in each case the salutation was ceremoniously returned. Slowly and with great dignity the condemned man mounted on to the raised floor, prostrated himself before the high altar twice, and seated[19] himself on the felt carpet with his back to the high altar, the *kaishaku* crouching on his left hand side. One of the three attendant officers then came forward, bearing a stand of the kind used in the temple for offerings,

---

[19] Seated himself-that is, in the Japanese fashion, his knees and toes touching the ground and his body resting on his heels. In this position, which is one of respect, he remained until his death.

に巻かれた九寸五分の脇差がのっている。とがった先までカミソリの刃のようにするどく研ぎすまされている。役人はこの脇差を、額づきながら渡した。滝善三郎はこれをうやうやしく受け取り、両手で頭の高さまでささげてから、自分の前に置いた。

　滝善三郎はもう一度深々と礼をすると、苦しい告白をする人間には当然の、感情の高ぶりとためらいが声に出たものの、そのほかには表情も所作も乱すことなく口上をのべた。

「神戸では、私、そして私一人が不用意に外国人への発砲を命じました。また逃亡しようとしたところに、再度発砲を命じました。この罪を負って、私は割腹いたします。居並ぶ方々、とくとご覧くだされますようお願い申し上げまする」。

　滝善三郎はもう一度礼をして着物をはだけ、上半身をあらわにした。そうしてうしろにひっくり返らないよう、慣例どおり袖を膝の下に押し込む。気高い日本

on which, wrapped in paper, lay the *wakizashi,* the short sword or dirk of the Japanese, nine inches and a half in length, with a point and an edge as sharp as a razor's. This he handed, prostrating himself, to the condemned man, who received it reverently, raising it to his head with both hands, and placed it in front of himself.

"After another profound obeisance, Taki Zenzaburo, in a voice which betrayed just so much emotion and hesitation as might be expected from a man who is making a painful confession, but with no sign of either in his face or manner, spoke as follows:—

'I, and I alone, unwarrantably gave the order to fire on the foreigners at Kobe, and again as they tried to escape. For this crime I disembowel myself, and I beg you who are present to do me the honor of witnessing the act.'

"Bowing once more, the speaker allowed his upper garments to slip down to his girdle, and remained naked to the waist. Carefully, according to custom, he tucked his sleeves under his knees to prevent himself from falling backward; for a noble

の侍は前に伏せて死なねばならぬのである。目の前の
脇差を、ふるえるでもなく、ゆっくりと手にとる。憧
れをふくんだ、ほとんど愛おしそうな目でそれを眺め
る。一瞬、最後の覚悟をするかのような表情をしたか
と思うと、刀を腹の左側に深々と突き立て、ゆっくり
と右側まで引く。そしてそのまま回して、わずかに切
り上げた。気の遠くなりそうなこの苦痛の所作のあい
だ、顔の筋肉一つ動かさない。そうして刀を抜くと前
にかがみ、首を差しのべた。このときはじめて苦痛の
表情が顔をよぎったが、うめき声一つたてない。この
瞬間、わきに屈んでこの所作の一々を食い入るように
見ていた介錯人がさっと立ち上がり、一瞬刀を空中に
静止させる。刃が一閃し、ずしりという醜悪な音とと
もに刀が振り下ろされる。一刀で首が体から離れた。

　深々と沈黙がおりる。我々の目の前にころがった、
動かぬ首から血がどくどくと流れ出る、身の毛のよだ
つ音だけがきこえる。一瞬前まで、肝のすわった折り
目正しい侍だったのに、なんという変わりようだろ
う。まことに見るにたえない光景であった。

　介錯人は深々と辞儀をして、用意してきた紙で刀を

Japanese gentleman should die falling forwards. Deliberately, with a steady hand he took the dirk that lay before him; he looked at it wistfully, almost affectionately; for a moment he seemed to collect his thoughts for the last time, and then stabbing himself deeply below the waist in the left-hand side, he drew the dirk slowly across to his right side, and turning it in the wound, gave a slight cut upwards. During this sickeningly painful operation he never moved a muscle of his face. When he drew out the dirk, he leaned forward and stretched out his neck; an expression of pain for the first time crossed his face, but he uttered no sound. At that moment the *kaishaku*, who, still crouching by his side, had been keenly watching his every movement, sprang to his feet, poised his sword for a second in the air; there was a flash, a heavy, ugly thud, a crashing fall; with one blow the head had been severed from the body.

"A dead silence followed, broken only by the hideous noise of the blood throbbing out of the inert head before us, which but a moment before had been a brave and chivalrous man. It was horrible.

"The *kaishaku* made a low bow, wiped his sword

ぬぐうと、畳の台からおりた。そしてよごれた脇差が
おごそかに運び去られた。処刑をあかす血まみれの証
拠であった。

　二人の天皇の使者が座をたち、外国の検使役の前ま
できて、滝善三郎の死罪がとどこおりなく行われた証
人となるよう、申し述べた。こうして儀式が終わり、
我々は堂を去った。

　切腹の生々しい描写は、様々の文献や、目撃談からい
くらでも引いてくることができようが、例はもう一つあ
げれば十分であろう。

　左近と内記という兄弟がいた。兄は二四歳、弟は一七
歳であったが、父親の憾みをはらすべく家康を暗殺しよ
うとした。ところが家康の陣に入る前に捕まってしまっ
た。家康は自分の生命が狙われたものの、この兄弟の心
意気をあっぱれに思って、侍らしく死ぬことを許した。
二人の弟の八麿は八歳の幼児であったが、同じ運命を命

with a piece of paper which he had ready for the purpose, and retired from the raised floor; and the stained dirk was solemnly borne away, a bloody proof of the execution.

"The two representatives of the Mikado then left their places, and crossing over to where the foreign witnesses sat, called to us to witness that the sentence of death upon Taki Zenzaburo had been faithfully carried out. The ceremony being at an end, we left the temple."

I might multiply any number of descriptions of seppuku from literature or from the relation of eye-witnesses; but one more instance will suffice.

Two brothers, Sakon and Naiki, respectively twenty-four and seventeen years of age, made an effort to kill Iyéyasu in order to avenge their father's wrongs; but before they could enter the camp they were made prisoners. The old general admired the pluck of the youths who dared an attempt on his life and ordered that they should be allowed to die an honorable death. Their little brother Hachimaro, a mere infant

じられた。一家の男子すべてに死罪が宣せられたのである。三人は刑が行われる寺に引いて行かれた。その場に立ち会った医者の日記が残っているので、この場面を翻訳しておこう。

　処刑のために一列に座らされると、左近は末の弟に向かって、「お前が最初だ。きちんとできるかどうか、おれが見届けてやる」と言った。弟が「今まで切腹を見たことがないので、兄上たちがなさるのを見て、真似をしたい」と答えると、上の二人は涙の下でにこりとほほ笑んで、「弟よ、よくぞ言った！それでこそ父上の子だ」と言った。二人は幼い弟を間に座らせ、まずは左近が刀を左の脇腹に突き刺す。そして「よく見るんだ！わかったか？　刀を突きすぎるなよ。ひっくり返るからな。うつむくんだ。膝をしっかりととじろ」と言った。内記がそれに続き、弟に向かって「目をつぶるなよ。つぶったら女みたいだぞ。刀が腹に入った

of eight summers, was condemned to a similar fate, as the sentence was pronounced on all the male members of the family, and the three were taken to a monastery where it was to be executed. A physician who was present on the occasion has left us a diary from which the following scene is translated.

"When they were all seated in a row for final despatch, Sakon turned to the youngest and said—'Go thou first, for I wish to be sure that thou doest it aright.' Upon the little one's replying that, as he had never seen *seppuku* performed, he would like to see his brothers do it and then he could follow them, the older brothers smiled between their tears:— 'Well said, little fellow! So canst thou well boast of being our father's child.' When they had placed him between them, Sakon thrust the dagger into the left side of his own abdomen and asked—'Look, brother! Dost understand now? Only, don't push the dagger too far, lest thou fall back. Lean forward, rather, and keep thy knees well composed.' Naiki did likewise and said to the boy—'Keep thy eyes open or else thou mayst look like a dying woman. If

ときに力がぬけたら、ふんばって二倍の力をだして横に切るんだ」と言った。八麿は二人を交互に見たが、兄たちが事切れると、落ち着きはらってもろ肌を脱ぎ、左右の手本にしたがった。

切腹が名誉なこととされると、その必要もないのに切腹したい者が出てくるのは自然のなりゆきであった。理も非もなく、死ぬほどのこともない理由で、血気にはやる若者が、夏の虫が火に飛び込むように死にいそいだ。女が尼寺の門をたたくよりも繁く、侍が不純で、あやしげな理由によって死地におもむいた。命は安かった。俗流の名誉の基準ではかられるので安っぽかった。無念至極なことに、死と引き換えになる名誉を金貨に譬えるなら、必ずしも純金ではなく、卑金属が混ざっていることもあるのだ。ダンテの描く地獄の第七圏には自殺者が放り込まれるが、地獄のどの場所より日本人の人口密度が高いことであろう！

しかしながら、真の侍にとって、死にいそいだり、死を求めたりするのは怯懦なふるまいであった。かつて、

thy dagger feels anything within and thy strength fails, take courage and double thy effort to cut across.' The child looked from one to the other, and when both had expired, he calmly half denuded himself and followed the example set him on either hand."

The glorification of *seppuku* offered, naturally enough, no small temptation to its **unwarranted committal**. For causes entirely incompatible with reason, or for reasons entirely undeserving of death, hot headed youths rushed into it as insects fly into fire; mixed and dubious motives drove more samurai to this deed than nuns into convent gates. **Life was cheap**—cheap as reckoned by the popular standard of honor. The saddest feature was that honor, which was always in the *agio*, so to speak, was not always solid gold, but alloyed with baser metals. No one circle in the Inferno will boast of greater density of Japanese population than the seventh, to which Dante consigns all victims of self-destruction!

And yet, for a true samurai to **hasten death** or to **court it**, was alike **cowardice**. A typical fighter, when

ある武士が戦いに負け続け、敵の追跡をうけて野から山へ、藪から洞穴へとのがれ、あげくのはてに、たった一人で、空腹をかかえながら暗い木の洞にひそんだ。刀の刃は毀れおち、弓は折れ、矢もつきている。ピリッポイでこのような運命におちた高貴なローマ人（マルクス・ユニウス・ブルータス）は、自らの剣で自害したが、この武人は死ぬのは怯懦であると考えた。そしてキリスト教の殉教者のような**強靭な精神力**でもって、

　　憂きことのなおこの上に積れかし
　　限りある身の力ためさん

という歌を即興で口ずさみ、自らを励ましたのであった。

　これが武士道の教えである。すなわち、**どんな苦難に出会っても、一心に立ち向かって耐えぬけ**、ということである。孟子いわく[20]——「天が人に大任を課すとき

---

[20] ここではレッジ博士の英訳を文字通りに訳している。

he lost battle after battle and was pursued from plain to hill and from bush to cavern, found himself hungry and alone in the dark hollow of a tree, his sword blunt with use, his bow broken and arrows exhausted—did not the noblest of the Romans fall upon his own sword in Phillippi under like circumstances?—deemed it cowardly to die, but with a **fortitude** approaching a Christian martyr's, cheered himself with an impromptu verse:

> "Come! evermore come,
> Ye dread sorrows and pains!
> And heap on my burden'd back;
> That I not one test may lack
> Of what strength in me remains!"

This, then, was the Bushido teaching—**Bear and face all calamities and adversities with patience and a pure conscience**; for as Mencius[20] taught, "When Heaven is about to confer a great office on

---

[20] I use Dr. Legge's translation verbatim.

には、まず苦しみをあたえて精神を鍛え、労苦をあたえ
て筋肉と骨格を鍛えさせる。肉体を飢餓にさらし、極貧
の境遇におとし、何を試みても失敗させる。このように
して精神が賦活（ふかつ）し、性質が強靭となり、足らざる能力が
補われる」。**真の名誉は天命を成就することにあり、そ
のために死ぬのは不名誉ではないが、天の定めを避ける
ために死ぬのは臆病者である！**サー・トーマス・ブラウ
ンによる天下の奇書『レリギオ・メディキ』には、武士
道で繰り返される教えとぴたりと重なり合う文章が英語
で記されているので、ここに引用しておこう。ブラウン
いわく、「死を軽んじるのは勇敢だが、死より生のほう
が恐ろしいときには、生きることこそ真の勇気である」。
十七世紀の著名な僧が辛辣な言葉を残している。「口は
達者でも、死んだことのない侍は肝心の時に逃げ隠れす
る。心の底で死んだことのある者は、真田の槍も、為朝
の矢も貫くことはできない」と。日本人のこのような考
え方は、「私のために命を失う者は、それを見出すであ
ろう」とイエス・キリストが教えたもうた神殿の門に、
きわめて近づいている！キリスト教と異教の違いをこと

anyone, it first exercises his mind with suffering and his sinews and bones with toil; it exposes his body to hunger and subjects him to extreme poverty; and it confounds his undertakings. In all these ways it stimulates his mind, hardens his nature, and supplies his incompetencies." **True honor lies in fulfilling Heaven's decree** and no death incurred in so doing is ignominious, whereas **death to avoid what Heaven has in store is cowardly** indeed! In that quaint book of Sir Thomas Browne's, *Religio Medici* there is an exact English equivalent for what is repeatedly taught in our Precepts. Let me quote it: "It is a brave act of valor to contemn death, but where life is more terrible than death, it is then the truest valor to dare to live." A renowned priest of the seventeenth century satirically observed—"Talk as he may, a samurai who ne'er has died is apt in decisive moments to flee or hide." Again— "Him who once has died in the bottom of his breast, no spears of Sanada nor all the arrows of Tametomo can pierce." How near we come to the portals of the temple whose Builder taught "he that loseth his life for my sake shall find it!" These are but a few of the numerous examples which tend to confirm

さらに強調しようとする者は多いが、実は、**人間の倫理感覚というのは人類共通である**ことが様々の例によって明らかであり、切腹もそうした例の一つにすぎないのである。

　以上、武士道における自害の制度は、乱用されたために**理不尽**で**野蛮**な風習のように見えるかもしれないが、その本質はそうではないということを示した。ここからは、切腹と対をなしている**仇討**──なんなら「**復讐**」という語を用いてもよいが──という社会制度について、**擁護できる点**があるかどうかを考えてみよう。とはいえ、それにはさして大げさな議論を必要としないだろう。類似の制度は（この語がしっくりこなければ「風習」といってもよいが）、世界中の民族に広く行き渡っており、今なお完全に廃れてはいないからである。その証拠に**決闘**や**私刑**が今でも行われているのである。**ドレフュスの汚名を雪**ぐために、アメリカ人の大尉がエスターハージーに決闘を申し込んだことは記憶に新しい。原始的な民族で、結婚の制度がないような場合には不倫という罪は存在しないので、女性を不義から守ることができるのは、愛する者の嫉妬のみである。刑事訴訟の法廷が存在しなかった時代には、殺人は罪ではなかったので、被害者の身内などがねばり強く復讐したからこそ、社会秩序が維持されたのである。エジプトの神話では、

the moral identity of the human species, notwithstanding an attempt so assiduously made to render the distinction between Christian and Pagan as great as possible.

We have thus seen that the Bushido institution of suicide was neither so **irrational** nor **barbarous** as its abuse strikes us at first sight. We will now see whether its sister institution of **Redress**—or call it **Revenge**, if you will—has its **mitigating features**. I hope I can dispose of this question in a few words, since a similar institution, or call it custom, if that suits you better, has at some time prevailed among all peoples and has not yet become entirely obsolete, as attested by the continuance of **duelling** and **lynching**. Why, has not an American captain recently challenged Esterhazy, that **the wrongs of Dreyfus be avenged**? Among a savage tribe which has no marriage, adultery is not a sin, and only the jealousy of a lover protects a woman from abuse: so in a time which has no criminal court, murder is not a crime, and only the vigilant vengeance of the victim's people preserves social order. "What is

オシリスがホルスに向かって「地上でもっとも美しいものは何か」と尋ねる。その答えは「**親の仇討ちをすること**」であったが、日本人ならこれに、「主君の仇討ちををすることも然^{しか}り」と付け加えるであろう。

　復讐にはどこか人の**正義感を満足させる**ものがある。**復讐する者**の理屈はこうである。「私の善良な父は、殺されるにあたいするようなことはしていない。父を殺した者は、父に対してひどい不正を加えた。かりに父が生きていたら、そのような行為は黙過しないだろう。そもそも不正を悪^{にく}むのは天である。よって不正をなす者の息の根を止めるのは、父の意志であると同時に天の意志でもある。奴は私の父に血を流させたのだから、父の血と肉を分けもった私の手にかかって死なねばならない。奴と私は『不倶戴天^{ふ ぐ たいてん}』——同じ天のもとに生きることはできない」。**この理屈は単純で子どもじみてさえいる**（ただしハムレットでさえこれより深い理屈づけはできていない）が、「**目には目を、歯には歯を**」という**本能的な正義のバランス感**が、ここには現れている。復讐についての我々の感覚は、数学的能力に劣らず厳密である。等式の両側が等しくならないことには、ものごとが片付いたように感じないのである。

　ユダヤ教の神は嫉妬深い。ギリシャ神話には復讐の女

the most beautiful thing on earth?" said Osiris to Horus. The reply was, "To **avenge a parent's wrongs,**"—to which a Japanese would have added "and a master's."

In revenge there is something which **satisfies one's sense of justice**. The **avenger** reasons:—"My good father did not deserve death. He who killed him did great evil. My father, if he were alive, would not tolerate a deed like this: Heaven itself hates wrong-doing. It is the will of my father; it is the will of Heaven that the evil-doer cease from his work. He must perish by my hand; because he shed my father's blood, I, who am his flesh and blood, must shed the murderer's. The same Heaven shall not shelter him and me." **The ratiocination is simple and childish** (though we know Hamlet did not reason much more deeply), nevertheless it shows **an innate sense of exact balance and equal justice "An eye for an eye, a tooth for a tooth."** Our sense of revenge is as exact as our mathematical faculty, and until both terms of the equation are satisfied we cannot get over the sense of something left undone.

In Judaism, which believed in a jealous God, or in

神ネメシスがいる。そこでは**人間を超えた存在に復讐が委ねられている**。これに対して武士道では、平凡な世俗智によって仇討という制度が与えられており、**倫理的な衡平裁判所**として機能している。通常の法によってさばくことのできない事柄を訴えることができるのである。四十七名の浪士の主君は死刑の裁きをうけた。主君には、**訴えるべき上級審はなかった**。**忠臣たち**は、唯一の最高審である「仇討」という手段に訴えた。この行為のために、彼ら自身は通常の法にしたがって死罪に処せられた。しかし、人々の本能はこれとは異なる判決をくだしたがゆえに、四十七士の記憶は泉岳寺の彼らの墓石とともに、今日にいたるまで色褪せることがないのである。

　老子は、**受けた害は親切で返せ**と教えたが、孔子はもっと声が大きく、**受けた害には正当なつぐないを求めよ**と説いた。ただし、復讐は**長上の者や恩人のために**限るとした。自分自身や妻子がこうむった不正は我慢して、赦さなければならなかった。したがって日本の武士は、祖国がこうむった不正に報いる誓いをたてたハンニバル

Greek mythology, which provided a Nemesis, **vengeance may be left to superhuman agencies**; but common sense furnished Bushido with the institution of redress as a kind of **ethical court of equity**, where people could take cases not to be judged in accordance with ordinary law. The master of the forty-seven Ronins was condemned to death;—**he had no court of higher instance to appeal to**; his **faithful retainers** addressed themselves to Vengeance, the only Supreme Court existing; they in their turn were condemned by common law,—but the popular instinct passed a different judgment and hence their memory is still kept as green and fragrant as are their graves at Sengakuji to this day.

Though Lao-tse taught to **recompense injury with kindness**, the voice of Confucius was very much louder, which counselled that **injury must be recompensed with justice**;—and yet revenge was justified only when it was undertaken **in behalf of our superiors and benefactors**. One's own wrongs, including injuries done to wife and children, were to be borne and forgiven. A samurai could therefore fully sympathize with Hannibal's oath to avenge his country's

には心から共感するだろうが、妻が摂政のマリ伯から被った不正を永遠に忘れず、自らの復讐心をかきたてるために、妻の墓の土を帯にはさんでもっていたというジェイムズ・ハミルトンは軽蔑することであろう。

これら腹切と仇討の制度は、**近代刑法**が定められて以降、**存在意義**を失ってしまった。現代ではもはや、うら若き乙女が変装して親のかたきを追い求めるというようなロマンティックな冒険物語は耳にしない。あるいは家と家の確執の中でおきる悲劇にも、お目にかかることはない。宮本武蔵の**武者修行**はもはや過去の物語となった。被害を被った者に代わって警察が犯人を探し出し、**法によって正義がもたらされる**。国と社会全体が、不正の正されることを保証する。こうして正義が回復したと感じるならば、もはや仇討の必要はない。仇討は、あるニューイングランドの神学者が述べているような「ひたすら犠牲者を血祭りにあげることを願い、それだけを生きがいにしている」願望に基づいた、野蛮な風習などではないのである。もしもそのようなものであったなら、刑法の数段の条文によって、こんなにきれいさっぱり消滅してしまうはずがないのである。

切腹については、法の上ではもはや存在しないが、それが行われたことを往々にして耳にする。過去の記憶が残っているあいだは、それが存在し続けることだろう。

wrongs, but he scorns James Hamilton for wearing in his girdle a handful of earth from his wife's grave, as an eternal incentive to avenge her wrongs on the Regent Murray.

Both of these institutions of suicide and redress lost their **raison d'être** at the promulgation of **the criminal code**. No more do we hear of romantic adventures of a fair maiden as she tracks in disguise the murderer of her parent. No more can we witness tragedies of family vendetta enacted. The **knight errantry** of Miyamoto Musashi is now a tale of the past. The well-ordered police spies out the criminal for the injured party and **the law metes out justice**. The whole state and society will see that wrong is righted. The sense of justice satisfied, there is no need of *kataki-uchi*. If this had meant that "hunger of the heart which feeds upon the hope of glutting that hunger with the life-blood of the victim," as a New England divine has described it, a few paragraphs in the Criminal Code would not so entirely have made an end of it.

As to *seppuku*, though it too has no existence *de jure*, we still hear of it from time to time, and shall continue to hear, I am afraid, as long as the past is re-

自殺志願者が世界中で恐ろしい勢いで増えているので、これからは自己を抹殺するために、苦痛がなく、時間もかからない様々な方法がはやることだろう。しかし、モルセリ教授も、切腹には貴族的な地位を認めないわけにはいかないであろう。モルセリ教授は、「自殺が強い痛みをともなう手段や、苦痛が長引く方法でなされるなら、その九九パーセントは狂信、狂気、病的な興奮による精神錯乱状態での実行であると分類されるだろう」と述べている[21]。しかし、正常な切腹は狂信、狂気、興奮とは無縁である。切腹をやり遂げるには、極度の冷静さが必要とされるからである。ストレイハン博士[22]は自殺を二分して、「理性的自殺、あるいは擬似的自殺」と「非理性的自殺、あるいは真性の自殺」に分類したが、切腹は前者の最高の例であるといえよう。

[21] Morselli, *Suicide*, p. 314.
[22] *Suicide and Insanity*.

membered. Many painless and time-saving methods of self-immolation will come in vogue, as its votaries are increasing with fearful rapidity throughout the world; but Professor Morselli will have to concede to *seppuku* an aristocratic position among them. He maintains that "when suicide is accomplished by very painful means or at the cost of prolonged agony, in ninety-nine cases out of a hundred, it may be assigned as the act of a mind disordered by fanaticism, by madness, or by morbid excitement."[21] But a normal *seppuku* does not savor of fanaticism, or madness or excitement, utmost *sang froid* being necessary to its successful accomplishment. Of the two kinds into which Dr. Strahan[22] divides suicide, the Rational or Quasi, and the Irrational or True, *seppuku* is the best example of the former type.

第 13 章

刀、
すなわち侍の魂

前章では腹切と仇討という二つの血なまぐさい制度を
論じたが、これに加えて武士道というものの全般的印象
から、刀が社会的規律、そして社会生活の中で重要な役
割を果たしたことは想像にかたくないだろう。俗に「刀
は**侍の魂**」と言われたが、いかにも刀は**力と勇気の象徴**
であった。モハメッドは「剣は天国と地獄の鍵」と豪語
したが、この言葉は日本人の気持ちそのものを表してい
る。侍の子は、幼少のみぎりから刀の扱いを教えられ
る。五歳になると**侍の装具一式**をまとわされ、碁盤のう
えに載せられ [23]、それまで遊んでいた**おもちゃの短剣**

---

[23] 碁は日本のチェッカーと呼ばれるが、それよりはるかに複雑なゲームである。碁
盤には 361 のます目があり、戦場を象徴しているとされる。より多くのます目を獲っ
た者が勝者である。

CHAPTER 13

THE SWORD,
THE SOUL OF THE SAMURAI

From these bloody institutions, as well as from the tenor of Bushido, it is easy to infer that the sword played an important part in social discipline and life. The saying passed as an axiom which called the sword **the soul of the samurai**, and made it **the emblem of power and prowess**. When Mahomet proclaimed that "The sword is the key of Heaven and of Hell," he only echoed a Japanese sentiment. Very early the samurai boy learned to wield it. It was a momentous occasion for him when at the age of five he was apparelled in **the paraphernalia of samurai costume**, placed upon a *go*-board[23] and initiated into the rights of the mili-

---

[23] The game of *go* is sometimes called Japanese checkers, but is much more intricate than the English game. The *go*-board contains 361 squares and is supposed to represent a battlefield- the object of the game being to occupy as much space as possible.

ではなく、**本物の刀**を帯にさしてもらって、武家の一員として認められることになる。この刀を授ける儀式のあとは、家を出るときには必ず、**武士の象徴**ともいうべき刀を帯びた。ふだんは**金属を張った短い木刀**であったが、数年後には常に、（なまくら刀だが）**真剣**を身につけるようになる。そうするとまがい物の刀は打ち捨てられ、この手に入れたばかりの刀の刃よりも鋭い喜びをもって、やたら木や石にむかって切れ味を試そうとする。十五歳で元服すると、**一人前の人間として自立**し、何でも切れる刀を誇らしく所持することになる。こうして危険な武器を所有しているということで、**自尊心と責任感**が生じ、それにふさわしい物腰がおのずと備わってくる。「だてに刀を持っているわけではない」というわけだ。腰にさしたものは、心に備わったもの、すなわち**忠義と名誉**の象徴である。長短二本の刀は——大刀と小刀、もしくは刀と脇差と呼ばれ——決して脇から遠ざけることがない。家にいるときは書斎や居間の上座をかざ

tary profession by having thrust into his girdle **a real sword**, instead of the **toy dirk** with which he had been playing. After this first ceremony of *adoptio per arma*, he was no more to be seen outside his father's gates without this **badge of his status**, even if it was usually substituted for every-day wear by **a gilded wooden dirk**. Not many years pass before he wears constantly **the genuine steel**, though blunt, and then the sham arms are thrown aside and with enjoyment keener than his newly acquired blades, he marches out to try their edge on wood and stone. When he reaches man's estate at the age of fifteen, **being given independence of action**, he can now pride himself upon the possession of arms sharp enough for any work. The very possession of the dangerous instrument imparts to him a feeling and an air of **self-respect** and **responsibility**. "He beareth not his sword in vain." What he carries in his belt is a symbol of what he carries in his mind and heart—**Loyalty** and **Honor**. The two swords, the longer and the shorter—called respectively *daito* and *shoto* or *katana* and *wakizashi*—never leave his side. When at home, they grace the most conspicuous place in study or parlor; by night

る。夜は枕から**手のとどくところ**において身をまもる。肌身はなさないので愛おしく、親しみのこもった名で呼ばれる。その大事にされるさまは、**ほとんど崇拝**といってよい。歴史の父ヘロドトスによって、スキタイ人が鉄の新月刀に生贄を捧げたという面白い話が記されている。日本の寺や旧家には刀が宝蔵され、うやまわれていることがよくある。ごく平凡な脇差しでさえうやまわれる。刀をあなどることは、持ち主を馬鹿にすることであった。床においた刀を不用意にまたぐなど、言語道断であった！

　刀はそれほど貴重なものだったので、ほどなく、芸術家が注目して製作しはじめた。また所有者にとっては、刀は大いなる自慢の対象であった。とくに世の中が平和なときにはそうであった。僧侶が錫杖をもち、国王が王笏をもつように、武士は刀を帯びたのである。柄には鮫皮や絹の布が巻かれ、鍔には金や銀の細工がほどこされ、鞘は漆できらびやかに彩られた。これによって死をまきちらす武器の恐怖がやわらいだものの、こうした装飾は刃そのものと比べれば遊びにすぎなかった。

　刀匠は単なる工人ではなく、霊感を授かった芸術家であった。そして、その工房は**神域**であった。刀鍛冶は日々仕事をはじめるにあたって、**神仏に祈り、斎戒沐浴**

they guard his pillow **within easy reach of his hand**. Constant companions, they are beloved, and proper names of endearment given them. Being venerated, **they are well-nigh worshiped**. The Father of History has recorded as a curious piece of information that the Scythians sacrificed to an iron scimitar. Many a temple and many a family in Japan hoards a sword as an object of adoration. Even the commonest dirk has due respect paid to it. Any insult to it is tantamount to personal affront. Woe to him who carelessly steps over a weapon lying on the floor!

So precious an object cannot long escape the notice and the skill of artists nor the vanity of its owner, especially in times of peace, when it is worn with no more use than a crosier by a bishop or a sceptre by a king. Shark-skin and finest silk for hilt, silver and gold for guard, lacquer of varied hues for scabbard, robbed the deadliest weapon of half its terror; but these appurtenances are playthings compared with the blade itself.

The **swordsmith** was not **a mere artisan** but **an inspired artist** and his workshop **a sanctuary**. Daily he commenced his craft with **prayer and purifica-**

をした。そしていわば「心魂気迫を打って錬鉄錬冶した」。大槌を振り下ろし、熱い刀身を水で冷却し、砥石でみがく。そうした動作の一つ一つが厳粛な祈りの行為であった。日本刀におそろしい魔力を授けるのは刀匠の魂だろうか? それとも刀匠を支える神であろうか? 日本刀はトレドやダマスカスの名剣にもひけをとることなく、一つの**芸術作品**となりおおせている。その完成度たるや人の技を超えている。鞘から抜き払ったその瞬間に、冷たい刃は空中の水滴を集めて白くにごる。一点くもりなき鋼(はがね)の刀身には青白い輝きがおどる。この比類なき鋭利な刃から、歴史や未来が生み出されるのだ。そりの入った背には、とてつもない強度と、この世のものとも思えぬ優美さが兼ね備わっている。日本刀は**力と美、畏れと恐怖**を感じさせ、見るものを魅了する。ただ見て美しく、楽しいだけなら、日本刀は無害なものにとどまるであろう! しかし、日本刀に手がとどくと、**むやみに使いたいという誘惑**にかられる。そのおとなしい鞘から刃がきらりと躍り出ることが、なんと多すぎたことか。試し切りのために首をはねられた、無辜の人がどれほどいたことか。

　しかしながら、ここでもっとも肝要な問題は、**刀をむやみに用いる**ことを武士道は是としたかということであ

tion, or, as the phrase was, "he committed his soul and spirit into the forging and tempering of the steel." Every swing of the sledge, every plunge into water, every friction on the grindstone, was a religious act of no slight import. Was it the spirit of the master or of his tutelary god that cast a formidable spell over our sword? Perfect as **a work of art**, setting at defiance its Toledo and Damascus rivals, there is more than art could impart. Its cold blade, collecting on its surface the moment it is drawn the vapors of the atmosphere; its immaculate texture, flashing light of bluish hue; its matchless edge, upon which histories and possibilities hang; the curve of its back, uniting exquisite grace with utmost strength;—all these thrill us with mixed feelings of **power and beauty**, of **awe and terror**. Harmless were its mission, if it only remained a thing of beauty and joy! But, ever within reach of the hand, it presented **no small temptation for abuse**. Too often did the blade flash forth from its peaceful sheath. The abuse sometimes went so far as to try the acquired steel on some harmless creature's neck.

The question that concerns us most is, however,—Did Bushido justify **the promiscuous use of the**

る。答えははっきりと否である！武士道は刀の正しい用い方を力説するとともに、あやまった使用については、それを嫌い、いましめている。必要もないのに刀を振り回すのは、腰抜けや威張り屋のすることである。冷静沈着な者は**いつ刀を抜くべきか**を知っているが、そのような機会は稀にしかおとずれない。先ごろ亡くなった勝伯爵（勝海舟）の言に耳を傾けてみよう。勝は日本史の中でもまれにみる乱世を生き抜いた人物である。その当時は暗殺や自害をはじめとする血なまぐさい出来事が、日常茶飯事であった。勝はかつてほぼすべての権力を一身に付託されていたがゆえに、たびたび暗殺の標的にされたが、みずからの刀を血でよごすことはたえてなかった。友人に語った回顧談で、勝は独特の庶民的な調子でこのように語っている。「私は人を殺すのが大嫌いで、一人でも殺したことはないよ。みんな逃して、殺すべきものでも、マアマアと言って放っておいた。川上彦斎（佐久間象山を暗殺した）が私に『あなたは、そう人を殺しなさらぬが、それはいけません。南瓜でも茄子でも、あなたはとっておあがんなさるだろう。あいつらはそんなものです』と教えてくれたが、それはヒドイ奴だったよ！しかし川上は殺されたよ。私が殺されなかったのは、無実の者を殺さなかった故かもしれんよ。刀でも、ひどく丈夫に結わえて、決して抜けないようにして

weapon? The answer is unequivocally, no! As it laid great stress on its proper use, so did it denounce and abhor its misuse. A dastard or a braggart was he who brandished his weapon on undeserved occasions. A self-possessed man knows **the right time to use it**, and such times come but rarely. Let us listen to the late Count Katsu, who passed through one of the most turbulent times of our history, when assassinations, suicides, and other sanguinary practices were the order of the day. Endowed as he once was with almost dictatorial powers, repeatedly marked out as an object for assassination, he never tarnished his sword with blood. In relating some of his reminiscences to a friend he says, in a quaint, plebeian way peculiar to him:—"I have a great dislike for killing people and so I haven't killed one single man. I have released those whose heads should have been chopped off. A friend said to me one day, 'You don't kill enough. Don't you eat pepper and eggplants?' Well, some people are no better! But you see that fellow was slain himself. My escape may be due to my dislike of killing. I had the hilt of my sword so tightly fastened to the scabbard that it was hard to draw the blade. I made up my

あった。人に斬られても、こちらは斬らぬという覚悟だった。ナニ蚤_(のみ)や虱_(しらみ)だと思えばいいのさ。肩につかまってチクリチクリ刺しても、ただ痒いだけだ。生命に関わりはしないよ」。武士道の修練が、燃えさかる炉のような逆境のなかで実地にためされ、勝ち抜いた人物の、重みのある言葉である。俗諺に「**負けるが勝ち**」というが、真に勝つことは、騒がしい敵と渡り合うところにはない、ということを言い表している。ほかにも「**最良の勝利は、血を流さずに得られる勝利である**」というような趣旨の言葉は数多くあるが、このようなことから考えても、武士道の究極の理想は不戦、すなわち**戦わざること**であるということが分かるのである。

mind that though they cut me, I will not cut. Yes, yes! some people are truly like fleas and mosquitoes and they bite—but what does their biting amount to? It itches a little, that's all; it won't endanger life." These are the words of one whose Bushido training was tried in the fiery furnace of adversity and triumph. The popular apothegm—**"To be beaten is to conquer,"** meaning true conquest consists in not opposing a riotous foe; and **"The best won victory is that obtained without shedding of blood,"** and others of similar import—will show that after all the ultimate ideal of knighthood was **Peace**.

第14章
女性の
教育と地位

　この「戦わず」という気高い理想は、もっぱら僧侶や道学者の説教に委ねられ、武士は素知らぬ顔で武門の技をみがき、それを称揚しつづけたのはなんと残念なことであろうか。あげくのはて、**女性の理想像**まで、アマゾン族の女傑のような色合いに染め上げてしまうこととなった。ここで数段落、女性の教育と地位について記してみるのも悪くないであろう。

　人類の半分を占める女性は、**矛盾の化身**（パラドックス）と呼ばれてきた。なぜなら女性心理は直感的で、男の「算術的な理解力」をこえているからである。漢字は象形文字だが、「神秘的」、「不可知」を意味する「妙」という文字は、「若い」という意味の「少」と、「女」という字が組み合わさってできている。これは**女性の肉体的な魅力と霊妙な精神作用**が、男性の粗雑な頭脳では説明しきれないというところから来ている。

CHAPTER 14

THE TRAINING AND POSITION OF WOMAN

It was a great pity that this high ideal was left exclusively to priests and moralists to preach, while the samurai went on practicing and extolling martial traits. In this they went so far as to tinge **the ideals of womanhood** with Amazonian character. Here we may profitably devote a few paragraphs to the subject of the training and position of woman.

The female half of our species has sometimes been called **the paragon of paradoxes**, because the intuitive working of its mind is beyond the comprehension of men's "arithmetical understanding." The Chinese ideogram denoting "the mysterious," "the unknowable," consists of two parts, one meaning "young" and the other "woman," because **the physical charms and delicate thoughts of the fair sex** are above the coarse mental calibre of our sex to explain.

しかしながら、武士道における女性の理想像に神秘性はほとんどなく、矛盾にしてもほんの見せかけにすぎない。上で「アマゾン族の女傑のようだ」と述べたが、それは半面の真理である。漢字では、妻は箒をもった女として表される。箒は防御であれ攻撃であれ、背の君にむけて振り回すためではなく、それに乗って空を飛ぶためでもなく、箒が発明されたそもそもの目的、すなわち無害で実用的な用途のためである。英語の「妻（wife<=weaver 機織り女」、「娘（daughter<=duhitar 乳搾りの女）」と同じく、家庭的な発想がもとになっているといえる。今上のドイツ皇帝閣下は、女性の活動の場はキッチン、教会、子ども（Küche, Kirche, Kinder）の三つのKに限るべしとしている。武士道ではそこまで言わないまでも、理想の女性像はすぐれて家庭的である。この見かけ上の矛盾——家庭的にして、しかもアマゾン的でもあるという特徴は、決して武士道の考え方と矛盾するものではないのである。

　武士道は主として男性のための教えなので、女性において褒めたたえる美徳も、当然のことながら女性固有のものからはほど遠い。ウィッケルマンは「ギリシャ芸術の最高の美は女性的ではなく男性的である」と述べ、レッキーがそれに付け加えて、芸術ばかりか倫理観につい

In the Bushido ideal of woman, however, there is little mystery and only a seeming paradox. I have said that it was Amazonian, but that is only half the truth. Ideographically the Chinese represent wife by a woman holding a broom—certainly not to brandish it offensively or defensively against her conjugal ally, neither for witchcraft, but for the more harmless uses for which the besom was first invented— the idea involved being thus not less homely than the etymological derivation of the English wife (weaver) and daughter (*duhitar*, milkmaid). Without confining the sphere of woman's activity to *Küche, Kirche, Kinder*, as the present German Kaiser is said to do, the Bushido ideal of womanhood was preeminently domestic. These seeming contradictions—Domesticity and Amazonian traits—are not inconsistent with the Precepts of Knighthood, as we shall see.

Bushido being a teaching primarily intended for the masculine sex, the virtues it prized in woman were naturally far from being distinctly feminine. Winckelmann remarks that "the supreme beauty of Greek art is rather male than female," and Lecky adds that it was true in the moral conception of the Greeks as in

ても同じことが言えると述べている。同様に武士道でも、「女性の弱さから自らを解放し、男性の強く雄々しい模範にふさわしいような、英雄的な気構えを示す者がもっとも評価される」[24]。したがって、ひとたび武家に生まれると娘時代には**感情をおさえ、ものに動じない神経を鍛え、武器をあつかうこと**を教えられる。その代表格は薙刀(なぎなた)という柄の長い刀剣で、不測の事態から身をまもるためである。ただし武術の鍛錬は、戦場(いくさば)での使用が主要な目的ではない。その目的は二つ、個人と家庭に関わっている。女性は直接主君に仕えるわけではないので、自ら身を守らねばならない。そして夫は主君が蹂躙(じゅうりん)されぬよう戦うように、妻は自らの身が犯されぬよう武器をふるうのである。武術の鍛錬の家庭的な用途というのは、家に生まれた男児の教育である。このことはまた後で触れることにしよう。

武術の鍛錬は実用に供されることは稀であったが、ふだんは座って暮らすことの多い女性には、格好の気晴らしであった。しかし、健康のみが目的で行われたのではない。いざ火急の際には、現実の役に立てられた。娘は成人すると懐剣（ふところ刀）を与えられた。襲いかか

---

[24] Lecky, *History of European Morals* II, p. 383.

their art. Bushido similarly praised those women most "who emancipated themselves from the frailty of their sex and displayed an heroic fortitude worthy of the strongest and the bravest of men."[24] Young girls therefore, were trained to **repress their feelings**, to **indurate their nerves**, to **manipulate weapons**,—especially the long-handled sword called *nagi-nata*, so as to be able to hold their own against unexpected odds. Yet the primary motive for exercises of this martial character was not for use in the field; it was twofold—personal and domestic. Woman owning no suzerain of her own, formed her own bodyguard. With her weapon she guarded her personal sanctity with as much zeal as her husband did his master's. The domestic utility of her warlike training was in the education of her sons, as we shall see later.

Fencing and similar exercises, if rarely of practical use, were a wholesome counterbalance to the otherwise sedentary habits of woman. But these exercises were not followed only for hygienic purposes. They could be turned into use in times of need. Girls, when they reached womanhood, were presented with dirks (*kai-ken*, pocket poniards), which might be directed

ってくる敵の胸を刺すこともあったが、必要とあらば自らの胸を刺すのにも用いられた。このように自害のために用いられることは多かったが、それを厳しい目で見ることは私にはできない。キリスト教徒の良心は自殺を嫌悪するが、自害した武家の女性には温かい目をそそいでくれるだろう。自らの生命を断ったペラギアとドムニナは純潔と敬虔ゆえに聖人に列せられているのであるから。日本のウィルギニアは貞節を脅かされても、父親が刺し殺してくれるのを待たない。自らの懐剣をつねに胸にひそめているからだ。**自害の正しい方法**を知らないことは、武家の女にとって恥である。人間の体についてはほとんど教わらないが、喉のどこを切ればよいか、正確に知っている。また、あらかじめ帯で両足を縛っておくことも必要な知識である。死の苦痛がどんなにひどくても、死骸は足をきちんとそろえた貞節の鑑のような姿で発見されなければならないからだ。これはキリスト教徒の聖ペルペトゥアや、ウェスタの処女コルネリアにも恥じない気構えとは言えないだろうか？　このように尋ねると唐突に聞こえるだろうが、私があえてここでそうしたのは、よりによって、日本人の入浴の風習などをもとに、日本人には恥じらいがないなどという誤解が蔓延しているからである[25]。恥じらいがないなど、とんでもない。それこそが武家の婦人が何よりも重んじる徳目

to the bosom of their assailants, or, if advisable, to their own. The latter was very often the case: and yet I will not judge them severely. Even the Christian conscience with its horror of self-immolation, will not be harsh with them, seeing Pelagia and Domnina, two suicides, were canonized for their purity and piety. When a Japanese Virginia saw her chastity menaced, she did not wait for her father's dagger. Her own weapon lay always in her bosom. It was a disgrace to her not to know **the proper way in which she had to perpetrate self-destruction**. For example, little as she was taught in anatomy, she must know the exact spot to cut in her throat: she must know how to tie her lower limbs together with a belt so that, whatever the agonies of death might be, her corpse be found in utmost modesty with the limbs properly composed. Is not a caution like this worthy of the Christian Perpetua or the Vestal Cornelia? I would not put such an abrupt interrogation, were it not for a misconception, based on our bathing customs and other trifles, that chastity is unknown among us.[25] On the contrary, chastity was a pre-eminent virtue of the samurai

で、**生命よりも大切にするもの**であったのだ。ある娘が敵にとらえられた。気の荒い足軽に乱暴されそうだと見てとるや、いかようにされるも運命だが、その前に、いくさのせいで離れ離れになった姉妹（きょうだい）たちへ文を認（したた）めさせてもらいたいといった。そして娘は書き終えるとそばの井戸に駆け寄り、身を投げて純潔を守ったのである。娘の文のむすびには、次のような歌が記されてあった。

　　世にへなばよしなき雲もおおひなん
　　いざ入りてまし山の端の月

　ここで男まさりであることだけが女のいちばんの理想であったという印象を、読者諸氏がもたれたとすれば、それは誤りである。むしろ逆である！女性には**種々の芸事**と、日々の生活を女性らしく彩るたしなみが求められた。**音曲、舞踊、詩文**もさかんであった。我が国の詩歌のうち、もっとも秀麗なものには女性の心を詠ったもの

[25]　裸体と入浴の風習については、フィンクの『日本における蓮の時』pp.286-297. に、冷静な説明がなされている。

woman, **held above life itself.** A young woman, taken prisoner, seeing herself in danger of violence at the hands of the rough soldiery, says she will obey their pleasure, provided she be first allowed to write a line to her sisters, whom war has dispersed in every direction. When the epistle is finished, off she runs to the nearest well and saves her honor by drowning. The letter she leaves behind ends with these verses;—

> "For fear lest clouds may dim her light,
>   Should she but graze this nether sphere,
>   The young moon poised above the height
>   Doth hastily betake to flight."

It would be unfair to give my readers an idea that masculinity alone was our highest ideal for woman. Far from it! **Accomplishments** and the gentler graces of life were required of them. **Music**, **dancing** and **literature** were not neglected. Some of the finest verses in our literature were expressions of feminine

[25] For a very sensible explanation of nudity and bathing see Finck's *Lotos Time in Japan*, pp. 286-297.

が含まれるが、むしろ日本の詞藻の伝統の中で女性のはたした役割はとても大きかったと言っておかねばならない。踊りが教えられたのは（ただし芸者ではなく、武家の娘の場合であるが）、**日常の立ち居ふるまいをなめらかにする**ためであった。また音曲が学ばれたのは、父親や夫君のつれづれを慰めるためである。したがって技量や芸術性を高めることを目指したわけではなかった。その究極の目的は、**心の浄化**にあった。**奏する者の心が己自身と調和して**はじめて、整った調べが出ると言われたのである。これは、若者の教育にも見られた考え方と共通している。若者のための様々の教育は、最終的には精神を高めるためのものであった。音曲と舞踏にも「ほど」が大事で、**生活を美しくし、彩りをあたえる**ことができれば十分であった。あだな自慢や、過度の熱中などもってのほかである。あるペルシャの皇子がロンドンでダンスの行われている広間に案内され、加わらないかと誘われたとき、自分の国では、そのようなことは女性の舞踏団が行うべきものときまっていると、にべもなく答えたというが、私はこの皇子に共感する。

　日本女性の技芸のたしなみは、人にほこったり、世で**出世する**ために行われたのではない。あくまでも**家庭の中での楽しみ**であった。社交的な場で発揮されたとして

sentiments; in fact, women played an important role in the history of Japanese *belles lettres*. Dancing was taught (I am speaking of samurai girls and not of *geisha*) only to **smooth the angularity of their movements**. Music was to regale the weary hours of their fathers and husbands; hence it was not for the technique, the art as such, that music was learned; for the ultimate object was **purification of heart**, since it was said that no harmony of sound is attainable without **the player's heart being in harmony with herself**. Here again we see the same idea prevailing which we notice in the training of youths—that accomplishments were ever kept subservient to moral worth. Just enough of music and dancing to **add grace and brightness to life**, but never to foster vanity and extravagance. I sympathize with the Persian prince, who, when taken into a ball-room in London and asked to take part in the merriment, bluntly remarked that in his country they provided a particular set of girls to do that kind of business for them.

The accomplishments of our women were not acquired for show or **social ascendency**. They were a **home diversion**; and if they shone in social parties, it

も、それは主婦としてのたしなみ、すなわち家として客をもてなす一部なのである。家庭的であるか、ということが教育の基準であった。古い日本の女性のたしなみは、文武いずれにせよ家庭が眼目であった。女性はいかに家から遠ざかろうと、気持ちはつねに家に向いていた。身を粉にして働き、自分の生活を犠牲にするのも、すべて家の名を守るためであった。昼夜をわかつことなく、毅然としながら心優しく、雄々しくそして悲しい声で、自分の巣に向かって囀りつづけたのである。娘は父のため、妻は夫のため、母は息子のためにわが身を捧げた。女性は物心がついたときから、自己犠牲を教えられた。女性の人生は独り立ちではなく、他に依存しつつ仕える人生であった。男を助けるのが役割で、男の出世を助けるなら表に立ち、妨げるなら裏に引っ込む。若者が家の女中が好きになり、相思相愛となったときに、女は相手が自分にうつつを抜かし、義務を怠っていると見ると、自分を忘れさせるために自らの器量をそこなうというようなことが、よくあった。武家の娘の鑑として、吾

was as the attributes of a hostess,—in other words, as a part of the household contrivance for hospitality. Domesticity guided their education. It may be said that the accomplishments of the women of Old Japan, be they martial or pacific in character, were mainly intended for the home; and, however far they might roam, they never lost sight of **the hearth** as the center. It was to **maintain its honor and integrity** that they slaved, drudged and gave up their lives. Night and day, in tones at once firm and tender, brave and plaintive, they sang to their little nests. As daughter, woman sacrificed herself for her father, as wife for her husband, and as mother for her son. Thus from earliest youth she was taught to deny herself. Her life was not one of independence, but of dependent service. Man's helpmeet, if her presence is helpful she stays on the stage with him: if it hinders his work, she retires behind the curtain. Not infrequently does it happen that a youth becomes enamored of a maiden who returns his love with equal ardor, but, when she realizes his interest in her makes him forgetful of his duties, disfigures her person that her attractions may cease. Adzuma, the ideal wife in the

妻のことを述べておこう。ある男が吾妻に懸想し、横取りするため夫君の殺害をたくらんだ。吾妻はこれに加担するふりをし、暗い夫の寝所にやすんだ。かくして男の刀は愛しい吾妻の寝首を掻き切ったのであった。

　以下は若い大名の妻が生命を断つ前に記した手紙である。贅言を費やさず、そのものをして語らしめよう。

　もはや何事がおきようと流れは変わらぬ、事は定めのとおり動いてゆくとお聞きしております。一樹の陰、一河の流れも他生の縁と申しますが、わずか二年前にとこしえの夫婦の契で結ばれてより、わが心は影の形に沿うがごとくあなた様に寄りしたがい、愛し愛され、心と心が分かちがたく結ばれています。このたび、来たるいくさがあなた様にはこの世の見納めとお聞きしましたので、お別れの一書をたてまつります。古の漢土の武士であった項羽は、愛妾の虞との別れ

minds of samurai girls, finds herself loved by a man who, in order to win her affection, conspires against her husband. Upon pretence of joining in the guilty plot, she manages in the dark to take her husband's place, and the sword of the lover assassin descends upon her own devoted head.

The following epistle written by the wife of a young *daimio*, before taking her own life, needs no comment:—

"Oft have I heard that no accident or chance ever mars the march of events here below, and that all moves in accordance with a plan. To take shelter under a common bough or a drink of the same river, is alike ordained from ages prior to our birth. Since we were joined in ties of eternal wedlock, now two short years ago, my heart hath followed thee, even as its shadow followeth an object, inseparably bound heart to heart, loving and being loved. Learning but recently, however, that the coming battle is to be the last of thy labor and life, take the farewell greeting of thy loving partner. I have heard that Kō-u, the mighty warrior of ancient China, lost a battle, loth

を惜しんでいくさに破れたとのこと。また源義仲も、猛き武士（もののふ）でありながら、妻に別れがいえず、大望を遂げられなかったとのことです。もはやこの世の望みも喜びも失せたこの私が、生きてあなた様の足手まといになっては申し訳がたちません。人と生まれたからには誰もが踏まねばならぬ道で、あなた様をお待ち申しております。ご主君の秀頼様からくだされたご恩をくれぐれもお忘れになりませぬよう。海よりも深く山よりも高いご恩ですので。

　女性が夫君や家のために身を捧げるのは、男が主君や国のために身を捧げるのと同じく、自らの意思で行い、名誉あることであった。いっさいの**人生の謎は自己放下（じこほうげ）をしなければ解決しない**が、この自己放下こそが男の忠義、家に対する女の献身の本質（エッセンス）である。男は主君の奴隷ではないが、女も夫君の奴隷というわけではない。女の役割は「内助」として正式に認められるものであった。主従関係は階層をなし、女は夫君のために自己を空しくし、男は主君のために自己を空しくし、主君は天に従う

to part with his favorite Gu. Yoshinaka, too, brave as he was, brought disaster to his cause, too weak to bid prompt farewell to his wife. Why should I, to whom earth no longer offers hope or joy—why should I detain thee or thy thoughts by living? Why should I not, rather, await thee on the road which all mortal kind must sometime tread? Never, prithee, never forget the many benefits which our good master Hideyori hath heaped upon thee. The gratitude we owe him is as deep as the sea and as high as the hills."

Woman's surrender of herself to the good of her husband, home and family, was as willing and honorable as the man's self-surrender to the good of his lord and country. **Self-renunciation, without which no life-enigma can be solved**, was the keynote of the Loyalty of man as well as of the Domesticity of woman. She was no more the slave of man than was her husband of his liege-lord, and the part she played was recognized as *Naijo*, "the inner help." In the ascending scale of service stood woman, who annihilated herself for man, that he might annihilate himself for the master, that he in turn might obey heaven. I know **the**

とされていたのである。たしかに、**このような教説には問題があり**、キリスト教がすぐれているのはまさにこの点にあるといえる。キリスト教では、この世にある一人ひとりの個人に、**直接創造主への責務を負う**ことを求めているからである。しかし、ここには、たとえ**個としての自己を殺して**でも、自らより高いものに仕えるという、**奉仕の概念**がある。キリストの教えのうちもっとも偉大で、キリストの地上の御業（みわざ）の聖なる核をなすものが、この奉仕の概念である。そしてそれを共有しているという点で、武士道は**永遠の真実**に根ざしているということができるのである。

　読者の皆さん、どうか、自らの意思で隷従することを不当に高く評価しているといって私を非難しないでいただきたい。私は、ヘーゲルが広い学識と深い思索をもって世に問うた「**歴史は自由が展開し実現されていく過程である**」という学説を、おおむね受け入れる者である。私の言わんとするのは、武士道には**自己犠牲の精神**が徹底して行き渡っているということ、女性ばかりでなく男性も同じであるということである。したがって、武士道の影響が完全に失せるまでは、アメリカの女権論者が性急に主張する「日本のすべての女性が古い慣習に反抗して立ち上がりますよう！」という事態が日本の社会に実

weakness of this teaching and that the superiority of Christianity is nowhere more manifest than here, in that it requires of each and every living soul **direct responsibility to its Creator**. Nevertheless, as far as **the doctrine of service**—the serving of a cause higher than one's own self, even **at the sacrifice of one's individuality**; I say the doctrine of service, which is the greatest that Christ preached and is the sacred keynote of his mission—as far as that is concerned, Bushido is based on **eternal truth**.

My readers will not accuse me of undue prejudice in favor of slavish surrender of volition. I accept in a large measure the view advanced with breadth of learning and defended with profundity of thought by Hegel, **that history is the unfolding and realization of freedom**. The point I wish to make is that the whole teaching of Bushido was so thoroughly imbued with **the spirit of self-sacrifice**, that it was required not only of woman but of man. Hence, until the influence of its Precepts is entirely done away with, our society will not realize the view rashly expressed by an American exponent of woman's rights, who exclaimed, "May all the daughters of Japan rise in revolt

現することはないであろう。このような反抗は成功する
だろうか？　**女性の地位が向上する**だろうか？　このよう
なせっかちな動きで得られた権利は、現在まで受け継が
れてきた**優しい心、美しい礼儀作法**が失われることに見
合うものだろうか？　ローマの婦人たちが家庭的でなく
なったとき、見るにたえない**倫理的腐敗**が生じたのでは
なかったか？　日本女性の反抗は歴史がたどる正しい道
筋だと、かのアメリカの女権論者は我々を納得させられ
るだろうか？　どれも難しい問題である。そもそも反抗
などしなくても、**変化は時がくればものごとの必然とし
て起きるものである！**よってそれはいずれ先のこととし
て、以下では、武士道の下での女性の地位が、反抗にあ
たいするほどひどいものであったのかどうか考えてみよ
う。

　ヨーロッパの騎士は「神と貴婦人」に、おおっぴらに
敬意を表したとよく言われる。神と貴婦人を並べると
は、何と不釣り合いなことであろうかと、ギボンは顔を
赤らめた。また、騎士道の倫理は粗雑で、**「騎士らしさ」**
には**不倫の愛**という意味が含まれているとハラムが述べ
ている。騎士道が女性にどのような影響をあたえたかと
いう問題について、哲学者があれこれ思索している。ギ
ゾー氏は封建制度と騎士道は社会に健全な影響をもたら
したと主張するのに対して、スペンサー氏は戦闘的な社

against ancient customs!" Can such a revolt succeed? Will it **improve the female status**? Will the rights they gain by such a summary process repay the loss of that **sweetness of disposition**, that **gentleness of manner**, which are their present heritage? Was not the loss of domesticity on the part of Roman matrons followed by **moral corruption** too gross to mention? Can the American reformer assure us that a revolt of our daughters is the true course for their historical development to take? These are grave questions. **Changes must and will come without revolts!** In the meantime let us see whether the status of the fair sex under the Bushido regimen was really so bad as to justify a revolt.

We hear much of the outward respect European knights paid to "God and the ladies,"—the incongruity of the two terms making Gibbon blush; we are also told by Hallam that the morality of Chivalry was coarse, that **gallantry** implied **illicit love**. The effect of Chivalry on the weaker vessel was food for reflection on the part of philosophers, M. Guizot contending that Feudalism and Chivalry wrought wholesome influences, while Mr. Spencer tells us that in a mili-

会では（封建制社会は言うまでもなく戦闘的である）、女性の地位は必然的に低く、産業社会になってはじめて向上すると述べている。日本にあてはまるのはギゾー氏の見方だろうか？　スペンサー氏の見解であろうか？　どちらも正しいというのが私の意見である。日本の戦闘的階級は武士に限られ、その数は約二百万人であった。その上に**貴族階級の武士**、すなわち大名や朝廷の**公卿たち**がいたが、これら上級の有閑貴族は**武人といっても名ばかり**であった。武士の下には多数の**庶民**、すなわち職人、商人、農民などがおり、平和な仕事で日々をおくっていた。したがって、ハーバート・スペンサーが戦闘的な社会の特徴と述べているものは、もっぱら武士階級に局限され、その上と下の階級には産業的な社会の特徴があてはまるといえる。このことは女性の地位にみごとに反映されている。武家の女性ほど不自由だった者はいない。おもしろいことに、**社会階層が低いほど**──たとえば、零細な職人を例にとってみればよいが──**妻と夫は平等である**。高い階層でも、男女の関係における差はそ

tant society (and what is feudal society if not militant?) the position of woman is necessarily low, improving only as society becomes more industrial. Now is M. Guizot's theory true of Japan, or is Mr. Spencer's? In reply I might aver that both are right. The military class in Japan was restricted to the samurai, comprising nearly 2,000,000 souls. Above them were the **military nobles**, the *daimio*, and **the court nobles**, the *kugé*—these higher, sybaritical nobles being **fighters only in name**. Below them were masses of the **common people**—mechanics, tradesmen, and peasants—whose life was devoted to arts of peace. Thus what Herbert Spencer gives as the characteristics of a militant type of society may be said to have been exclusively confined to the samurai class, while those of the industrial type were applicable to the classes above and below it. This is well illustrated by the position of woman; for in no class did she experience less freedom than among the samurai. Strange to say, **the lower the social class**—as, for instance, among small artisans—**the more equal was the position of husband and wife**. Among the higher nobility, too, the difference in the relations of the sexes was less marked,

れほど目立っていない。その主要な要因は、**有閑の貴人は文字どおり女性化した**ので、本来の女性との距離が目立つことが少なかったのだろう。このようにスペンサーの説は古い日本には完全に妥当する。ギゾーのほうについていうと、その封建社会の説明を読めば分かるが、主として氏の念頭にあるのは上層の貴族である。したがって、ギゾーの説は大名と公卿に当てはまるのである。

ここまでの記述から、武士道の下で女性の地位がきわめて低かったという印象を持たれたとすれば、私は歴史の真実をゆがめたことになる。**女性は男性と同じように扱われなかった**ということは、まちがいなく言える。しかし、「違い」と「不平等」は異なるものであることをきちんと理解しないことには、この問題についての誤解はたえないだろう。

男性そのものが、今でも例えば法廷や選挙の投票などで、とうてい平等とはいえないということを考えると、男女間の平等の問題を論じることが虚しく感じられる。**アメリカの独立宣言**では、**すべての人間は生まれながらにして平等である**と述べられたが、精神的、あるいは肉体的な面での生まれながらの才能については触れられていない。ローマの政治学者ウルピアヌスがはるか昔に述べたこと、すなわち**法の前ですべての人間が平等である**

chiefly because there were few occasions to bring the differences of sex into prominence, the **leisurely nobleman having become literally effeminate**. Thus Spencer's dictum was fully exemplified in Old Japan. As to Guizot's, those who read his presentation of a feudal community will remember that he had the higher nobility especially under consideration, so that his generalization applies to the *daimio* and the *kugé*.

I shall be guilty of gross injustice to historical truth if my words give one a very low opinion of the status of woman under Bushido. I do not hesitate to state that **she was not treated as man's equal**; but until we learn to discriminate between difference and inequalities, there will always be misunderstandings upon this subject.

When we think in how few respects men are equal among themselves, e.g., before law courts or voting polls, it seems idle to trouble ourselves with a discussion on the equality of sexes. When, the **American Declaration of Independence** said that **all men were created equal**, it had no reference to their mental or physical gifts: it simply repeated what Ulpian long ago announced, that **before the law all men are equal**.

ということを蒸し返しているにすぎない。この場合、**法的権利**が、平等かどうかを決める尺度であった。社会における女性の地位を調べるのに、法的権利のみが尺度であるなら、それがどのあたりなのかを述べることは、体重をポンドとオンスで述べると同じくらい容易いことであろう。だが問題は、**男と女の社会的地位を相対的に比べる正確な基準が存在するかどうか**、ということである。金と銀の価値を比べて結果を数値化するように、女性と男性の地位を比較することが正しいのだろうか？ それで十分なのだろうか？ そのような計算方法では、人間に備わっているもっとも貴重な価値、すなわち**人間としての本性**を考慮の外においてしまうのではないだろうか？ 男性女性それぞれが、この地上での役目を果たすにはおよそ様々の条件が必要であることを考えると、男性と女性の地位を比較するのに用いる基準は、複合的なものでなければならないだろう。経済学の言葉を借りるなら、「**多重的な基準**」ということになる。武士道にはそれ独自の、二項的な基準があった。女性の価値を、**戦場**と**家庭**という二つの基準で測った。戦場では価値がなく、家庭での価値がすべてであった。女性の待遇は、この二つの判定に対応していた。社会・政治的単位とし

Legal rights were in this case the measure of their equality. Were the law the only scale by which to measure the position of woman in a community, it would be as easy to tell where she stands as to give her avoirdupois in pounds and ounces. But the question is: **Is there a correct standard in comparing the relative social position of the sexes?** Is it right, is it enough, to compare woman's status to man's as the value of silver is compared with that of gold, and give the ratio numerically? Such a method of calculation excludes from consideration the most important kind of value which a human being possesses; namely, **the intrinsic**. In view of the manifold variety of requisites for making each sex fulfil its earthly mission, the standard to be adopted in measuring its relative position must be of a composite character; or, to borrow from economic language, it must be a **multiple standard**. Bushido had a standard of its own and it was binomial. It tried to guage the value of woman on **the battle-field** and by **the hearth**. There she counted for very little; here for all. The treatment accorded her corresponded to this double measurement;—as a social-political unit not much, while **as wife and moth-**

ての扱いは小さかったが、**妻・母として最大の敬意と深い愛情を受けた**。ローマのような軍事的な国家で、婦人がなぜあれほどの尊敬を受けたのだろうか？ それは、マトローナ、すなわち母親だったからではなかろうか？ 戦士、立法家ではなく、母親として男の前に立って、平伏させたのである。武士道でも同じことである。父や夫たる者が戦場や野営地に出て不在のときには、すべて**家を取り仕切る**のを任されたのは母や妻であった。子の教育ばかりか、子を敵の手から守る仕事でさえ母親に委ねられたのである。先に述べた女性の**武術修練**は、子の教育を賢く監視し、実施することができることを主たる目的としていたのだ。

なまかじりの知識の外国人の間で、とても浅はかな考えが広まっている。日本では妻のことを「荊妻」などと呼ぶが、これは女性が軽んじられている証拠だ、というのである。日本語では家族をさして「愚父」や「豚児」、自分のことを「拙者」などと謙遜するのが普通であるといえば、分かってもらえるだろうか？

日本人の結婚観は、「夫と妻は一つの肉たるべし」という点において、いわゆるキリスト教徒の先をいくよう

er she received highest respect and deepest affection. Why among so military a nation as the Romans, were their matrons so highly venerated? Was it not because they were *matrona*, mothers? Not as fighters or law-givers, but as their mothers did men bow before them. So with us. While fathers and husbands were absent in field or camp, **the government of the household** was left entirely in the hands of mothers and wives. The education of the young, even their defence, was entrusted to them. **The warlike exercises** of women, of which I have spoken, were primarily to enable them intelligently to direct and follow the education of their children.

I have noticed a rather superficial notion prevailing among half-informed foreigners, that because the common Japanese expression for one's wife is "my rustic wife" and the like, she is despised and held in little esteem. When it is told that such phrases as "my foolish father," "my swinish son," "my awkward self," etc., are in current use, is not the answer clear enough?

To me it seems that our idea of marital union goes in some ways further than the so-called Christian. "Man and woman shall be one flesh." **The individu-**

に思われる。**アングロサクソンの個人主義**は、夫と妻が別々の人間であるという感覚を捨てきれない。それゆえ仲違いすると**別々の「権利」**を意識し、仲がよいときは言葉のかぎりをつくして**およそ馬鹿げた愛称や愚にもつかない甘い言葉**をべたべたと用いる。夫か妻が他人に向かって、つれ合いのことを「わたしのよき半身（better half）」が美しいだの、賢いだの、温かいなどと褒めそやすのは、**日本人の耳にはたいへん理性にもとる**所作である。自分自身のことをさして、「聡明なわたし」とか「愛すべき人柄」などと言うのは悪趣味もよいところではないか？　日本人には自分の妻や夫を褒めるのは、**自分自身のことを褒める**のと同じだという感覚がある。そして自己を褒めるのは、控えめにいってもよい趣味とはいえないと、日本人は感じる。願わくば、キリスト教徒の国々でもそうであってほしいものだ！このようにくだくだと脱線に及んだのは、**妻のことを謙遜する礼儀**は、武士にとってはきわめて普通のことであるからだ。

　チュートン系の民族では、部族の歴史の初期には、女性を**畏怖する迷信**があった（ただし現在のドイツではほとんど消えつつある）。そしてアメリカで社会が成立した当初は、女性不足[26] が痛いほど意識されていた（お気の毒なことに現在では数が増え、植民地時代の母親た

alism of the Anglo-Saxon cannot let go of the idea that husband and wife are two persons;—hence when they disagree, **their separate rights** are recognized, and when they agree, they exhaust their vocabulary in all sorts of **silly pet-names** and— **nonsensical blandishments**. It sounds highly **irrational to our ears**, when a husband or wife speaks to a third party of his other half— better or worse—as being lovely, bright, kind, and what not. Is it good taste to speak of one's self as "my bright self," "my lovely disposition," and so forth? We think praising one's own wife or one's own husband is **praising a part of one's own self**, and self-praise is regarded, to say the least, as bad taste among us,—and I hope, among Christian nations too! I have diverged at some length because **the polite debasement of one's consort** was a usage most in vogue among the samurai.

The Teutonic races beginning their tribal life with a **superstitious awe** of the fair sex (though this is really wearing off in Germany!), and the Americans beginning their social life under the painful consciousness of the numerical insufficiency of women[26] (who, now increasing, are, I am afraid, fast losing the pres-

ちが持っていた権威が急速に失せつつある）。そのせいで、西欧文明では、男性が女性に敬意をはらうのが、**基本的な道徳の標準**となっていた。これに対して武士道は武門の倫理であるがゆえに、善悪を分ける分水嶺は別のところに求められた。それは、人を自分自身の神性、及び他者と結びつけるために生じてくる様々の義務に沿って定義づけられている。この本の最初のほうで挙げた「五倫」がこれにあたり、その中でも特に「君臣の義」について詳しく述べておいたが、その他のものについては、とくに武士道のみに当てはまるものではないので、機に応じて触れてきた。それらはすべて**自然な情愛に基づくもの**なので、**人類に共通するもの**である。ただし、教え方によってとくに強く意識されるようになったものと、そうでないものとがある。これに関連して触れておかねばならないのは、**男同士の友情がきわめて強く、細やかであったということだ。結社**などの絆に、ロマンチックな愛着の色合いがともなうのはそのせいである。こ

---

[26] ここで触れているのは、女性がイギリスから連れてこられて、何ポンドかのタバコ等と交換されて結婚させられた時代のことである。

tige their colonial mothers enjoyed), the respect man pays to woman has in Western civilization become **the chief standard of morality**. But in the martial ethics of Bushido, the main water-shed dividing the good and the bad was sought elsewhere. It was located along the line of duty which bound man to his own divine soul and then to other souls, in the five relations I have mentioned in the early part of this paper. Of these we have brought to our reader's notice, Loyalty, the relation between one man as vassal and another as lord. Upon the rest, I have only dwelt incidentally as occasion presented itself; because they were not peculiar to Bushido. **Being founded on natural affections**, they could but be **common to all mankind**, though in some particulars they may have been accentuated by conditions which its teachings induced. In this connection, there comes before me the peculiar **strength and tenderness of friendship between man and man**, which often added to the bond of **brotherhood** a romantic attachment doubt-

[26] I refer to those days when girls were imported from England and given in marriage for so many pounds of tobacco, etc.

れは**若年の時期に男女が分けられたこと**によって、強められたことはまちがいない。西洋の騎士道で許されていた男女の愛、アングロサクソンの国々の自由な異性との触れ合いは、武士道文化の中では禁じられていたので、自然な愛情の流れが阻害されたからである。ダモンとピュテアス、アキレスとパトロクロスの物語の日本版はいくらでもひいてくることができる。あるいはダヴィデとヨナタンを結びつけたかたい絆を、武士道流に述べることもできよう。

　しかしながら、武士道ならではの美徳や教えは、武家の階級のみにとどまらなかったことは、さして驚くことではない。よって、ここからは武士道が国全体へと及ぼした影響について考えてみよう。

less intensified by **the separation of the sexes in youth**,—a separation which denied to affection the natural channel open to it in Western chivalry or in the free intercourse of Anglo-Saxon lands. I might fill pages with Japanese versions of the story of Damon and Pythias or Achilles and Patroclos, or tell in Bushido parlance of ties as sympathetic as those which bound David and Jonathan.

It is not surprising, however, that the virtues and teachings unique in the Precepts of Knighthood did not remain circumscribed to the military class. This makes us hasten to the consideration of the influence of Bushido on the nation at large.

第 **15** 章
武士道の影響

　武士道の様々の美徳は大きな山脈のようにつらなり、我が国民の一般の徳性をはるかに超えて堂々とそびえている。そして、本書のここまでのところでは、中でもとくに抜きん出た山頂をいくつかご覧いただいた。朝日が昇るとき、まずもってもっとも秀でた頂が明々と染まり、やがて谷の下へ下へと光が及んでいく。それと同じように、気高い道徳律はまず武人の階級を照らし、しかるのちに一般の庶民からも信奉者を得ることとなったのである。**民主主義は生来の君主の器を育てあげ**、指導者をつくる。**貴族の政治は一般大衆の中に君主的な精神を注ぎ込む**。悪しき習わしと同じく、美徳も人から人へと広まっていく。「賢者が一人いればよい。それで皆が賢くなる。驚くべき感染力である」とはエマーソンの言である。**徳風があまねく行き渡る圧倒的な力**には、社会のどんな階級もカーストも勝てない。

　アングロサクソンの自由の理念はたしかに勝利をおさ

CHAPTER 15

THE INFLUENCE OF BUSHIDO

We have brought into view only a few of the more prominent peaks which rise above the range of knightly virtues, in themselves so much more elevated than the general level of our national life. As the sun in its rising first tips the highest peaks with russet hue, and then gradually casts its rays on the valley below, so the ethical system which first enlightened the military order drew in course of time followers from amongst the masses. **Democracy** raises up **a natural prince** for its leader, and **aristocracy** infuses **a princely spirit** among the people. **Virtues are no less contagious than vices.** "There needs but one wise man in a company, and all are wise, so rapid is the contagion," says Emerson. No social class or caste can resist **the diffusive power of moral influence**.

Prate as we may of the triumphant march of **An-**

めてきた。しかしその原動力は大衆から得られたもので
はない。むしろ、それは地主階級や「ジェントルマン」
によって成し遂げられたのである。テーヌ氏の「英仏海
峡の向こうで用いられるこの一語に、英国社会の歴史が
要約されている」という言葉がすべてを物語っている。
このように言われると、民主主義は自信たっぷりに反論
し、「アダムが耕しイブが紡いでいたとき、ジェントル
マンなどどこにいたのだ」と反問するだろう。そう、ま
さにそこなのだ。エデンの園にジェントルマンがいなか
ったことこそが無念なのである！ジェントルマンがいな
かったがゆえに、人類の祖であるアダムとイブは高い代
償を払わねばならなかったのである。ジェントルマンが
そこにいたなら、エデンの園はもっと趣味よく手入れさ
れたであろうことはいうまでもないが、アダムとイブ
は、**エホバに逆らうのは忠義にもとる不名誉**であり、**裏
切りであり反乱である**ことを、つらい経験をすることな
く、教わることができたはずなのである。

　過去の日本は武士によって作られた。武士は**国の華**で
あったのみならず、根でもあった。すばらしい天来の徳
はすべて、武士をとおしてもたらされた。武士は**超然と
していて、庶民と社交的にまじわることはなかったが、
倫理の基準をあたえ、模範を示すことで衆をみちびい
た。**武士道には**秘儀**としての面にくわえて、**俗世間への**

glo-Saxon liberty, rarely has it received impetus from the masses. Was it not rather the work of the squires and *gentlemen*? Very truly does M. Taine say, "These three syllables, as used across the channel, summarize the history of English society." Democracy may make self-confident retorts to such a statement and fling back the question—"When Adam delved and Eve span, where then was the gentleman?" All the more pity that a gentleman was not present in Eden! The first parents missed him sorely and paid a high price for his absence. Had he been there, not only would the garden have been more tastefully dressed, but they would have learned without painful experience that **disobedience to Jehovah** was **disloyalty and dishonor, treason and rebellion**.

What Japan was she owed to the samurai. They were not only **the flower of the nation** but its root as well. All the gracious gifts of Heaven flowed through them. Though they **kept themselves socially aloof from the populace**, they **set a moral standard** for them and **guided them by their example**. I admit Bushido had its **esoteric** and **exoteric teachings**;

教えという二つの顔がある。後者は衆生に安寧と幸福をあたえようとする「**幸福主義**」である。前者は、**徳なるがゆえに徳を行う**という、「**徳倫理学**」である。

　ヨーロッパで騎士道がもっとも盛んであったころ、騎士は数の上ではごく少数に過ぎなかったが、「サー・フィリップ・シドニーからサー・ウォルター・スコットにいたるまで、英文学の戯曲の半分と、小説のすべてが、このような人物（すなわちジェントルマン）を描いている」とエマーソンは言った。ここでシドニーとスコットのかわりに近松と馬琴の名を入れれば、日本の文学史のあらましを述べたことになる。

　庶民の娯楽や教育の手段は、**芝居、講談、説法、浄瑠璃、小説**など様々であったが、主なテーマは武士の物語であった。粗末な小屋でいろりを囲んだ農民たちは、義経と弁慶の主従の美談や、蘇我兄弟の勇敢な仇討ち話を繰り返し聞いて飽きることがなかった。うす汚れた子どもたちもそんな物語を、木が燃え尽き、燃えさしの灰が暗くなるまで夢中になって聞き、終わったあとも、かっかと燃える心がなかなか冷めることがなかった。商家の

these were **eudemonistic**, looking after the welfare and happiness of the commonalty, while those were **aretaic**, emphasizing **the practice of virtues for their own sake**.

In the most chivalrous days of Europe, Knights formed numerically but a small fraction of the population, but, as Emerson says—"In English Literature half the drama and all the novels, from Sir Philip Sidney to Sir Walter Scott, paint this figure (gentleman)." Write in place of Sidney and Scott, Chikamatsu and Bakin, and you have in a nutshell the main features of the literary history of Japan.

The innumerable avenues of popular amusement and instruction— **the theatres, the story-teller's booths, the preacher's dais, the musical recitations, the novels**—have taken for their chief theme the stories of the samurai. The peasants round the open fire in their huts never tire of repeating the achievements of Yoshitsuné and his faithful retainer Benkei, or of the two brave Soga brothers; the dusky urchins listen with gaping mouths until the last stick burns out and the fire dies in its embers, still leaving their hearts aglow with the tale that is told. The clerks and the

番頭・手代や小僧たちも、一日の仕事がすんで雨戸[27]をたてると、一所に集まって信長や秀吉の話を夜の更けるまで楽しみ、やがて疲れた目が睡魔に襲われると、夢の世界で帳場の労苦からいくさ場の武勇へと運ばれていくというありさまだった。幼児はよちよち歩きはじめると、鬼ヶ島で鬼を退治した桃太郎のあっぱれな物語をたどたどしく語ることを教わる。女子でさえ、武人の立派なふるまいや心構えへのあこがれに心がいっぱいで、デズデモーナのごとく、侍の物語に真剣に耳をかたむけ、貪るように聞くのが常であった。

侍は**日本人の最高の理想**となった。「花は桜、人は武士」と庶民は謳った。武士に経済的活動は禁じられていたので、直接、商売の道を助けることはなかった。しかし人間としての活動や思想で、いささかなりとも**武士道の影響**を受けていないものはない。今の日本人の知と徳は、直接的にも間接的にも武士道によって作られたものである。

---

[27] 外の鎧戸

shop-boys, after their day's work is over and the *ama-do*[27] of the store are closed, gather together to relate the story of Nobunaga and Hidéyoshi far into the night, until slumber overtakes their weary eyes and transports them from the drudgery of the counter to the exploits of the field. The very babe just beginning to toddle is taught to lisp the adventures of Momotaro, the daring conqueror of ogre-land. Even girls are so imbued with the love of knightly deeds and virtues that, like Desdemona, they would seriously incline to devour with greedy ear the romance of the samurai.

The samurai grew to be **the *beau ideal* of the whole race**. "As among flowers the cherry is queen, so among men the samurai is lord," so sang the populace. Debarred from commercial pursuits, the military class itself did not aid commerce; but there was no channel of human activity, no avenue of thought, which did not receive in some measure **an impetus from Bushido**. Intellectual and moral Japan was directly or indirectly the work of Knighthood.

---

[27] Outside shutters.

マロック氏の『貴族階級と進化』というとても示唆に富む本で、「生物としての進化は別として、社会の進化は偉人の思想や意図から、意図せざる結果として生じてくるものと定義することができよう」と述べられている。さらに、歴史の進歩とは「一般の人々の生きる努力ではなく、少数エリートの、衆を最良の形に導き、方向づけ、用いようとする努力から」生み出されるものだという。マロックの本の立論が健全なものかどうか、それはしばらく措くとして、ここに述べられている文言の正しさは、少なくとも我が国の社会の進歩において、武士道が大きな役割を果たしてきたことによって、十分に立証されているといえよう。

　武士道精神が、いかに日本社会のすべての階層に浸透していたか、それは「男伊達」と呼ばれる者たちが登場したことにも表れている。「男伊達」とは、**庶民のなかで頭角をあらわす、リーダーの素質を持って生まれた者**のことで、志操堅固にして、全身、男らしい強さにあふれていた。彼らはつねに**庶民の心情を語り、庶民を守護しようとする**。それぞれに何千何百もの心酔者がいて、武士が大名に忠義を尽くすように、「身命、浮世の財や名の一切」を喜んで捧げる覚悟ができていた。このよう

Mr. Mallock, in his exceedingly suggestive book, *Aristocracy and Evolution*, has eloquently told us that "social evolution, in so far as it is other than biological, may be defined as the unintended result of the intentions of great men;" further, that historical progress is produced by a struggle "not among the community generally, to live, but a struggle amongst a small section of the community to lead, to direct, to employ, the majority in the best way." Whatever may be said about the soundness of his argument, these statements are amply verified in the part played by bushi in the social progress, as far as it went, of our Empire.

How the spirit of Bushido permeated all social classes is also shown in the development of a certain order of men, known as *otoko-daté*, the **natural leaders of democracy**. Staunch fellows were they, every inch of them strong with the strength of massive manhood. At once **the spokesmen and the guardians of popular rights**, they had each a following of hundreds and thousands of souls who proffered in the same fashion that samurai did to *daimio*, the willing service of "limb and life, of body, chattels and earthly honor."

な**生まれながらの「親分」**は、気がみじかく、手のはや
い職人連中の圧倒的な支持をうけていたので、二本差し
の階級の者たちが権力を傘にきて専横な振る舞いをしよ
うにも、それを牽制する大きな力となったのである。

　武士道は、それが生み出された階級から様々の形で下
の階級へと伝播していき、庶民のなかで酵母のような働
きをし、民族全体に倫理の基準をもたらした。武士道は
誕生したときにはエリート階級がおびる名誉の徴であっ
たが、時代が下るとともに**日本のすべての民にとってめ
ざすべき目標、奮いたたせる理想**となったのである。そ
して、たとえ気高い者たちの精神の高みに、庶民が達す
るのは無理であるにしても、やまと魂はこの島国の「民
族精神」を表すものとなったのだ。もしも宗教が、マシ
ュー・アーノルドが述べたように「感情に彩られた道
徳」にすぎないとすれば、道徳律は様々にあれど、その
中でも武士道こそまさしく「宗教」の名にふさわしいも
のといえよう。本居宣長は、日本人が暗黙のうちに了解
していたことを言葉にあらわして、このように詠った。

　　しき嶋のやまとごゝろを人とはゞ
　　朝日ににほふ山ざくら花

Backed by a vast multitude of rash and impetuous working-men, those **born "bosses"** formed a formidable check to the rampancy of the two-sworded order.

In manifold ways has Bushido filtered down from the social class where it originated, and acted as leaven among the masses, furnishing a moral standard for the whole people. The Precepts of Knighthood, begun at first as the glory of the *elite*, became in time **an aspiration and inspiration to the nation at large**; and though the populace could not attain the moral height of those loftier souls, yet *Yamato Damashii*, the Soul of Japan, ultimately came to express the *Volksgeist* of the Island Realm. If religion is no more than "Morality touched by emotion," as Matthew Arnold defines it, few ethical systems are better entitled to the rank of religion than Bushido. Motoori has put the mute utterance of the nation into words when he sings:—

"Isles of blest Japan!
  Should your Yamato spirit
  Strangers seek to scan,
  Say—scenting morn's sunlit air,
  Blows the cherry wild and fair!"

まさに言い得て妙ではないか。桜[28]は昔から**日本人が
もっとも好む花**であり、**我が国民性の象徴**であった。と
くに、「やまと魂とは？」という問いに答えている、「朝日
ににほふ山ざくら花」という言葉に注目しておこう。

　やまと魂は大事に育てられたひよわな草ではなく、野
に育つ、野生の樹木である。**日本の土壌に自生する植物
である**。その花としての特徴は、他国の花にも同じもの
があるだろうが、桜は本来、我が国の土と水から自然に
生えた、固有の植物である。しかし、日本人が桜を愛す
るのは、自生の植物であるからというばかりではない。
桜の花の洗練された美しさ、上品さは日本人の美感にう
ったえるが、他の花ではこうはいかない。ヨーロッパ人
が愛でるバラは、日本人にこんな感興をあたえない。桜
は**単純素朴**なところが身上だが、バラにはそれが欠けて
いる。くわえて、バラは美しい花の下にトゲを隠し、い
つまでも生に執着して散ろうとしない。死を悪み恐れる
がごとく、腐るがままに茎の上にとどまって生き恥をさ
らすのである。しかも、これ見よがしのどぎつい色彩
と、濃厚な匂いを持っている。すべて桜とは正反対であ
る。桜は美しい顔の下に短剣も毒もひそめることなく、

---

[28]　（学名）*Cerasus pseudo-cerasus,* Lndley.

Yes, the *sakura*[28] has for ages been **the favorite of our people** and **the emblem of our character**. Mark particularly the terms of definition which the poet uses, the words the *wild cherry flower scenting the morning sun.*

The Yamato spirit is not a tame, tender plant, but a wild—in the sense of natural—growth; **it is indigenous to the soil**; its accidental qualities it may share with the flowers of other lands, but in its essence it remains the original, spontaneous outgrowth of our clime. But its nativity is not its sole claim to our affection. **The refinement and grace of its beauty** appeal to *our* **aesthetic sense** as no other flower can. We cannot share the admiration of the Europeans for their roses, which lack the **simplicity** of our flower. Then, too, the thorns that are hidden beneath the sweetness of the rose, the tenacity with which she clings to life, as though loth or afraid to die rather than drop untimely, preferring to rot on her stem; her showy colors and heavy odors—all these are traits so unlike our flower, which carries no dagger or poison

[28] *Cerasus pseudo-cerasus*, Lindley.

**自然の声にしたがって生に別れるのをためらうこともな
く、その色彩も厚化粧ではなく、あわい香りはいつまで
も飽きることがない。色と形の美しさを見せようとする
ことには限度がある。それは本来、変化することなく存
在し続ける性質のものだからである。これに対して、香
りはいずれ消えるもの、生命ある者の息のようにうつろ
いやすい。**どの宗教の儀式でも、乳香や没薬などの薫香
が用いられるのはそれが理由だ。**香りは魂に語りかけ
る。**地球をめぐる太陽がまず極東の島々を明るく照らし
出し、桜のかぐわしい香りが朝の空気に生命のいぶきを
注ぐとき、美しい朝日から生まれたかのような息を胸い
っぱいに吸い込む。これほど心を平和にし、生き生きと
した活力をあたえてくれるものがあるだろうか？

　創造主でさえ、甘い香りをかいだとき、心に新たな決
意をもったと伝えられている（創世記8：21）。桜の花
がかぐわしい季節に、日本人が小さな住まいから飛び出
してくることに、なんの不思議があろうか？　そんな一
時、彼らの手足が労働を忘れ、心が苦しみや悲しみから
遠ざかったといって責めるなかれ。須臾の楽しみが終わ
ると、彼らは新たな活力と新たな気力をもって、日々の
仕事にもどる。このような意味でも、桜は国の華なので
ある。

under its beauty, which is ever **ready to depart life at the call of nature**, whose colors are never gorgeous, and whose light fragrance never palls. Beauty of color and of form is limited in its showing; it is a fixed quality of existence, whereas fragrance is volatile, **ethereal as the breathing of life**. So in all religious ceremonies frankincense and myrrh play a prominent part. **There is something spirituelle in redolence**. When the delicious perfume of the *sakura* quickens the morning air, as the sun in its course rises to illumine first the isles of the Far East, few sensations are more serenely exhilarating than to inhale, as it were, the very breath of beauteous day.

When the Creator himself is pictured as making new resolutions in his heart upon smelling a sweet savor (Gen. VIII, 21), is it any wonder that the sweet-smelling season of the cherry blossom should call forth the whole nation from their little habitations? Blame them not, if for a time their limbs forget their toil and moil and their hearts their pangs and sorrows. Their brief pleasure ended, they return to their daily tasks with new strength and new resolutions. Thus in ways more than one is the *sakura* the flower of the nation.

桜はかくもかぐわしく、はかない。風の吹くがままになびき、香りをはなち、たちまち散ってしまう。このような花が、やまと魂を象徴しているのだろうか？ 日本の魂は、かくももろく、死と縁が深いものなのだろうか？

Is, then, this flower, so sweet and evanescent, blown whithersoever the wind listeth, and, shedding a puff of perfume, ready to vanish forever, is this flower the type of the Yamato spirit? Is the Soul of Japan so frailly mortal?

武士道は
今も生きているか?

　それとも、西洋文明が国中に広まった結果、武士道は
すでにみじんの痕跡を残すこともなく拭い去られてしま
ったのだろうか?

　一国の魂ともあろうものがそれほど早々と死にたえて
しまうような、みじめな話などあるものではない。やま
と魂は、そんなに容易く外からの影響に屈してしまうほ
ど、貧弱なものではない。国民の性格は様々な心理的な
要素が集まって一つのまとまりをなし、いわゆる**「国民
性」**と呼ばれているが、それは容易に変化するものでは
ない。「魚のヒレ、鳥の嘴、肉食獣の歯などのような、
それ以上還元できない種としての特徴」と等しく不変で
ある。ルボン氏 [29] の近著はあれこれ底の浅い断定と、
はでな一般化に満ちみちた書物であるが、その中で、

---

[29] *The Psychology of Peoples*, p. 33.

CHAPTER 16

IS BUSHIDO
STILL ALIVE?

Or has Western civilization, in its march through the land, already wiped out every trace of its ancient discipline?

It were a sad thing if a nation's soul could die so fast. That were a poor soul that could succumb so easily to extraneous influences. The aggregate of psychological elements which constitute **a national character**, is as tenacious as the "irreducible elements of species, of the fins of fish, of the beak of the bird, of the tooth of the carnivorous animal." In his recent book, full of shallow asseverations and brilliant generalizations, M. LeBon[29] says, "The discoveries due

「知性による発見は、人類共通の遺産である。性格上の
資質や欠陥は、それぞれの民族に固有の遺産である。そ
れは盤石の岩のごときものであり、幾世紀ものあいだ
日々大洋の波が洗っても、せいぜいとがった角がすりへ
るだけだ」と述べられている。大胆しごくな断定で、い
かにも熟考にあたいするかのようにも見えるが、それぞ
れの民族に「固有の遺産」であるような資質や欠陥なる
ものがそもそも存在するのかどうか、そこが大いに疑問
である。この手の図式は、ルボンのこの本を待つまでも
なくはるか昔からおなじみのものであり、もうずいぶん
前にセオドア・ウェイツとヒュー・マレイによってこっ
ぱ微塵にされている。本書では、ここまで武士道によっ
てもたらされた数々の美徳を研究してきたが、その際に
ヨーロッパの文献をふんだんに引用して、比較し、例を
示した。これによって明らかとなったのは、**どのような
資質も武士道に「固有の」ものではない**ということであ
る。様々の倫理的資質が集まって一つのまとまりをなし
ているのを見ると、たしかに、民族に独自のものと見え
るかもしれない。この「まとまり」のことをさして、エ
マーソンは「あらゆる大きな力が流れ込んで成立してい
る複合体」と呼んだ。しかし、それが人種や民族に固有
の遺産であるとするルボンとは違って、コンコードの哲
人エマーソンは「あらゆる国の、もっともすぐれた人格

to the intelligence are the common patrimony of humanity; qualities or defects of character constitute the exclusive patrimony of each people: they are the firm rock which the waters must wash day by day for centuries, before they can wear away even its external asperities." These are strong words and would be highly worth pondering over, provided there were qualities and defects of character which *constitute the exclusive patrimony* of each people. Schematizing theories of this sort had been advanced long before LeBon began to write his book, and they were exploded long ago by Theodor Waitz and Hugh Murray. In studying the various virtues instilled by Bushido, we have drawn upon European sources for comparison and illustrations, and we have seen that **no one quality of character was its *exclusive* patrimony**. It is true the aggregate of moral qualities presents a quite unique aspect. It is this aggregate which Emerson names a "compound result into which every great force enters as an ingredient." But, instead of making it, as LeBon does, an exclusive patrimony of a race or people, the Concord philosopher calls it "an element

者を結びつける特徴であり、それによって彼らはお互い
を理解し、融和し合う。それはきわめて明瞭なものであ
り、フリーメイソンの標を帯びている人間なのかどうか
はすぐに分かってしまう」と述べている。

　武士道によって日本、とくに武士に刻みこまれた性格
は、「それ以上還元できない種としての特徴」であると
まではいえないが、現在にいたるも強い生命力を持ち続
けていることは疑いえない。武士道が単に物理的な力だ
としても、**過去七百年の間に積もってきた勢い**がこれほ
ど急に止まってしまうということはありえない。また、
かりに遺伝によって伝わるものなら、その影響はとてつ
もなく広汎に及んでいるはずだ。フランスの経済学者シ
ェイソン氏の計算したところによると、一世紀の間に三
つの世代があるとするなら、「紀元千年に生きていた、
少なくとも二千万の人の血が現在の個々の人間の血管に
流れている」ことになる。「時の重みを負いかねて」地
面に這いつくばっているどんな農民でも、血管の中には
永劫の時代の血がめぐっているがゆえに、我々とも兄弟
であるばかりか、「ウシとも」血縁なのである。

　武士道は、それと意識されない、抗えない影響力を及
ぼすことで、国や個々の人を動かしてきた。現代日本を

which unites the most forcible persons of every country; makes them intelligible and agreeable to each other; and is somewhat so precise that it is at once felt if an individual lack the Masonic sign."

The character which Bushido stamped on our nation and on the samurai in particular, cannot be said to form "an irreducible element of species," but nevertheless as to the vitality which it retains there is no doubt. Were Bushido a mere physical force, the **momentum it has gained in the last seven hundred years** could not stop so abruptly. Were it transmitted only by heredity, its influence must be immensely widespread. Just think, as M. Cheysson, a French economist, has calculated, that supposing there be three generations in a century, "each of us would have in his veins the blood of at least twenty millions of the people living in the year 1000 A.D." The merest peasant that grubs the soil, "bowed by the weight of centuries," has in his veins the blood of ages, and is thus a brother to us as much as "to the ox."

An unconscious and irresistible power, Bushido has been moving the nation and individuals. It was an

切り開いた最高の知性であった吉田松陰は、処刑前夜に
このように詠んだ。

　　かくすればかくなるものと知りながら
　　已むに已まれぬ大和魂

これは日本民族にとっての、偽らざる心情の表出にほか
ならない。武士道は**きちんとした体系をなしてはいない**
ものの、過去において精神的支柱として**我が国を動かし
てきた**し、現在でもそうなのである。

　ランサム氏は「**三つの異なる日本が同時に存在してい
る**。いまだ死にたえていない古い日本、変化がいまだ精
神のみにとどまっている新生日本、そして目下はげしい
陣痛に悩んでいる、出産途上の日本の三つだ」と述べて
いる。この分析は概して正しい。とくに有形の、具体的
な制度についてはまさにそのとおりである。しかし、基
本的な倫理観については、多少の修正が必要だ。「古い
日本」を作り、またそれによって作られもした武士道
は、依然として**変化を導く基本原理**となっており、今後
も、**新たな時代を作り出していく原動力**となっていくこ
とと思われる。

　日本という国の舵をとって、**大政奉還**の嵐と**明治維新**

honest confession of the race when Yoshida Shoin, one of the most brilliant pioneers of Modern Japan, wrote on the eve of his execution the following stanza;—

> "Full well I knew this course must end in death;
> It was Yamato spirit urged me on
> To dare whate'er betide."

Unformulated, Bushido was and still is the animating spirit, **the motor force of our country**.

Mr. Ransome says that "there are three distinct Japans in existence side by side to-day,—the old, which has not wholly died out; the new, hardly yet born except in spirit; and the transition, passing now through its most critical throes." While this is very true in most respects, and particularly as regards tangible and concrete institutions, the statement, as applied to fundamental ethical notions, requires some modification; for Bushido, the maker and product of Old Japan, is still **the guiding principle of the transition** and will prove **the formative force of the new era**.

The great statesmen who steered the ship of our

の大波をくぐり抜けた偉大な政治家たちは、武士道より
ほかに精神教育を受けていない者たちであった。近年、
キリスト教の布教活動が、新生日本を作るのにそうとう
の貢献があったことを証明しようとする者がいる[30]。
私は、然るべき方面にきちんと功績を認めるのに吝かで
はないが、善意にあふれていたとはいえ、宣教師たちに
この功績を認めるのはいかがなものであろうか。根拠の
ないことをむりに主張するより、「名誉は互いに譲りあ
うべし」という聖書の教えを肝に銘じておくことこそ、
宗教人たる彼らの職にふさわしいのではなかろうか。私
自身は、キリスト教の宣教師が日本のために大きな仕事
をしてくれていると思う。教育、とくに倫理教育の面で
そうである。それはそれとして、神の玄妙なる御業はま
ちがいなく達せられるにせよ、いまだ人の目には見えが
たい。宣教師たちの仕事の成果は、いまだ表には出てい
ない。そう、キリスト教宣教師の仕事は、**新生日本の国
柄をつくる**うえで、今のところ、何か目に見えるものを
もたらしたとはいえない。むしろ、良かれ悪しかれ我々
を衝き動かしてきたのは、純粋で単純な武士道なのであ
る。近代日本を作った人々の伝記を開いてみよう。佐久

---

[30] Speer; *Missions and Politics in Asia,* Lecture *IV,* pp. 189-190; Dennis: *Christian Missions and Social Progress,* Vol. I, p. 32, Vol. II, p. 70, etc.

state through the hurricane of **the Restoration** and the whirlpool of **national rejuvenation**, were men who knew no other moral teaching than the Precepts of Knighthood. Some writers[30] have lately tried to prove that the Christian missionaries contributed an appreciable quota to the making of New Japan. I would fain render honor to whom honor is due: but this honor can hardly be accorded to the good missionaries. More fitting it will be to their profession to stick to the scriptural injunction of preferring one another in honor, than to advance a claim in which they have no proofs to back them. For myself, I believe that Christian missionaries are doing great things for Japan—in the domain of education, and especially of moral education:—only, the mysterious though not the less certain working of the Spirit is still hidden in divine secrecy. Whatever they do is still of indirect effect. No, as yet Christian missions have effected but little visible in **moulding the character of New Japan**. No, it was Bushido, pure and simple, that urged us on for weal or woe. Open the biographies of the makers of Modern Japan—of Sakuma, of Saigo, of

間象山、西郷隆盛、大久保利通、木戸孝允、くわえて伊藤博文、大隈重信、板垣退助など現存の人たちの回顧談を見るがよい。彼らが**武士としての本能にしたがってものを考え、働いていた**ということが手にとるように分かるだろう。ヘンリー・ノーマン氏は極東を研究し観察してきた成果として、「日本では、人類の歴史で類をみないほど**厳格で高踏的、几帳面な名誉の規範**が、国民の行動を導く指針となっており、日本はこの一点で他のアジアの専制国家と分かたれている」と述べている[31]。このノーマンの観察は、新生日本を現在の姿へと作り上げてきた、まさにその原動力をとらえているといえよう。そして、このような規範によって導かれていくのが、将来の日本の運命となるであろう。

　日本の変貌は、世界全体に知られている出来事である。これほどの大事業をなすには、いくつもの動因が絡み合っていることはいうまでもないが、中でも最重要のものを挙げるとすれば、それは武士道であると述べることに何のためらいもない。**国を開いて海外との交易をはじめ、生活の全般に最新の進歩を取り入れ、**西洋の政治と科学を学びはじめた当初の動機は、**兵を強くしたり、**

---

[31] *The Far East*, p. 375.

Okubo, of Kido, not to mention the reminiscences of living men such as Ito, Okuma, Itagaki, etc.:—and you will find that it was **under the impetus of samurai-hood that they thought and wrought**. When Mr. Henry Norman declared, after his study and observation of the Far East,[31] that only the respect in which Japan differed from other oriental despotisms lay in "the ruling influence among her people of **the strictest, loftiest, and the most punctilious codes of honor** that man has ever devised," he touched the main spring which has made new Japan what she is and which will make her what she is destined to be.

The transformation of Japan is a fact patent to the whole world. In a work of such magnitude various motives naturally entered; but if one were to name the principal, one would not hesitate to name Bushido. When we **opened the whole country to foreign trade**, when we **introduced the latest improvements in every department of life**, when we began to study Western politics and sciences, our guiding motive was

国を富ませたりすることではなかった。ましてや、西洋の習俗を**やみくもに模倣すること**ではなかった。アジアの国々の制度や民族をつぶさに観察してきた、ある西洋人がこのように書いている。「日本はヨーロッパの影響を受けていると、耳にたこができるくらい聞かされるが、事実は、この島国で起きている変化がまったく**自発性のもの**で、ヨーロッパが日本を教えたというより、日本自身が積極的に政府や軍隊を組織する方法をヨーロッパから学び取り成功をおさめてきたということである。トルコがかつてヨーロッパの砲術を取り入れたように、日本はヨーロッパの科学的な技術を輸入した。このことをさして影響というのは正確ではない。イギリスが中国から茶を買ったからといって、それが影響であるなどとは言わないからである。ヨーロッパの宣教師、哲学者、政治家、煽動家で、日本を作り直したといえる者などいるだろうか?」[32]。タウンセンド氏は、**日本を変貌させている行動の源**が、**日本人自身のうち**にあったということをきちんと見据えているのである。そして、さらにもう一歩、**日本人の心**の中にまで踏み込めば、**この源はほかならぬ武士道である**ことを、氏の慧眼は容易に見抜い

---

[32] Meredith Townsend, *Asia and Europe*, N.Y., 1900, 28.

not **the development of our physical resources and the increase of wealth**; much less was it **a blind imitation** of Western customs. A close observer of oriental institutions and peoples has written:—"We are told every day how Europe has influenced Japan, and forget that the change in those islands was entirely **self-generated**, that Europeans did not teach Japan, but that Japan of herself chose to learn from Europe methods of organization, civil and military, which have so far proved successful. She imported European mechanical science, as the Turks years before imported European artillery. That is not exactly influence," continues Mr. Townsend, "unless, indeed, England is influenced by purchasing tea of China. Where is the European apostle," asks our author, "or philosopher or statesman or agitator who has re-made Japan?"[32] Mr. Townsend has well perceived that **the spring of action which brought about the changes in Japan** lay entirely **within our own selves**; and if he had only probed into **our psychology**, his keen powers of observation would easily have convinced him that that **spring was no other than Bushido**. The sense of

たことであろう。**劣等国**として蔑まれてはならないとい
う名誉心、それこそがもっとも強い動機であったのだ。
国を富ませ、産業を振興させようという考えは、変貌を
遂げていく中で生じてきたものなのである。

　武士道の影響は今でもなお、いたるところに見られ
る。日本人の生活をちらとでも見れば、そのことは歴然
としている。例えばラフカディオ・ハーン。**日本の心**を
忠実に汲み取り、雄弁な筆に託したこの作家の作品を読
めば、日本人の心の作用は、とりもなおさず武士道のそ
れであることが分かる。日本人は誰でも礼儀正しいとい
うのも**武士道の遺産**だが、これはよく知られていること
なので煩をさけて略そう。「ちんちくりんの日本人」が
示す**身体的な我慢強さ、精神の芯の強さ、勇敢さ**は日清
戦争でじゅうぶんに証明されている[33]。多くの人が
「日本ほど忠誠心と愛国心に富む国があるだろうか？」
という問いを発している。胸を張って「否」という答え
を出せるのは、まさに武士道のおかげなのである。

　その一方で、ひいきの引き倒しにならぬよう、武士道
のせいでもたらされている、日本人の国民性の不足や欠

---

[33] これについて書かれた本は多数あるが、とくにエストレイクとヤマダの『英雄的
な日本』とダイオシーの『新たな極東』を挙げておこう。

honor which cannot bear being looked down upon as **an inferior power**,—that was the strongest of motives. Pecuniary or industrial considerations were awakened later in the process of transformation.

The influence of Bushido is still so palpable that he who runs may read. A glimpse into Japanese life will make it manifest. Read Hearn, the most eloquent and truthful interpreter of **the Japanese mind**, and you see the working of that mind to be an example of the working of Bushido. The universal politeness of the people, which is **the legacy of knightly ways**, is too well known to be repeated anew. **The physical endurance**, **fortitude** and **bravery** that "the little Jap" possesses, were sufficiently proved in the China-Japanese war.[33] "Is there any nation more loyal and patriotic?" is a question asked by many; and for the proud answer, "There is not," we must thank the Precepts of Knighthood.

On the other hand, it is fair to recognize that for the very faults and defects of our character, Bushido is

---

[33] Among other works on the subject, read Eastlake and Yamada on *Heroic Japan*, and Diosy on *The New Far East*.

陥というべきものをも認めておくべきであろう。我が国には高級な哲学の理論が存在しない。科学研究で国際的な評価をえている若手の研究者はすでに出始めているが、哲学でそのような業績をあげている者は一人もいない。これは武士道の教育に、**形而上学的な知的訓練**が欠けていることに起因する。また、名を重んじるところから、**日本人は過度に潔癖で、短気**になるきらいがある。日本人は**気取っている**という外国人がいるが、これも**名へのこだわりが異常なまでに昂じた結果**であろう。

　日本を旅すると、蓬髪を風になびかせ痩身を粗衣にくるみ、手に大杖か本をもった若者が、世の出来事など眼中にないといった顔で道を歩いているのに出会うかもしれない。書生と呼ばれる人種（すなわち学生）である。彼らにとっては**地はあまりに狭く、天はあまりに低い**。書生は独自の世界観と人生観をもっている。空中の楼閣に住み、霞のような智慧の言葉を食っている。眼には野心の炎が燃え、心は知識を求めて飢えている。書生にとって、洗うがごとき赤貧は、前へと駆り立てるムチにすぎず、浮世の財は高潔な志への足かせにほかならない。**書生は忠義と愛国心の権化である**。みずから買って出

largely responsible. Our lack of **abstruse philosophy**—while some of our young men have already gained international reputation in scientific researches, not one has achieved anything in philosophical lines—is traceable to the neglect of **metaphysical training** under Bushido's regimen of education. Our sense of honor is responsible for **our exaggerated sensitiveness and touchiness**; and if there is the **conceit** in us with which some foreigners charge us, that, too, is **a pathological outcome of honor**.

Have you seen in your tour of Japan many a young man with unkempt hair, dressed in shabbiest garb, carrying in his hand a large cane or a book, stalking about the streets with an air of utter indifference to mundane things? He is the *shosei* (student), to whom **the earth is too small and the Heavens are not high enough**. He has his own theories of the universe and of life. He dwells in castles of air and feeds on ethereal words of wisdom. In his eyes beams the fire of ambition; his mind is athirst for knowledge. Penury is only a stimulus to drive him onward; worldly goods are in his sight shackles to his character. He is **the repository of Loyalty and Patriotism**. He is **the self-imposed**

た、国の名誉の守護者である。徳も不徳もひっくるめて、書生こそは武士の末裔である。

　武士道はいまなお根深く、強い影響力を及ぼしているが、それは**無意識であり、無言の影響**であると述べた。人々の心というものは、なぜかその理由が分からないままに、生まれながらに受け継いできたものに反応するものである。したがって同じ倫理でも、あらたな言葉で言い換えられたものと、旧来の武士道の言葉で述べられたものとでは、その及ぼす効果が大きく異なってくる。『天路歴程』のクリスチャンは牧師にいくら説教されても堕ちていくばかりだったが、忠誠心にうったえて、汝はかつて天の主に忠誠を誓ったではないかと言われることで、堕落の道からのがれ出ることができた。「忠誠心」という言葉によって、**だらけるがままに放置されていた**心に、**高貴な感情**がふたたび熱く燃え始めたのである。反抗的な大学生たちが徒党をくみ、ある教師が気に入らないからといって、「学生のストライキ」をだらだらといつまでも続けていたのが、学長に二つの単純明快な質問をされて、さっさと矛を収めてしまったという事件があった。学長いわく「その先生は非の打ちどころのない人格者なのか？　ならばその人は敬って、ぜひとも大学にいてもらわなければ困る。それとも、弱い人間なのか？　であるなら、そんな倒れそうな人間の背中を押す

guardian of national honor. With all his virtues and his faults, he is the last fragment of Bushido.

Deep-rooted and powerful as is still the effect of Bushido, I have said that it is an **unconscious and mute influence**. The heart of the people responds, without knowing the reason why, to any appeal made to what it has inherited, and hence the same moral idea expressed in a newly translated term and in an old Bushido term, has a vastly different degree of efficacy. A backsliding Christian, whom no pastoral persuasion could help from downward tendency, was reverted from his course by an appeal made to his loyalty, the fidelity he once swore to his Master. The word "Loyalty" revived all **the noble sentiments** that **were permitted to grow lukewarm**. A band of unruly youths engaged in a long continued "students' strike" in a college, on account of their dissatisfaction with a certain teacher, disbanded at two simple questions put by the Director,—"Is your professor a blameless character? If so, you ought to respect him and keep him in the school. Is he weak? If so, it is not

など、男のやることか？」。事の発端はこの教師が科学者として無能であったということだが、このように**人の道を問われれば**、そんな問題なんぞ霞んでしまったのである。**武士道によって養われた感情**をかきたてることで、大きな**倫理的な刷新**が成し遂げられるであろう。

　キリスト教の布教が日本でうまく行かなかった最大の理由は、宣教師たちがあまりに日本の歴史を知らなさすぎたということである。「異教徒の過去の記録などどうでもいい」という者もいて、そのために、彼らの教えが、我々や過去の日本人が何百年も慣れ親しんできた考え方から離れることになった。**一国の歴史を軽んじる**など、とんでもないことである！どんな民族の歴史も——たとえ記録をもたないアフリカの未開部族でさえ、神の手によって記された、全人類の歴史の一ページなのだ。失われた民族でさえ、見る人が見ればきちんと解読して、その姿を浮かび上がらせることができる。それぞれの人種には、神の記した文字が、白や黒の肌色と同じくはっきりと残されていることは、知を愛する宗教者には一目瞭然なのである。そして、この比喩をさらに続けるなら、黄色人種は黄金の象形文字で記された、貴重な一ページをなしているのである！宣教師たちは**民族の過去の歴史をまるで無視**して、キリスト教があらたな宗教で

manly to push a falling man." The scientific incapacity of the professor, which was the beginning of the trouble, dwindled into insignificance in comparison with **the moral issues hinted at**. By arousing **the sentiments nurtured by Bushido, moral renovation** of great magnitude can be accomplished.

One cause of the failure of mission work is that most of the missionaries are grossly ignorant of our history—"What do we care for heathen records?" some say—and consequently estrange their religion from the habits of thought we and our forefathers have been accustomed to for centuries past. **Mocking a nation's history!**—as though the career of any people—even of the lowest African savages possessing no record—were not a page in the general history of mankind, written by the hand of God Himself. The very lost races are a palimpsest to be deciphered by a seeing eye. To a philosophic and pious mind, the races themselves are marks of Divine chirography clearly traced in black and white as on their skin; and if this simile holds good, the yellow race forms a precious page inscribed in hieroglyphics of gold! **Ignoring the past career of a people**, missionaries claim that

あると主張する。しかし、日本人の目には、それは
「昔、昔の物語」であり、もしも彼らに理解できる言葉
で記されていれば——すなわち民族の倫理的進化を記す
ときの言葉で表現されていれば、**人種や国籍には関係な
く、彼らの心にも容易に受け入れられた**ことであろう。
アメリカやイギリスのキリスト教は——キリストの恩寵
や純潔よりも、アングロサクソン的な奇癖や気まぐれが
目立つので ——武士道という台木に接ぎ木するには、
おそまつな若芽であった。かりに、あらたな信仰を広め
ようとして、武士道を根こそぎ取り払い、ひっかき回し
た土壌に福音の種をまいたとすれば、どうなっていたで
あろうか? このように蛮勇をふるうことは可能かもし
れない。ハワイでは、教会の戦士が土着の民族を皆殺し
にして、莫大な富を略奪したといわれている。しかしこ
のようなことは、日本では絶対に起こり得ないことであ
った。このような方法は、地上に自らの王国をうち樹て
ようとしたキリストその人が絶対に肯じなかったであろ
う。ある敬虔なキリスト教徒であり、学殖豊かな聖職者
の言を、しっかりと胸に刻みつけなければならない。
——「人は世界を異教の国とキリスト教の国に分け、異
教の国にどれほどの善がかくされ、キリスト教の国にど

Christianity is a new religion, whereas, to my mind, it is an "old, old story," which, if presented in intelligible words,—that is to say, if expressed in the vocabulary familiar in the moral development of a people—will **find easy lodgment in their hearts, irrespective of race or nationality**. Christianity in its American or English form—with more of Anglo-Saxon freaks and fancies than grace and purity of its founder—is a poor scion to graft on Bushido stock. Should the propagator of the new faith uproot the entire stock, root and branches, and plant the seeds of the Gospel on the ravaged soil? Such a heroic process may be possible—in Hawaii, where, it is alleged, the church militant had complete success in amassing spoils of wealth itself, and in annihilating the aboriginal race: such a process is most decidedly impossible in Japan—nay, it is a process which Jesus himself would never have employed in founding his kingdom on earth. It behooves us to take more to heart the following words of a saintly man, devout Christian and profound scholar:—"Men have divided the world into heathen and Christian, without considering how much good may have been hidden in the one, or how much evil may

れほどの悪が混在しているか考えもしない。彼らは**自ら
の最善の部分と、隣人の最悪の部分を比較**している。キ
リスト教の理想と、ギリシャや東方諸国の腐敗を比べて
いるのである。**公平にものを考えよう**などとは思いもし
ないで、自らの賛美になること、他の宗教の不利なこと
ばかりをこれでもかと積み重ねているのである」[34]。

　しかしながら、個々の宣教師がおかした過ちはともか
くとして、彼らが標榜する宗教の基本的な原理は重要な
ものであり、武士道の将来について考えようとするな
ら、無視することはできない。武士道は**もはや命運が尽
きているように見える**。その未来を物語るかのような、
不吉な兆候が存在する。いや兆候にはとどまらず、それ
を脅かす強い流れがすでに生じている。

---

[34]　Jowett, *Sermons on Faith and Doctrine*, II.

have been mingled with the other. They have **compared the best part of themselves with the worst of their neighbors**, the ideal of Christianity with the corruption of Greece or the East. They have not **aimed at impartiality**, but have been contented to accumulate all that could be said in praise of their own, and in dispraise of other forms of religion."[34]

But, whatever may be the error committed by individuals, there is little doubt that the fundamental principle of the religion they profess is a power which we must take into account in reckoning the future of Bushido, **whose days seem to be already numbered**. Ominous signs are in the air, that betoken its future. Not only signs, but redoubtable forces are at work to threaten it.

第 17 章

武士道の将来

　東西の歴史を比較するのは陳腐だが、ヨーロッパの騎士道と日本の武士道を並べてみて、これほど好個の一対はない。**歴史が繰り返す**なら、騎士道にふりかかった運命は、必ずや武士道にも起きるであろう。騎士道を廃らせた原因として、特定の時代や地域に根ざすものをセント・パレイエが挙げているが、これは言うまでもなく日本には当てはまらない。だが、**中世**以降、**騎士道を衰弱させることになった**、もっと**巨視的で一般的な原因**が、日本の武士道をも衰退させる方向へと作用していることはまちがいない。

　ヨーロッパで起きたことを日本と比べてみると、一つ大きく異なっているところがあるのに気づく。ヨーロッパでは、騎士道は封建制度の懐を去ると、こんどは教会に抱かれ、そこで**あらたな生を得る**こととなった。対する日本では、武士道を包容するほどの大きな宗教が存在

CHAPTER 17

THE FUTURE OF BUSHIDO

Few historical comparisons can be more judiciously made than between the Chivalry of Europe and the Bushido of Japan, and, if **history repeats itself**, it certainly will do with the fate of the latter what it did with that of the former. The particular and local causes for the decay of Chivalry which St. Palaye gives, have, of course, little application to Japanese conditions; but **the larger and more general causes** that **helped to undermine Knighthood and Chivalry** in and after **the Middle Ages** are as surely working for the decline of Bushido.

One remarkable difference between the experience of Europe and of Japan is, that, whereas in Europe when Chivalry was weaned from Feudalism and was adopted by the Church, it obtained **a fresh lease of life**, in Japan no religion was large enough to nourish

しなかったので、封建制という母なる制度が去ると、武士道はいわば孤児として取り残され、**独り立ちする**ほかなかった。**高度に発達を遂げた現在の軍隊組織**は武士道を庇護するかもしれないが、現代の戦争には、武士道を成長発展させるだけの余地はない。**神道**は揺籃期^{ようらんき}の武士道を育てたが、今日ではもはやかつての影響力はなく、中国古代の聖人の教えも、新参の知識人すなわち、ベンサム、ミルといった輩によって主役の座を追われてしまった。武士道の代わりに、**心地よいたぐいの俗流道徳**が発明され、提唱されている。**現代のショーヴィニズム的風潮**にとって都合のよいものなので、**時代のニーズに合ってはいる**のだろうが、今のところ、**大衆紙の紙面**でヒステリックな声をあげているばかりである。

　世界の主要な国々は、こぞって武士道的な戒律を根絶やしにしようとしている。ヴェブレンの言葉を借りるなら、すでに「産業にたずさわる階級で、**折り目ただしい行動規律が衰退**（言い換えれば、**生活が卑俗化**）してきている。これは、すぐれた感性を持つ人々には、近代の文明が犯した大罪の一つとして映る」。民主主義が勝利をおさめ、抗しがたい流れとして広まってきた。武士階

it; hence, when the mother institution, Feudalism, was gone, Bushido, left an orphan, had to **shift for itself**. **The present elaborate military organization** might take it under its patronage, but we know that modern warfare can afford little room for its continuous growth. **Shintoism**, which fostered it in its infancy, is itself superannuated. The hoary sages of ancient China are being supplanted by the intellectual parvenu of the type of Bentham and Mill. **Moral theories of a comfortable kind**, flattering to **the Chauvinistic tendencies of the time**, and therefore thought **well-adapted to the need of this day**, have been invented and propounded; but as yet we hear only their shrill voices echoing through **the columns of yellow journalism**.

Principalities and powers are arrayed against the Precepts of Knighthood. Already, as Veblen says, "**the decay of the ceremonial code**—or, as it is otherwise called, **the vulgarization of life**—among the industrial classes proper, has become one of the chief enormities of latter-day civilization in the eyes of all persons of delicate sensibilities." The irresistible tide of triumphant democracy, which can tolerate no form or

級とは、**知的、文化的財産を独占**し、**世の倫理的な価値や等級付けの源泉**としての役割をはたす者たちの集団であるが、このような階級に権力を委託するというような考え方は、民主主義では絶対に容認されない。したがって現代社会では、このような民主主義だけでも、**武士道の残っている痕跡**を一掃するにじゅうぶんである。現代の社会的趨勢（すうせい）は、狭量な階級意識を目の敵にしている。そしてフリーマンが厳しく糾弾するように、武士道はまさに階級意識そのものである。近代社会は、国を統合する原理として、「排他的な階級を利するための、純粋に個人的な義務」を容認することはできない[35]。これに加えて、**大衆教育**が普及し、産業の技術や慣習が発達し、富や都会生活が社会全体に広まりつつある。こうなると、侍がいかに鋭い刀を振るおうと、武士道がいかに大胆に矢を射かけようと、もはや蟷螂（とうろう）の斧（おの）である。**名誉の岩盤の上に築かれ、名誉という刀で守られてきた国**は──ドイツ語で「エーレンシュタット（名誉の国）」、もしくはカーライルの顰（ひそみ）にならって「英雄支配政治」と呼ぶべきかもしれないが──屁理屈で武装した、巧言令色の三百代言や嘘八百の政治家の掌中に、今や怖ろしい勢

---

[35] *Norman Conquest*, Vol. V, p. 482.

shape of trust—and Bushido was a trust organized by those who **monopolized reserve capital of intellect and culture**, **fixing the grades and value of moral qualities**— is alone powerful enough to engulf **the remnant of Bushido**. The present societary forces are antagonistic to petty class spirit, and Chivalry is, as Freeman severely criticizes, a class spirit. Modern society, if it pretends to any unity, cannot admit "purely personal obligations devised in the interests of an exclusive class."[35] Add to this the progress of **popular instruction**, of industrial arts and habits, of wealth and city-life,—then we can easily see that neither the keenest cuts of samurai's sword nor the sharpest shafts shot from Bushido's boldest bows can aught avail. **The state built upon the rock of Honor and fortified by the same**—shall we call it the *Ehrenstaat* or, after the manner of Carlyle, the Heroarchy?—is fast falling into the hands of quibbling lawyers and gibbering politicians armed with logic-chopping engines

いで堕ちつつある。ある思想家が、聖テレサとアンティゴネの運命について語った言葉がそのまま日本の侍に当てはまる。すなわち「彼らの情熱の行動が可能であった環境が永遠に消え去ってしまった」のである。

武人の美徳、**侍魂**（さむらいだましい）が地上から消滅するのは、なんと悲しいことだろう！ 戦（いくさ）のラッパと太鼓とともに誕生した武人の徳は、「武将と王が去るとともに」消える運命にあるのだ。

歴史から教訓を得るとするなら、スパルタのような都市国家にせよ、ローマのような大帝国にせよ、**武人の徳の上に樹てられた国**は、この地上で「永遠の都市」とはなりえないということである。**戦いの本能**は、人類共通の生得の性質であり、**高貴な感情**と、**男性的な美徳**を生み出す源泉となったが、人間はそれだけで出来ているわけではない。この本能の下には、**もっと神に近い、愛するという本能**がひそんでいる。すでに示したように、神道でも、孟子でも、王陽明でも、このことははっきりと示されている。しかし武士道をはじめとする世界の武人流の倫理では、目の前の必要にどう対処すべきかということに忙しく、「愛」に正しい考慮をあたえることを怠りがちであった。**近代になって、人間の生が多様になってきた。**今日では、武人よりも広い見識にかかわる、誉の高い職業を選ぶことも可能である。拡大した人生観、

of war. The words which a great thinker used in speaking of Theresa and Antigone may aptly be repeated of the samurai, that "the medium in which their ardent deeds took shape is forever gone."

Alas for knightly virtues! alas for **samurai pride!** Morality ushered into the world with the sound of bugles and drums, is destined to fade away as "the captains and the kings depart."

If history can teach us anything, **the state built on martial virtues**— be it a city like Sparta or an Empire like Rome—can never make on earth a "continuing city." Universal and natural as is the **fighting instinct** in man, fruitful as it has proved to be of **noble sentiments** and **manly virtues**, it does not comprehend the whole man. Beneath the instinct to fight there lurks **a diviner instinct to love**. We have seen that Shintoism, Mencius and Wan Yang Ming, have all clearly taught it; but Bushido and all other militant schools of ethics, engrossed, doubtless, with questions of immediate practical need, too often forgot duly to emphasize this fact. **Life has grown larger in these latter times**. Callings nobler and broader than a warrior's claim our attention to-day. With an enlarged

民主主義の成長、そして他の民族や国家のことをより知るようになる中で、**孔子の「仁」の思想は**——そしてあえて言うなら、**仏教の慈悲の思想が**——**キリスト教の「愛」の概念**へと拡大していくことだろう。人はもはや「臣民」を超えて、「市民」へと進化した。いや市民というより「人間」となった。

　現在、地平線の上には戦争の暗雲が重くたれこめているが、平和の天使がその翼で払いのけてくれるものと信じる。世界の歴史は、「従順なる者が地を引き継ぐであろう」という予言の実現を見ることであろう。平和という生得の権利を売りとばす国、産業化の最前線から後退して、しがない軍事国家に成り下がるのは、なんと割に合わない選択であろうか！

　社会の状況がこれほどまでに変化し、**武士道を嫌うどころか、それを敵視するまでになった**からには、武士道は**名誉ある埋葬**にそなえなければならない。武士道がいつ死ぬかは、いつ誕生したのかと同じく、正確に述べることは難しい。ミラー博士によると、西洋の騎士道が正式に廃されたのは、一五五九年、フランスのアンリ二世が馬上槍試合で死んだときだという。日本では、一八七〇年に幕藩体制を廃止する詔勅が出たが、これが武士道

view of life, with the growth of democracy, with better knowledge of other peoples and nations, **the Confucian idea of Benevolence**—dare I also add **the Buddhist idea of Pity?**—will expand into **the Christian conception of Love**. Men have become more than subjects, having grown to the estate of citizens: nay, they are more than citizens, being men.

Though war clouds hang heavy upon our horizon, we will believe that the wings of the angel of peace can disperse them. The history of the world confirms the prophecy that "the meek shall inherit the earth." A nation that sells its birthright of peace, and backslides from the front rank of Industrialism into the file of Filibusterism, makes a poor bargain indeed!

When the conditions of society are so changed that they have **become not only adverse but hostile to Bushido**, it is time for it to prepare for **an honorable burial**. It is just as difficult to point out when chivalry dies, as to determine the exact time of its inception. Dr. Miller says that Chivalry was formally abolished in the year 1559, when Henry II. of France was slain in a tournament. With us, the edict formally abolishing Feudalism in 1870 was the signal to toll the knell

の弔いの鐘であった。その二年後の**廃刀令**によって、「生まれながらの身分、安上がりの国の守り、男らしい感情と英雄的な行動の育成」といった旧いものが葬りさられ、「詭弁と理財と計算」をもっぱらとする新時代が招き入れられたのである。

　日本が日清戦争に勝ったのは、村田銃と、クルップ砲のおかげだといわれる。また、**近代的な学校制度**の賜物だとも言われる。しかし、これは真実の半分にも満たない。エアバーやスタインウェイの技術の粋をつくしたピアノであっても、名手が弾かないことには、リストの狂詩曲やベートーヴェンのソナタを奏でることはない。もしも**銃砲が戦（いくさ）を制する**というなら、機関銃を持っていたルイ・ナポレオンはなぜプロシャに負けたのか？　モーゼル銃を持っていたスペイン軍が、旧式のレミントン銃しか持たないフィリピン人になぜ負けたのか？　言い古された言葉だが、人が魂を入れないことには、どんなによい道具も宝の持ち腐れなのである。**いかに改良が進んでも、銃や大砲が自分で撃ってくれるわけではない。どんなに近代的な教育をほどこしても、臆病者を英雄には変えない。**それは絶対に否である！鴨緑江（おうりょくこう）、朝鮮、満

of Bushido. The **edict**, issued two years later, **prohibiting the wearing of swords**, rang out the old, "the unbought grace of life, the cheap defence of nations, the nurse of manly sentiment and heroic enterprise," it rang in the new age of "sophisters, economists, and calculators."

It has been said that Japan won her late war with China by means of Murata guns and Krupp cannon; it has been said the victory was the work of **a modern school system**; but these are less than half-truths. Does ever a piano, be it of the choicest workmanship of Ehrbar or Steinway, burst forth into the Rhapsodies of Liszt or the Sonatas of Beethoven, without a master's hand? Or, if **guns win battles**, why did not Louis Napoleon beat the Prussians with his *Mitrailleuse*, or the Spaniards with their Mausers the Filipinos, whose arms were no better than the old-fashioned Remingtons? Needless to repeat what has grown a trite saying that it is the spirit that quickeneth, without which the best of implements profiteth but little. **The most improved guns and cannon do not shoot of their own accord; the most modern educational system does not make a coward a hero.** No! What

州の戦闘で勝ったのは、**父祖の霊魂**が我らの手をみちびき、心の臓を高鳴らせてくれたからである。父祖の霊、戦を事としたわが先祖の魂は死んではいない。見る目のある人には、はっきりと見えるのである。日本人はどんなに進歩的な考えをもった人でも、一皮むけばその下から侍が出てくる。名誉、勇気をはじめとする武人の徳は、偉大な遺産として「我々に託されている。これは逝きし者たち、そして未来の世代の奪うべからざる財産であり、我々にはこの大切な預かりものを**大事に守って伝える義務がある**」とはクラム教授の言である。まことに言い得て妙である。この遺産を守り、昔の精神をわずかなりとも減らさないことが、**現代に生きる者の義務**である。そして、柔軟な思考によって、それを人生のあらゆる分野に応用していくのが未来の世代の義務である。

　かつて、封建日本の倫理は城や城壁のように崩れ去り、新生日本を進歩の道へとみちびく**新たな道徳が不死鳥のように立ち上がってくる**だろうと予言され、過去半世紀の流れのなかでこの予言は見事的中した。そもそもが実現しそうな予言ではあり、それが望ましい結果でもあったが、ここで忘れてならないのは、**不死鳥は自らの灰から復活してくる**ものだ、ということである。不死鳥は渡り鳥でもなければ、他の鳥の羽根を借りて飛ぶわけ

won the battles on the Yalu, in Corea and Manchuria, was **the ghosts of our fathers**, guiding our hands and beating in our hearts. They are not dead, those ghosts, **the spirits of our warlike ancestors**. To those who have eyes to see, they are clearly visible. Scratch a Japanese of the most advanced ideas, and he will show a samurai. The great inheritance of honor, of valor and of all martial virtues is, as Professor Cramb very fitly expresses it, "but ours on trust, the fief inalienable of the dead and of the generation to come," and **the summons of the present** is to **guard this heritage**, nor to bate one jot of the ancient spirit; the summons of the future will be so to widen its scope as to apply it in all walks and relations of life.

It has been predicted—and predictions have been corroborated by the events of the last half century—that the moral system of Feudal Japan, like its castles and its armories, will crumble into dust, and **new ethics rise phoenix-like** to lead New Japan in her path of progress. Desirable and probable as the fulfilment of such a prophecy is, we must not forget that **a phoenix rises only from its own ashes**, and that it is not a bird of passage, neither does it fly on pinions

でもない。「神の王国は汝自身の中にある」という。高い山から下ってくるわけでも、広い海を渡ってくるわけでもない。「神はあらゆる民に、それぞれの言葉で語る預言者をあたえたもうた」とコーランに言う。日本人の心が証し、とらえた神の王国の種は、武士道という花を咲かせた。今や、無念にも**果実を結ぶことなく**その終焉のときが近づき、日本人はそれに代わるものを模索している真っ最中である。**優しさと光、力とやすらぎをもたらすもの**を求めるも、日本の中ではいまだ見つかっていない。功利主義と実利主義は**損得勘定の哲学**を唱えるが、それを好むのは、心の狭い屁理屈屋ばかりである。功利主義と実利主義に対抗できるほどの力を持っているのはキリスト教のみだが、これと比べると、武士道は、救世主が「消さずに炎を掻き立てよ」と言った「暗く燃える灯心」のようなありさまである。武士道はキリスト以前の預言者、とくにイザヤ、エレミア、アモス、ハバククに似て、**君主や公人、そして国家そのものの振る舞いの倫理性**に重きをおいている。これとは対照的に、キ

borrowed from other birds. "The Kingdom of God is within you." It does not come rolling down the mountains, however lofty; it does not come sailing across the seas, however broad. "God has granted," says the Koran, "to every people a prophet in its own tongue." The seeds of the Kingdom, as vouched for and apprehended by the Japanese mind, blossomed in Bushido. Now its days are closing—sad to say, **before its full fruition**—and we turn in every direction for other **sources of sweetness and light, of strength and comfort**, but among them there is as yet nothing found to take its place. **The profit and loss philosophy** of Utilitarians and Materialists finds favor among logic-choppers with half a soul. The only other ethical system which is powerful enough to cope with Utilitarianism and Materialism is Christianity, in comparison with which Bushido, it must be confessed, is like "a dimly burning wick" which the Messiah was proclaimed not to quench but to fan into a flame. Like His Hebrew precursors, the prophets—notably Isaiah, Jeremiah, Amos and Habakkuk—Bushido laid particular stress on **the moral conduct of rulers and public men and of nations**,

リストの倫理はもっぱら個人、キリストに追随する者たちに関わっていた。よって近代社会で**個人主義が道徳の重要な要素となる**につれて、キリスト教倫理がますます実生活に用いられるようになる。**ニーチェ**の尊大で身勝手な**「主人の道徳」**と称するものは、ある意味で武士道に似ていなくもないが、私の見込み違いでなければ、すぐに姿を消すであろう。**ナザレ人の慎ましく、自己犠牲をよしとする道徳**が、ニーチェの歪んだ目には「奴隷の道徳」と映り、ニーチェはそれに一時的な反発をしてみせたにすぎないからである。

キリスト教と（**功利主義を含む**）**実利主義**が——将来これは「ヘブライズムとヘレニズム」という古代の対立図式へと還元されるかもしれないが——世界を二分することになるだろう。**その他諸々の弱小の道徳律**は、生き残るために、この二つのどちらかに結びつくだろう。武士道はどちらに即くだろうか？ **守らねばならない教義も経典もない**ので、まるごと消滅するも可である。桜の花のように朝一番の風とともに散るのはむしろ本望であろう。しかし、完璧な消滅は武士道の運命にはないだろう。**禁欲主義**が消滅したといえるだろうか？ 一つの道徳律としては死んだ。しかし、一つの徳としては生きている。今なお人生の様々の道筋で——西洋諸国の哲学の

whereas the Ethics of Christ, which deal almost solely with individuals and His personal followers, will find more and more practical application as **individualism, in its capacity of a moral factor, grows in potency**. The domineering, self-assertive, so-called **master-morality** of **Nietzsche**, itself akin in some respects to Bushido, is, if I am not greatly mistaken, a passing phase or temporary reaction against what he terms, by morbid distortion, **the humble, self-denying slave-morality of the Nazarene**.

Christianity and **Materialism** (including **Utilitarianism**)—or will the future reduce them to still more archaic forms of **Hebraism** and **Hellenism**?—will divide the world between them. **Lesser systems of morals** will ally themselves on either side for their preservation. On which side will Bushido enlist? Having **no set dogma or formula to defend**, it can afford to disappear as an entity; like the cherry blossom, it is willing to die at the first gust of the morning breeze. But a total extinction will never be its lot. Who can say that **stoicism** is dead? It is dead as a system; but it is alive as a virtue: its energy and vitality are still felt through many channels of life—in the

中で、文明世界の法体系の中で、そのエネルギーとバイタリティーは健在である。そればかりか、人が自分に勝とうと懸命に努力するとき、努力によって精神が肉体を支配するにいたるとき、禁欲というゼノンの不滅の原理がそこに作用しているのがありありと見えるのである。

　武士道は独立した倫理の体系としては消え去った。しかし、**その影響は地上から失せることはないだろう**。武勇の学校、名誉の学校は取り壊されても、その燦きと栄光は廃墟の上に末永く生き残るであろう。武士道を象徴する桜の花のように、花びらは風に散ろうとも、その香りは人類を祝福し、人生を豊かにしてくれる。長い年月がたってその慣習が葬られ、武士道という名すらも忘れ去られても、その薫りが馥郁と漂ってくるだろう。まるで「ふとかたへに目をやると」、目に見えない遠くの丘の薫りが感じられるように。クエーカー教徒のある詩人の美しい言葉を借りるなら、

　　旅人は、いずこ知らねど、
　　甘い薫りに心はしゃぎ、
　　足をとめ、帽をぬいで、
　　空気の祝福をうけとめる。

philosophy of Western nations, in the jurisprudence of all the civilized world. Nay, wherever man struggles to raise himself above himself, wherever his spirit masters his flesh by his own exertions, there we see the immortal discipline of Zeno at work.

Bushido as an independent code of ethics may vanish, but **its power will not perish from the earth**; its schools of martial prowess or civic honor may be demolished, but its light and its glory will long survive their ruins. Like its symbolic flower, after it is blown to the four winds, it will still bless mankind with the perfume with which it will enrich life. Ages after, when its customaries shall have been buried and its very name forgotten, its odors will come floating in the air as from a far-off unseen hill, "the wayside gaze beyond;"—then in the beautiful language of the Quaker poet,

> "The traveler owns the grateful sense
>   Of sweetness near he knows not whence,
>   And, pausing, takes with forehead bare
>   The benediction of the air."

訳者のことば

　21世紀に入り、人類は10年ごとに試練のときを迎えている。

　2008年の信用不安、2020年に始まった新型コロナウイルスのパンデミック——どちらも世界全体を不安と混乱の渦に巻き込んだ。現代は高度に文明が発達し、科学技術がどんな難問でも解決してくれるかのように見える。しかしそれにもかかわらず、いつ予想もしない大事件が起きて、我々の生活や人生そのものが脅かされるか分からない。

　このような時代に『武士道』は、人は世にいかに処すべきか、人生いかに生きるべきかといった大問題を、考えるヒントをあたえてくれる。それはなぜだろう？

＊　　＊　　＊

　新渡戸稲造は名実ともに日本で最初の国際人であった。

　生まれたのは1862年、江戸時代の末期である。当時の日本は二五〇年の太平の眠りからさめたばかり、急速に前時代の衣を脱ぎすて、大政奉還、明治維新へと突き進もうとする真っ最中であった。それこそ寸暇を惜しんで、西欧の近代に追いつこうと奮闘していた。そんな近代日本の思春期ともいうべき時代に、新渡戸は十代の多感な時期を過ごし、成長した。札幌農学校を卒業後、東京大学に学ぶが、そこでの学問にあきたらず、私費で渡米してジョンズ・ホプキンス大学に学ぶも数年後に中退し、後にドイツに留学しハレ大学より博士号を得た。

帰国後は札幌農学校に迎えられ、専門の農政学を教えるかたわら執筆や講演活動に忙しい日々をおくり、『日米関係史』をジョンズ・ホプキンス大学から出版し、名誉博士号をあたえられた。しかし身辺の煩忙ゆえか精神の不調におちいり、職を辞して療養することになった。そして、その間に英語で執筆されたのが *Bushido* であった。

　Bushido の初版は1900年に出版された。そして世界的なベストセラーとなった。折しも日本の軍事力が海外へと向かおうとし始めたときにあたり、にわかに国際舞台に躍り出た日本が、漸く世界の人びとの耳目をひきつけようとしていた。そして1894〜5年には、「眠れる巨人」と言われていた中国を日清戦争で破ったことで、日本への国際的な関心がいやが上にも高まった。前近代社会そのものであった日本を、20年あまりで世界の列強に比肩しうる国力をたくわえるほどに押し上げた原動力はなんだったのだろう？　そんな当然の疑問が世界中の人の心をとらえた。そして、その答えが *Bushido* だったのだ。

＊　　＊　　＊

　「武士道は日本の国の華。国の象徴である桜とともに、日本の土壌に生えた純潔の華である」。『武士道』の冒頭の第一句である。すなわち日本固有のものであることが、まず強調される。

　しかしまもなく、西欧の人間にとって理解しやすいように、武士道は騎士道と同じように封建社会で生み出されたものであり、同じような精神を持っていることが述べられる。そしてさ

らに、イギリス人にとっておなじみの『トム・ブラウンの学校生活』が引用される。「小さな少年を虐めることなく、大きな少年を前にたじろぐこともなかったと後々賞賛されたい」という気持ち、フェアプレイの精神こそが武士道の基本精神であるという。

この第1章のあらましだけでもすでに明らかだが、Bushidoは単に日本の独自性を、もの珍しく外国人に紹介しようとした本ではない。むしろ、表面的には日本固有の制度・慣習であり、西欧人の目にはとても奇妙に映るかもしれないが、その根本的な考え方は西欧のもの、とりわけキリスト教の精神と共通しているというのが、新渡戸のもっとも重要なメッセージである。

新渡戸はそのことを、世界史、世界文化や文学の驚くべき知識、西欧の名だたる論客にも決して負けない知性と教養を縦横無尽に駆使しながら、証明して見せる。そうして幕末に来日した西欧人に由来する「野蛮な」日本という常識をくつがえしてみせる。

日本の独自性とは、日本西欧を問わず普遍的に存在する高邁な精神を、高度に発達させて一つの制度としたばかりか、それを明治に至るまで何世紀にもわたって維持し続けてきたことにある。そのおかげで、武士道精神で重んじられている自制心、他者への思いやり、公私の峻別、潔いふるまい、公正を重んじる心、謙虚さなど、誇るべき精神の遺産が、現在の日本人の中にも息づいているのである。

＊　＊　＊

世界に次々と襲いかかってくる危機的な状況に際し、日本は他国にくらべて比較的冷静に対処することができている。国を構成する一人ひとりの日本人が、このような武士道の精神を遺伝子として受け継いでいるからではなかろうか？

　武士道精神とは何か？　それは世がどんなに乱れても右往左往することなく、ぶれない自分をしっかりと保つための心構えのことである。新渡戸稲造の *Bushido* は、世界史の流れの全体を上から眺め、人類にとって普遍的な価値、人間が人間であるかぎり重要であるものが何かを教えてくれる名著である。

　なお、原著は達意の英語で書かれている。新渡戸の洋の東西を問わない深い教養があふれ、独自の比喩表現がふんだんに用いられた名文である。対訳の日本語は、原文の内容が理解しやすいようにとの思いで作成された。皆様のお役に立つことができれば幸いである。

　本書は 1905 年刊行の改訂版を底本としている。テクストのうち重要な語句については、本文理解に資するよう太字にして強調した。また原注のうち、英語の書名についてはもとの標記のままにしたことを付記しておこう。

　最後になったが、本書の企画・制作のすべてにわたって、朝日新聞出版書籍編集部の齋藤太郎氏にひとかたならぬお世話になった。心よりお礼を申し上げたい。

2021 年 7 月

山本史郎

新渡戸稲造 にとべ・いなぞう

1862年、岩手県盛岡市生まれ。13歳で東京英語学校(のちの東京大学)入学後、札幌農学校(のちの北海道大学)に学ぶ。その後アメリカ、ドイツの大学に留学。帰国後、札幌農学校教授、京都帝国大学教授、東京帝国大学教授、第一高等学校校長、東京女子大学学長、国際連盟事務次長など歴任。1933年没。著書に『農業本論』『一日一言』など多数。

山本史郎 やまもと・しろう

1954年、和歌山県生まれ。東京大学名誉教授。昭和女子大学特命教授。英文学者。翻訳家。東京大学教養学部教養学科卒業。著書に『翻訳の授業』『読み切り世界文学』『名作英文学を読み直す』『東大の教室で「赤毛のアン」を読む』など、共著に『毎日の日本 英語で話す! まるごとJAPAN』『教養英語読本Ⅰ・Ⅱ』など、訳書に『ホビット』『アーサー王と円卓の騎士』『完全版 赤毛のアン』『自分で考えてみる哲学』など多数。

朝日新書
823

対訳　武士道
たい やく　ぶ し どう

2021年7月30日第1刷発行

著　者	新渡戸稲造　著
	山本史郎　訳

発行者	三宮博信
カバーデザイン	アンスガー・フォルマー　田嶋佳子
印刷所	凸版印刷株式会社
発行所	朝日新聞出版

〒104-8011　東京都中央区築地5-3-2
電話　03-5541-8832(編集)
　　　03-5540-7793(販売)

©2021 Nitobe Inazo, Yamamoto Shiro
Published in Japan by Asahi Shimbun Publications Inc.
ISBN 978-4-02-295132-8
定価はカバーに表示してあります。

落丁・乱丁の場合は弊社業務部(電話03-5540-7800)へご連絡ください。
送料弊社負担にてお取り替えいたします。